Energy Trading and Risk Management

Founded in 1807, John Wiley & Sons is the oldest independent publishing company in the United States. With offices in North America, Europe, Australia and Asia, Wiley is globally committed to developing and marketing print and electronic products and services for our customers' professional and personal knowledge and understanding.

The Wiley Finance series contains books written specifically for finance and investment professionals as well as sophisticated individual investors and their financial advisors. Book topics range from portfolio management to e-commerce, risk management, financial engineering, valuation and financial instrument analysis, as well as much more.

For a list of available titles, visit our Web site at www.WileyFinance.com.

Energy Trading and Risk Management

A Practical Approach to Hedging, Trading, and Portfolio Diversification

IRIS MACK

WILEY

Other Wiley Editorial Offices
John Wiley & Sons, 111 River Street, Hoboken, NJ 07030, USA
John Wiley & Sons, The Atrium, Southern Gate, Chichester, West Sussex, P019 8SQ, United Kingdom
John Wiley & Sons (Canada) Ltd., 5353 Dundas Street West, Suite 400, Toronto, Ontario, M9B 6HB, Canada
John Wiley & Sons Australia Ltd., 42 McDougall Street, Milton, Queensland 4064, Australia
Wiley-VCH, Boschstrasse 12, D-69469 Weinheim, Germany

ISBN 978-1-118-33933-6 (Hardcover)
ISBN 978-1-118-33936-7 (ePDF)
ISBN 978-1-118-33934-3 (ePub)

Typeset in 10/12 pt, Sabon LT Std by Aptara

Printed and bound by CPI Group (UK) Ltd, Croydon, CR0 4YY

C9781118339336_170924

In loving memory of my parents:
Dorothy Mack Watson (mom)
U.S. Army Veteran Willie Mack, Jr. (dad)
Fred Watson Sr. (stepdad)

Contents

Preface

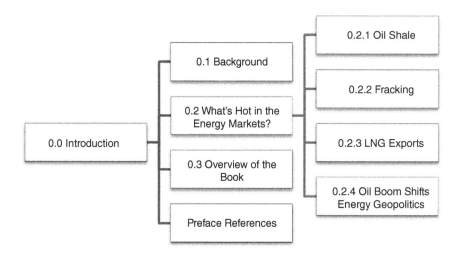

The Preface presents a preview of what the reader will find if he or she keeps turning the pages of this book. More specifically, I discuss why the book was written and some of the current hot topics in the energy markets. I also give an overview of how this book is organized.

0.1 BACKGROUND

I grew up in New Orleans, which is in a state with a fairly sizable energy industry. Although Louisiana's energy industry suffered because of Hurricane Katrina and the BP oil spill, it is still thriving. For example, the existence of oil shale in the Gulf of Mexico and advances in fracking technology have opened new possibilities for Louisiana's energy industry. Hopefully this book will be useful to energy market participants in my home state as they still attempt to recover from the devastation of Hurricane Katrina and the BP oil spill (EIA 2012; Good 2011).

For a substantial part of my academic studies and professional life, I have been involved in energy-related work.

- The mathematics and computer models developed in my Harvard doctoral thesis are utilized to study the transient stability analysis of electrical power systems (Mack 1986).
- I conducted some of my Harvard doctoral thesis research at Sandia National Laboratories. Lockheed Martin manages Sandia for the U.S. Department of Energy's National Nuclear Security Administration.
- My London Business School MBA thesis included applications to electricity and weather derivatives (Mack 1999).
- As a university faculty member, I worked on a consulting/research contract for Lockheed Martin Energy Systems.
- For a couple of years, I worked on real options applications to valuation of aircraft investments and fuel cost hedging when I was a faculty member of the MIT Sloan School, a Boeing Welliver Fellow, and a Boeing faculty researcher (Mack 2011a), (Mack 2011b).
- Some of my work at financial institutions in the United States, London, and Asia involved the structuring and trading of energy and commodities derivatives. This included a stint as a power options trader at Enron.
- I currently consult, advise, and/or lecture on energy and commodities derivatives in the United States, United Kingdom, and Asia for
  - Fitch 7City Certificate in Quantitative Finance Programme (http://cqf.com/lecturers?page=2)
  - Fitch 7City Corporate and Finance Consulting Division (www.fitchlearning.com/uk/corporate-and-finance-division)
  - AlgoAnalytics Trading and Financial Analytics (http://algoanalytics.com)
  - Market Express Financial News and Research (http://www.marketexpress.in)
  - Terrapinn Group Singapore (www.terrapinntraining.com/our-faculty/dr.%20iris%20mack)

0.2 WHAT'S HOT IN THE ENERGY MARKETS?

Energy producers are confronted with a host of challenges in trying to provide safe and affordable energy sources to consumers. Technological breakthroughs coupled with a thirst for the next major energy find are unlocking the door to potentially "hot" energy sources all across the globe. In this section we discuss the following hot topics in the energy markets:

- Discovery of new oil shale sources
- Advances in fracking technology

- Liquefied natural gas (LNG) exports
- Oil boom shifting global energy geopolitics

0.2.1 Shale

Natural gas and crude oil are important primary fossil fuels. The common use of petroleum is often restricted to the liquid oil form, that is, crude oil. Crude oil is a complex mixture of hydrocarbons derived from the geologic transformation and decomposition of plants and animals that lived hundreds of millions of years ago.

Shale oil is an alternative to conventional crude oil. Shale (shown in Figure P.1) is a dark fine-grained laminated sedimentary rock formed by compression of successive layers of clay-rich sediment. Oil shale is a fine-grained shale containing oil. When heated, oil shale yields petroleum or natural gas. Figure P.2 shows a schematic overview of why shale may be an interesting source of energy in the U.S. market.

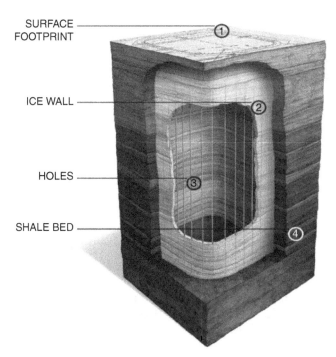

FIGURE P.1 Shale
Source: U.S. Bureau of Land Management.

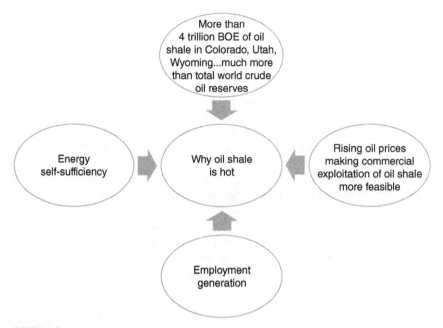

FIGURE P.2 U.S. Shale Oil Resources

Note: Barrel of oil equivalent (BOE) is a unit of energy based on the approximate energy released by burning one barrel (42 U.S. gallons) of crude oil.

SHALE OIL

Shale oil is an alternative to conventional crude oil. Shale is a dark fine-grained laminated sedimentary rock formed by compression of successive layers of clay-rich sediment.

0.2.2   Fracking

Hydraulic fracturing ("fracking"), illustrated in Figure P.3, involves the use of a high-pressure blend of chemicals, water, and sand injected into gas-bearing rock formations deep underground to free trapped gas and bring it to the surface. Critics of fracking argue that this extraction process can pollute the air and ground water. Conversely, proponents of fracking maintain that it is safe when performed properly (Drajem 2013; Edwards 2013; Fox 2010; McElroy and Lu 2013; Nearing 2012).

HYDRAULIC FRACTURING (FRACKING)

Hydraulic fracturing ("fracking") involves the use of a high-pressure blend of chemicals, water, and sand injected into gas-bearing rock formations deep underground to free trapped gas and bring it to the surface.

Some of the forecasted benefits of shale exploration are as follows (MarketWatch 2013):

- The United States is projected to become the largest producer of oil by 2020.
- By 2030 the United States is projected to become a net exporter of oil.
- It is projected that by 2035, the United States should be fairly self-sufficient in energy.
- The prospects of many U.S. energy companies should greatly improve.

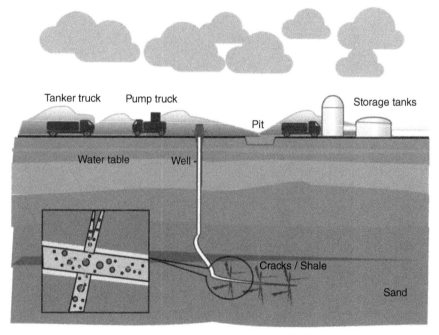

FIGURE P.3   Fracking

0.2.3   Liquefied Natural Gas Exports

Liquefied natural gas (LNG) is natural gas that has been cooled to approximately –256 degrees Fahrenheit so that it can be transported from regions with a surplus of natural gas to those with a deficit. In its liquefied state, natural gas takes up 1/600th of the space of uncooled gas. Figure P.4 shows the complete LNG production process. LNG is much easier to ship and store when pipeline transport is not feasible. As world energy consumption increases, experts anticipate that the LNG trade will grow in importance.

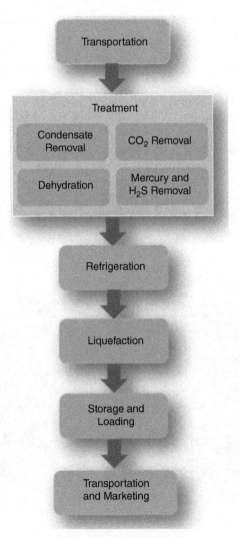

FIGURE P.4   Liquefied Natural Gas (LNG) Production Process

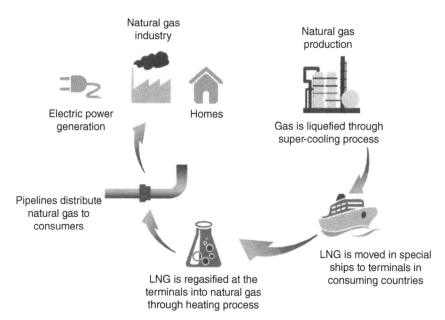

FIGURE P.5 How Liquefied Natural Gas (LNG) Reaches Gas Customers

Shale development has led to an increase in the U.S. domestic natural gas production. There are more than 110 LNG facilities operating in the United States. Depending on location and use, an LNG facility may be regulated by various federal and state agencies. U.S. producers are making moves to export LNG due to an oversupply in the U.S. natural gas markets and because the global demand for LNG is increasing. In Figure P.5 we illustrate how LNG reaches gas customers (FERC 2013).

LIQUEFIED NATURAL GAS (LNG)

Liquefied natural gas (LNG) is natural gas that has been cooled to approximately –256 degrees Fahrenheit so that it can be transported from regions with a surplus of natural gas to those with a deficit.

LNG facilities may provide one or more of the following services:

- Export natural gas.
- Provide natural gas supply to the interstate pipeline system.
- Provide natural gas to local distribution companies.

- Store natural gas for periods of peak demand.
- Produce LNG for vehicle fuel or for industrial use.

0.2.4   Oil Boom Shifts Energy Geopolitics

> *We have a revolution here. This is the equivalent of a Category 5 hurricane.*
>
> Larry Goldstein, Director of the
> Energy Policy Research Foundation

Large quantities of oil and gas have been discovered in the Americas—from Canada, to the United States, to Colombia, to Brazil. Most of these newly discovered energy resources are embedded in shale rock. This energy boom is shifting global energy geopolitics, potentially resulting in energy independence for various countries in the Americas (Forero 2012).

In 2005 the United States imported 60 percent of its liquid fuels. Later in 2011, the U.S. liquid fuels imports declined to 45 percent. This downward trend was due in part to:

- The economic downturn in the United States
- Improvements in automobile efficiency
- Reliance on biofuels
- Fracking

0.3   OVERVIEW OF THE BOOK

An *energy derivative* is a derivatives contract based on (derived from) an underlying asset such as crude oil, natural gas, electricity, and so forth. Some energy derivatives are traded on an exchange. There are also over-the-counter (privately negotiated) energy derivatives such as forwards or swap agreements. The value of an energy derivative will vary based on the changes in the price of the underlying energy product. In this book I present three ways energy derivatives are utilized by energy market participants (see Figure P.6).

ENERGY DERIVATIVE

An *energy derivative* is a derivatives contract based on (derived from) an underlying asset such as crude oil, natural gas, electricity, and so forth.

FIGURE P.6   Applications of Energy Derivatives

Some of the key features of this book are the numerous examples, industrial case studies, and illustrations of various theoretical concepts from the energy markets. This book should make for a handy resource manual for energy market participants, Wall Street and hedge fund traders, consultants, academic researchers, regulators, and students interested in careers in energy trading and risk management.

The structure of the chapters of this book is as follows:

Chapter 1: Energy Markets Fundamentals—physical forward, futures, spot, intraday, balancing and reserve markets; congestion and transmission rights

Chapter 2: Quant Models in the Energy Markets—stochastic models for estimating electricity spot and forward prices

Chapter 3: Plain Vanilla Energy Derivatives—global commodity exchanges, stochastic pricing models for vanilla derivatives, their roles and limitations in the energy markets

Chapter 4: Exotic Energy Derivatives—stochastic pricing models for exotic derivatives, their roles and limitations in the energy markets

Chapter 5: Risk Management and Hedging Strategies—hedging strategies for the energy markets, risk management, the "Greeks," quant models utilized to manage energy risk

Chapter 6: Illustrations of Hedging with Energy Derivatives—examples and case studies of how energy market participants can use energy derivatives to protect against large price fluctuations

Chapter 7: Speculation—key trading terminology, fundamental and technical analysis; speculation in the oil, natural gas, and electricity markets

Chapter 8: Energy Portfolios—modern portfolio theory (MPT), energy portfolio management (EPM), portfolio optimization, economic load dispatch case study

Chapter 9: Hedging Non-Linear Pay-Offs Using Options—a wind energy case study designed and coauthored by Dario Raffaele

Chapter 10: Case Study: Hydropower Generation and Behavioral Finance in the U.S. Pacific Northwest—a hydroelectric case study designed and coauthored by Bill Dickens

Back-of-book content—a compilation of all the references listed at the end of each chapter

It is our hope that our readers utilize this book as a resource to help grapple with the very interesting and oftentimes complex issues that arise in energy trading and risk management. Please note that it was my goal to include a chapter on energy regulations in this edition of my book. However, due to the current political gridlock in Washington, D.C., over the implementation of the Dodd-Frank Wall Street Reform and Consumer Protection Act, many regulatory issues are currently in flux. As a result, most of the research I conducted on the regulations chapter was basically obsolete by the time this book went to press (CFTC 2010).

REFERENCES

Drajem, Mark. 2013. "Methane in Water Seen Sixfold Higher Near Fracking Sites." Bloomberg. www.bloomberg.com/news/2013-06-24/methane-in-water-seen-sixfold-higher-near-fracking-sites.html.

Edwards, Lin. 2013. "Fracking Risks to Ground Water Assessed." PHYS.org. http://phys.org/news/2013-05-fracking-ground.html.

Federal Energy Regulatory Commission (FERC). 2013 (June). "Industries: LNG." http://ferc.gov/industries/gas/indus-act/lng.asp.

Forero, Juan. 2012. "Oil Boom in the Americas Shifts Energy Geopolitics." Global Association of Risk Professionals. www.garp.org/risk-news-and-resources/risk-headlines/story.aspx?newsid=47220.

GasLand. Directed by Josh Fox. http://www.amazon.com/GasLand-Josh-Fox/dp/B005C0DHEY/ref=sr_1_1?ie=UTF8&qid=1393640152&sr=8-1&keywords=gasland.

Good, Allison. 2011. "New Possibilities Are Opening for Louisiana's Energy Industry." *The Times Picayune* www.nola.com/business/index.ssf/2011/08/new_possibilities_are_opening.html.

Mack, Iris, and Harrison Rowe. 1981. "Coupled Modes with Random Propagation Constants." Radio *Science Journal*, 16(4), 485-493, July-August 1981.

Mack, Iris. 1986. "Block Implicit One-Step Methods for Solving Smooth and Discontinuous Systems of Differential/Algebraic Equations: Applications to Transient Stability of Electrical Power Systems." PhD diss., Harvard University Press.

———. 1999. "Day-Ahead Lunch-Time Electricity Demand Forecasting: Applications to Electricity and Weather Derivatives." Master's Thesis, London Business School.

Mack, Iris, and Sloan School of Management. 2011a. "Generalized Picard-Lindelf theory." (White paper). Available at http://amzn.to/1fbHxEX.

Mack, Iris, and Sloan School of Management. 2011b. "Convergence analysis of block implicit one-step methods for solving differential/algebraic equation." (White paper). Available at http://amzn.to/1igEnaF.

MarketWatch. 2013. "Potential Hidden Opportunities in the Fracking Industry." *Wall Street Journal.* www.marketwatch.com/story/potential-hidden-opportunities-in-the-fracking-industry-2013-02-05.

McElroy, Michael, and Xi Lu. 2013. "Fracking's Future." *Harvard Magazine*. http://harvardmagazine.com/2013/01/frackings-future#article-images.

Nearing, Brian. 2012. "Report Finds Little Drilling Damage." *GARP*. www.garp.org/risk-news-and-resources/risk-headlines/story.aspx?newsid=46723.

U.S. Commodity Futures Trading Commission (CFTC). 2010. "Dodd-Frank Wall Street Reform and Consumer Protection Act." U.S. Congress, H.R. 4172. www.cftc.gov/ucm/groups/public/@swaps/documents/file/hr4173_enrolledbill.pdf.

U.S. Energy Information Administration (EIA). 2012. "Louisiana: Profile Overview." www.eia.gov/state/?sid=la.

Acknowledgments

I wish to thank John Wiley Global Finance Publishers in Singapore for giving me the wonderful opportunity to write this book. Thank you to my publisher Nick Wallwork and to my editors Emilie Herman and Gemma Diaz.

Mr. Dario Raffaele and Mr. Bill Dickens helped to make this book attractive to practitioners by collaborating to design and develop wind and hydropower case studies, respectively. These case studies can be found in the last two chapters of this book.

I wish to thank Suresh Pabbisetty—a former student in the *Certificate in Quantitative Finance* program and an *ERCOT* energy regulator—for his keen proofreading and industry feedback. In addition, I wish to thank the following individuals for their contributions to this book project: Vynogradov Dmytro V. of the *National Academy of Sciences of Ukraine*; Ezilarsan PKP, Founder of *Market Express Financial News and Research*; and Mohammad Asif of *JaZaa Financial Services*.

About the Author

Iris Mack, PhD, EMBA earned a Harvard doctorate in Applied Mathematics and a London Business School Sloan Fellow MBA. She is a former MIT professor. Dr. Mack is also a former Derivatives Quant/Trader who has worked in financial institutions in the U.S., London, and Asia. In addition, Dr. Mack has also spent some of her professional career at NASA, Boeing, and AT&T Bell Laboratories—where she obtained a patent for research on optical fibers (Mack, 1981).

Dr. Mack lectures and consults on Energy Derivatives, Quantitative Finance and High Frequency Trading for

1. *Fitch 7City Certificate of Quantitative Finance Program* in NYC
2. *Fitch 7City Corporate Finance Consulting Group* in Singapore
3. *The Terrapinn Group* in Singapore, Hong Kong, Indonesia, and London

In addition, Dr. Mack serves on various boards:

- *National Academy of Sciences Transportation Research Board*
- *The Edwin Moses Global Institute*
- *AlgoAnalytics Trading and Financial Analytics* (India)
- *MarketExpress Financial News and Research* (India)

Dr. Mack founded Phat Math Inc. and The Global Energy Post in Miami, Florida. In 2007 she and her colleagues at Phat Math launched their prototype mathematics edutainment social network PhatMath.com. Students in grades K-12 and college have access to free 24/7 online math homework help on PhatMath.com—named one of the Top 50 Social Sites for Educators and Academics and 25 Useful Networking Sites for Grad Students.

Dr. Mack has been an astronaut semifinalist, one of *Glamour* magazine's "Top 10" college students, one of *Glamour's* "Top 10" working women, an investment banker, an Enron Energy Trader, and an MIT professor. In addition, she was the second African-American female to earn a doctorate in Applied Mathematics from Harvard. Later she became a mathematics and business school professor, while simultaneously running a consulting firm.

About the Contributors

Bill Dickens designed and coauthored the hydro-electric power case study in Chapter 10. Mr. Dickens is an economist with nearly 25 years of professional experience as a researcher, instructor, op-ed columnist, and expert witness in hydro-electric economics, natural gas market fundamentals, smart grid technologies, and alternative energy supply resources. Prior to working for Tacoma Power, he was a staff economist for the Florida Public Service Commission (1998–2008) and a Member of the Florida Governor's Council of Economic Advisors (2000–2007). His graduate education in economics (1979–1986) was completed at American University in Washington, D.C. Mr. Dickens is a former W. E. B. Dubois Fellow at Harvard University (1987) and past HBCU Faculty Fellow at the Pentagon (1987–1998). He is a member of the International Association for Energy Economics, National Economic Association, Association of Christian Economists, and the American Association of Blacks in Energy. He is currently completing a new book titled, *Economics for the Hood: Hip-Hop Culture Meets General Equilibrium.*

Dario Raffaele designed and coauthored the wind power case study in Chapter 9. Mr. Raffaele is an ETRM professional, with energy trading front-office experience, and currently works for a leading management and technology consulting firm. Inspired by the field of finance, he has grounded his academic and professional training in this field. He holds a Master of Science in Finance and Investments from Rotterdam School of Management and has obtained the *Certificate in Quantitative Finance* designation. To this very day, Mr. Raffaele is driven by a strong interest for quantitative and modeling problems in the field of energy finance and is currently active with financial engineering research applied to the energy industry.

CHAPTER 1

Energy Markets Fundamentals

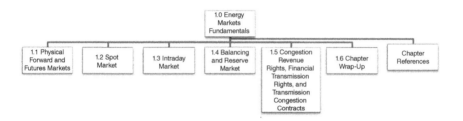

For sake of clarity, we will focus quite a bit of our attention on electricity markets because the generation and transmission of electricity are two of the primary reasons for the existence of energy markets. In addition, I have spent a part of my professional and academic career studying and working in the electricity markets (Mack 1986, 1999). However, please note that other energy products (oil, gas, etc.) will be discussed as well.

> *The generation and transmission of electricity are two of the essential reasons for the existence of energy markets.*

Power and energy are two words often confusingly interchanged. These two key terms are summarized in Figure 1.1 and more rigorously defined as follows:

- *Power* is the metered net electrical transfer rate at any given moment. It is measured in megawatts (MW). A watt is equal to one joule per second. The joule is a derived unit of energy, work, or amount of heat in the International System of Units.

- *Energy* is electricity that flows through a metered point for a given period and is measured in megawatt-hours.
- *Electric power* is the rate at which electric energy is transferred by an electric circuit. The instantaneous electrical power P delivered to a component is given by

$$P(t) = I(t) \cdot V(t)$$

Where $P(t)$ is the instantaneous power (measured in *watts*)

$V(t)$ is the potential difference (or voltage drop) across the component (measured in *volts*)

$I(t)$ is the current (measured in *amperes*)

MWh (megawatt-hour) is a unit of energy

MW (megawatt) is a unit of power

Consumer energy demand, load profiling and forecasting drive power generation and transmission. Specifically, power transmission patterns are determined by location and size of load. In addition, transmission congestion is responsible for significant price volatility in electricity markets and in fact is a primary market driver.

Electricity derivatives may be structured to protect market participants from exposure to price fluctuations, volume risks, high volatility, and so

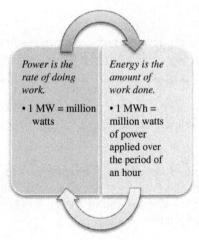

FIGURE 1.1   Power and Energy

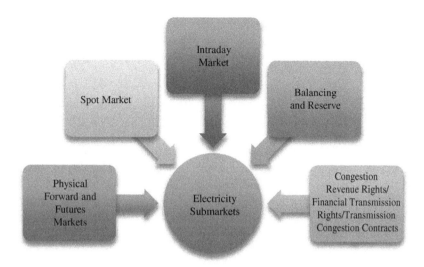

FIGURE 1.2   Electricity Submarkets

forth. Some examples of electricity derivatives are options, price swaps, basis swaps, futures, and forward contracts. We will discuss electricity derivatives and their pricing models in great detail in Chapters 3 and 4.

The electricity markets are segmented into the submarkets highlighted in Figure 1.2 (Burger, Graeber, and Schindlmayr 2007).

1. Physical forward and futures markets
2. Spot market
3. Intra-Day market
4. Balancing and reserve
5. Congestion revenue rights (CRRs), financial transmission rights (FTRs), and transmission congestion contracts (TCCs)

We will now take a closer look at these segments of the electricity markets.

1.1   PHYSICAL FORWARD AND FUTURES MARKETS

A *forward contract* is a nonstandardized contract between two parties to buy or to sell an asset at a specified future time at a price agreed upon today. An *electricity forward contract* can be either a financial contract or a physical contract (Figure 1.3).

- If a forward contract is settled before its maturity date, it is a *financial forward contract* since no electric power is physically delivered.
- A forward contract is a *physical contract* if the electric power is delivered physically.

The seller of a physical forward contract is obligated to physically deliver power to a location specified in the power contract (the hub). The forward contract does not specify the location at which the power is generated or consumed. However, the power contract states that the seller is responsible for delivering the power from the generator location to the hub, and the buyer is responsible for delivering the power from the hub to the load location. For both counterparties, this may involve purchasing additional transmission contracts, or purchasing/selling power through the spot market (Skantze and Ilic 2000).

A *futures contract* is a standardized contract between two parties to buy or sell a specified asset of standardized quantity and quality for a price agreed upon today with delivery and payment occurring at a specified future date. The contracts are negotiated at a futures exchange, which acts as an intermediary between the two parties.

A futures contract trader has two options, either to close the contract on or before the maturity date or roll over the contract. This roll over of contracts is referred to as a *swap* (Figure 1.4). With swaps, a trader would simultaneously execute two contracts, close the initial contract and open another longer term maturity date contract. Rolling over of contracts has some cost associated with it.

Electricity futures contracts are exchange-traded legally binding and negotiable contracts that call for the future delivery of electricity products.

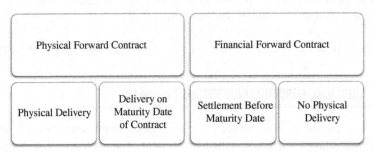

FIGURE 1.3   Forward Contract

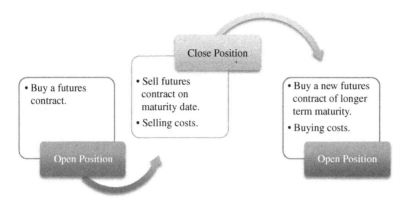

FIGURE 1.4   Swaps

Often times, physical delivery does not take place, and the futures contract is closed by buying or selling a futures contract on or near the delivery date (Stoft et al. 1998).

Forwards, futures, and swaps will be more rigorously defined and modelled in Chapter 3. However, for now the takeaway for the reader is the following:

- Forward contracts are bilateral agreements between a buyer and a seller. They are not exchange-traded.
- Futures contracts are standardized agreements. They are traded on an exchange.
- The forward and futures markets are key markets for trading, speculation, and risk management, allowing market participants opportunities to manage (hedge) price risks.
- The contract delivery dates or acceptance period of forward and futures markets includes dates occurring after the next trading day.

1.2   SPOT MARKET

The *spot market* is a commodities or securities market in which goods are sold for cash and delivered immediately. Contracts bought and sold on these markets are immediately effective.

Due to physical and financial constraints, there are relatively few players in regional electricity spot markets. Hence electricity markets are essentially oligopolies and not *free markets* as in the financial sense. Participants in North American electricity markets trade spot products on a power exchange or through an *independent system operator* (ISO). An ISO is a neutral operator primarily responsible for maintaining reliability of the electric power grid system (Figure 1.5). The ISO performs its function by controlling the dispatch of flexible power plants to ensure that loads match resources available to the system (ISO/RTO Council, 2001).

ISO

An ISO is a neutral operator primarily responsible for maintaining reliability of the electric power grid system. The ISO performs its function by controlling the dispatch of flexible power plants to ensure that loads match resources available to the system.

Please note that we utilize several schematic diagrams in this book to illustrate concepts and processes in the energy industry. We try to be consistent in these diagrams—with regards to symbols and directions of the arrows. However, the directions of the arrows may vary from diagram to diagram—depending on the context.

Key players in the electricity spot markets are listed in Figure 1.6. These market participants submit bids, generally on a *day-ahead* basis. *Day-ahead* products are the most common electricity spot products. A market maker clears the market and announces hourly settlement point prices. Trade on

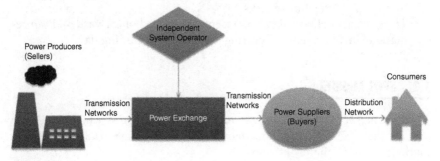

FIGURE 1.5   Role of the Independent System Operator (ISO) in the Electricity Markets

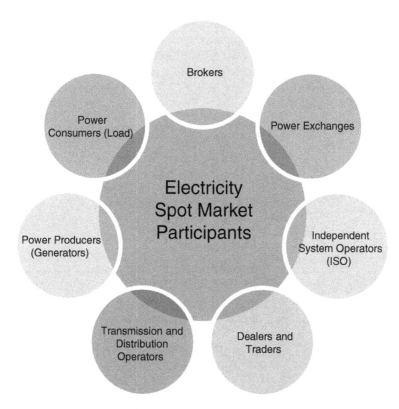

FIGURE 1.6   Spot Market Participants

the spot market is *physical*, meaning that physical delivery is expected. If a market participant defaults on delivery, it is required to pay the price differential between corresponding day-ahead market and real time market settlement point prices.

> *In the* day-ahead *market, electricity products are traded for the delivery on the next operating day.*

In the *day-ahead* market, electricity products are traded and delivered the next day. If the next day is not a trading day, then electricity products can be delivered between the next day and the next trading day. *Day-ahead* products are the underlying assets of futures contracts on a power exchange.

Electric power markets possess some of the characteristics of more matured commodity and financial securities markets. However there are some unique characteristics of the operation of the wholesale electric spot market that have implications for energy trading. Some of these unique characteristics are listed in Table 1.1 (KPMG 2006; Pilipovic 2007; Weron and Misiorek 2005).

TABLE 1.1   Some Unique Characteristics of Electricity Markets

Prices	Quantifiable exogenous variables that may affect electricity prices: ■ *Transmission constraints* ■ *Weather-induced demand spikes* ■ *Generator bidding patterns* ■ *Seasonality of load*
	Psychological and sociological factors may cause an unexpected buyout of certain contracts, leading to price fluctuations.
	Electricity spot prices exhibit strong *mean-reversion,* which is gravitation toward a "normal" equilibrium price level that is usually governed by the cost of production and level of demand. ■ Electric energy is a *secondary energy* source. ■ It's generated from the conversion of other *primary energy products*: oil, natural gas, coal, wind, nuclear, solar, hydro, etc. ■ Hence, the price of electric power is affected by the prices and availability of these primary energy sources.
Production, storage, and transmission	Volume and cost constraints on production, storage, and transmission of electricity. ■ Necessity for regional transmission networks prohibits the creation of a global power market. ■ Since there is *no global electricity market*, electricity products can vary from one regional electricity market to another.
	Electricity cannot be easily stored and must be available on demand. Exceptions are hydroelectricity (hydro-pumped power) and battery farms, which create storable energy.
	Storage constraints produce volatile day-to-day behavior.
	Nonstorability requires continuous balancing of supply and demand.
Volatility	Electricity spot prices can be much more volatile than prices of natural gas and other commodities.
	The high volatility of spot prices is a result of the nonstorability of electricity.

TABLE 1.1 (*continued*)

Market Maturity	Financial and some commodities markets are more mature.
Deregulation	Since the 1970s, some regional electricity markets have undergone significant restructuring, in part, due to market deregulation.
	Worldwide deregulation of electricity markets led to the restructuring of the generation, transmission, distribution, and pricing of electricity and other energy derivatives.
Seasonality of price process is multi-scale	▪ Intraday ▪ Weekly ▪ Monthly ▪ Annual
Non-normality of electricity spot prices (Figure 1.7)	▪ *Positive skewness:* Skewness or skew refers to the extent to which a distribution is not symmetrical. ▪ *Leptokurtosis:* The condition of a probability density curve to have fatter tails and a higher peak at the mean than the normal distribution.

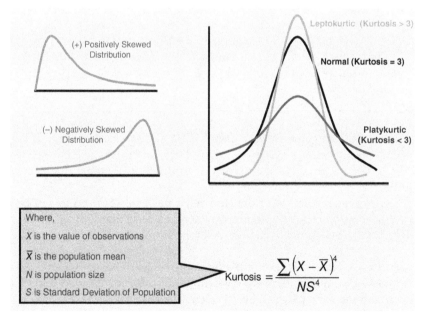

FIGURE 1.7 Nonnormality of Electricity Spot Prices Graphs

1.3 INTRADAY MARKET

The intraday market is for electricity products with a delivery on the same day. This market can be utilized to satisfy short-term needs of electricity or to sell short-term overcapacities. This market is also most commonly referred to as the *real time market*.

Energy market participants can utilize the intraday market as follows:

- To optimize their position to reduce risks associated with unexpected price fluctuations
- As a portfolio management tool

1.4 BALANCING AND RESERVE MARKET

Balancing and reserve markets are influenced by national regulation. In the *reserve market* an ISO is allowed to purchase electricity products to compensate for imbalances between supply and demand in the system. The *balancing market* allows electricity firms and traders to submit offers to sell and bids to buy energy from the system by altering generation or consumption.

> *The **balancing market** allows electricity firms and traders to submit offers to sell and bids to buy energy from the system by altering generation or consumption.*

Transmission system operators (TSOs) are entrusted with the task of guaranteeing power system security. They procure balancing services in the balancing or real-time market accordingly (Tractebel Engineering 2009).

Since the deregulation of the electricity markets, TSOs no longer hold power generation resources in direct ownership. To maintain the power system balance, TSOs procure balancing services from:

- *Power generators*—they are the main providers of balancing services.
- *Load*—through contractual switching-off schemes. Due to technical limitations, load plays a limited role in the balancing market.

Various types of balancing services are listed in Table 1.2.

TABLE 1.2   Types of Balancing Services

Primary Frequency Control	A joint action of generating units and loads spread evenly across an interconnected network.
	Local automatic control that adjusts generation and consumption levels to stabilize a power system frequency following a disturbance.
	Activated within 30 seconds.
Secondary Frequency Control	Goal is to bring the power system's frequency back to its target value following a disturbance.
	This control is supplied by the generating units located in the control area where the imbalance originated.
	Activated within 15 minutes.
Tertiary Frequency Control	Refers to all automatic or manual changes in generation and load levels.
	Assist secondary control in performing its task.
	Restore secondary control reserves, or optimally redispatch secondary control power according to economic considerations.

1.5 CONGESTION REVENUE RIGHTS, FINANCIAL TRANSMISSION RIGHTS, AND TRANSMISSION CONGESTION CONTRACTS

The following financial instruments are used by energy market participants to manage variability in congestion costs between one point and another, based on *locational marginal pricing* (LMP).

- Congestion revenue rights (CRR)
- Financial transmission rights (FTR)
- Transmission congestion contracts (TCC)

LOCATIONAL PRICE

Note: A power generator receives the locational price at the point where it injects power into the market. In addition, a load pays the locational price at the point where it withdraws power from the market.

Congestion revenue rights (CRR) are defined as financial instruments, made available through the CRR allocation, CRR auction, and Secondary Registration System, that enable CRR holders to manage variability in congestion costs based on the LMP. CRRs are acquired primarily, although not solely, for the purpose of offsetting integrated forward market congestion costs that occur in the day-ahead market (CAISO 2013).

Financial transmission rights (FTRs) are defined as financial instruments entitling an energy market participant to a stream of revenues (or charges) based on the hourly congestion price differences across a transmission path in the day-ahead market. FTRs allow energy market participants to hedge against their congestion costs by acquiring FTRs that are consistent with their energy deliveries (Kristiansen 2004; PJM 2013).

Transmission congestion contracts (TCCs) enable energy market participants to hedge transmission price fluctuations. A TCC holder has the right to collect or the obligation to pay congestion rents in the day-ahead market for energy associated with transmission between specified points of injection and withdrawal (NYISO 2013).

The financial contracts—CRRs, FTRs, and TCCs—are summarized in this section for the sake of completeness in describing the power submarkets. However, they will not be discussed any further in this book.

1.6 CHAPTER WRAP-UP

This chapter gives the reader an overview of how the electricity markets are segmented into the following submarkets.

1. Physical forward and futures markets
2. Spot market
3. Intraday market
4. Balancing and reserve
5. Congestion revenue rights (CRRs), financial transmission rights (FTRs), and transmission congestion contracts (TCCs)

The first two submarkets, involving physical forwards, futures, and the spot markets, lay the foundation for the subsequent chapters. These concepts will be defined more rigorously from a quantitative modeling perspective. In addition, I will provide a variety of examples and case studies to illustrate how these energy submarkets work.

REFERENCES

Burger, M., B. Graeber, and G. Schindlmayr. 2007. *Managing Energy Risk*. Chichester, England: Wiley Finance.

California ISO (CAISO). 2013. "Congestion Revenue Rights." www.caiso.com/market/Pages/ProductsServices/CongestionRevenueRights/Default.aspx.

ISO/RTO Council. 2001. www.isorto.org.

KPMG Energy Reform Implementation Group. 2006. "Review of Energy Related Financial Markets: Electricity Trading." www.ret.gov.au/energy/Documents/erig/Financial_markets_review_KPMG20070413120316.pdf.

Kristiansen, Tarjei. 2004. "Markets for Financial Transmission Rights." *Energy Studies Review* 13(1). http://digitalcommons.mcmaster.ca/cgi/viewcontent.cgi?article=1250&context=esr.

Mack, Iris. 1986. "Block Implicit One-Step Methods for Solving Smooth and Discontinuous Systems of Differential/Algebraic Equations: Applications to Transient Stability of Electrical Power Systems." PhD diss., Harvard University Press.

———. 1999. "Day-Ahead Lunch-Time Electricity Demand Forecasting: Applications to Electricity and Weather Derivatives." Master's thesis, London Business School.

New York ISO (NYISO). 2013. "Transmission Congestion Contracts." www.nyiso.com/public/markets_operations/market_data/tcc/index.jsp.

Pilipovic, Dragana. 2007. *Energy Risk: Valuing and Managing Energy Derivatives*, 2nd ed. New York: McGraw-Hill.

PJM. 2013. "Financial Transmission Rights." PJM Markets and Operation. www.pjm.com/markets-and-operations/ftr.aspx.

Skantze, Petter, and Marija Ilic. 2000. "The Joint Dynamics of Electricity Spot and Forward Markets: Implications of Formulating Dynamic Hedging Strategies." Energy Laboratory Report No. MIT-EL 00-005. http://web.mit.edu/energylab/www/pubs/el00-005.pdf.

Stoft, S., T. Belden, C. Goldman, and S. Pickle. 1998. "Primer on Electricity Futures and Other Derivatives." Environmental Energy Technologies Division: Ernest Orlando Lawrence Berkeley National Laboratory, LBNL-41098, UC-1321. http://eetd.lbl.gov/ea/emp/reports/41098.pdf.

Tractebel Engineering. 2009. "Study on Interaction and Dependencies of Balancing Markets, Intraday Trade and Automatically Activated Reserves, Final Report." Katholieke Universiteit Leuven, TREN/C2/84/2007. http://ec.europa.eu/energy/gas_electricity/studies/doc/electricity/2009_balancing_markets.pdf.

Weron, R., and A. Misiorek. 2005. "Forecasting Spot Electricity Prices with Time Series Models." International Conference of The European Electricity Markets EEM-05, www.mendeley.com/research/forecasting-spot-electricity-prices-time-series-models.

CHAPTER 2

Quant Models in the Energy Markets

Role and Limitations

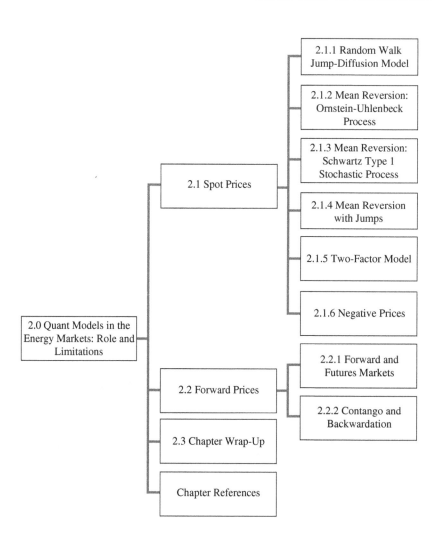

I n this chapter we will examine fundamental concepts of electricity price models. There are two common approaches to modeling electricity price dynamics:

1. Movements of the forward curve and behavior of forward prices
2. Spot price dynamics and derivation of forward prices from the model

Either approach may be employed. Properly calibrated, one can transform one method into the other (Riedhauser 2003).

> *It is important to have an understanding of the dynamics of electricity prices in order to develop effective trading and risk management strategies.*

It is important to have an understanding of the dynamics of electricity prices in order to develop effective trading and risk management strategies. Electricity—a secondary energy source—is generated from the conversion of other energy sources such as oil, natural gas, nuclear power, wind power, hydroelectric power, and so forth. Hence the price of electricity is affected by the prices of these primary energy sources.

There is no global electricity market. Hence, electricity products may vary from one regional electricity market to another. Since the 1970s some regional markets have undergone significant restructuring, in part, due to market deregulation. Worldwide deregulation of electricity markets led to the restructuring of the generation, transmission, distribution, and pricing of electricity.

As previously stated, there is quite a bit of political gridlock in Washington, D.C., over the implementation of the *Dodd-Frank Wall Street Reform and Consumer Protection Act,* and many regulatory issues are currently in flux. As a result, we will need to defer a more in-depth discussion of regulatory issues for a future edition of this book. However, for now, you should note that market deregulation eradicated electricity price constraints and led to the proliferation of financial engineering products for all of the following:

- Modeling electricity prices
- Forecasting electricity prices
- Trading energy products
- Structuring energy products
- Hedging market risks

2.1 SPOT PRICES

An *electricity spot transaction* is a physical transaction with nearby delivery of electrical power. The *spot price*, $S(t)$, is the current market price at which electricity is bought or sold for immediate payment and delivery. As summarized in Table 2.1, electricity spot prices exhibit unique features.

> **SPOT PRICE**
>
> The **spot price**, $S(t)$, is the current market price at which electricity is bought or sold for immediate payment and delivery.

Figure 2.1 illustrates the APX average monthly spot prices between 2000 and 2011. This data is utilized in a wind energy case study in Chapter 9.

> **STOCHASTIC (OR RANDOM) PROCESS**
>
> A **stochastic** (or **random**) process is the probabilistic counterpart to a **deterministic** process. It is a statistical process involving random variables that are dependent on a variable parameter (such as time).

A *stochastic* (or random) process is the probabilistic counterpart to a *deterministic* process. It is a statistical process involving random variables

TABLE 2.1 Unique Features of Electricity Spot Prices

Mean-Reversion	Seasonality	Spikes
This is the tendency of spot prices to converge toward their long-term level.	■ Electricity prices are influenced by various factors, such as business, economic, and weather conditions. ■ These factors are the primary cause of seasonality in electricity price data: intraday, weekly, monthly, and annual.	These are sudden increases in the amount of electricity that a system produces.

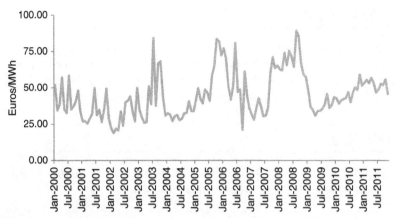

FIGURE 2.1   APX Historical Average Monthly Spot Prices
Source: APX Group (www.apxgroup.com/trading-clearing/apx-power-uk/).

that are dependent on a variable parameter (such as time) (Figures 2.2 and 2.3).

We will take a look at the following *stochastic processes* commonly utilized to model electricity spot prices:

- Random Walk *Jump-Diffusion* Model
- Mean Reversion: Ornstein-Uhlenbeck Process
- Mean Reversion: Schwartz Type 1 Stochastic Process
- Mean Reversion with Jumps
- Two-Factor Model

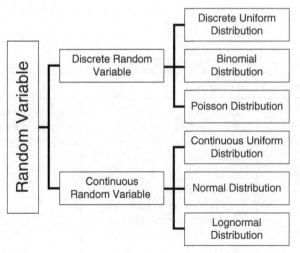

FIGURE 2.2   Random Variables of Stochastic Processes

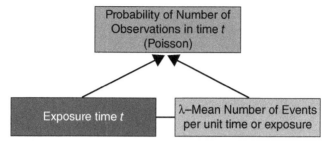

FIGURE 2.3 Poisson Process: A Type of Stochastic Process

Stochastic processes that are utilized to model electricity spot prices:

- *Random Walk* Jump-Diffusion *Model*
- *Mean Reversion: Ornstein-Uhlenbeck Process*
- *Mean Reversion: Schwartz Type 1 Stochastic Process*
- *Mean Reversion with Jumps*
- *Two-Factor Model*

In this chapter we will introduce some theory and intuition regarding the *stochastic differential equations* (SDEs), which are used to model electricity spot prices. Please don't feel you have to be a PhD mathematician to understand this chapter. If you wish to learn more about the stochastic calculus used to derive these SDEs, you may refer to Dr. Paul Wilmott's books on quantitative finance, such as *Paul Wilmott Introduces Quantitative Finance* (2007).

Note: Please keep in mind that the mathematical equations in this book are utilized to model various phenomena, based on certain finance and economic assumptions and data. They are in essence to be used as rules of thumb, *guestimates*, and guidelines. Common sense and understanding of the markets should also be taken into consideration when applying financial engineering models.

2.1.1 Random Walk Jump-Diffusion Model

Looking at the name of this model might make a novice want to stop reading right here. So before we introduce any mathematical equations, let us just try to understand the intuition behind this financial engineering model.

What is diffusion?

Diffusion is the scattering of molecular particles in the atmosphere. Diffusion works by transportation of molecules from higher concentration, more tightly packed, to lesser concentration. Molecules move this way naturally, so that a substance eventually becomes uniform in composition.

How does a diffusion process work?

An example of how diffusion works is by spraying cologne into the air. As the cologne spreads out into the air, it diffuses. Eventually its smell is very light and diminishes compared to how it smells if you sniff it directly from a bottle.

How do we make the leap from applying diffusion processes to problems in physics to those in finance?

The heat equation is used to model the diffusion of particles, heat, and various other diffusive processes. Diffusion processes have also been applied to model some phenomena arising in finance and economics: Black-Scholes options pricing model, the Ornstein-Uhlenbeck stochastic process, and so forth.

The heat equation is used to determine the three-dimensional spatial change with time in any function. For any function $u(x,y,z,t)$, the heat equation is given by:

$$\frac{\partial u}{\partial t} - \alpha \nabla^2 u = 0$$

Where $u(x,y,z,t)$ is a function of three spatial variables (x,y,z) and the time variable t

             α is a positive constant

             ∇^2 denotes the *Laplace operator*

What is a jump-diffusion process?

A *jump-diffusion process* is a stochastic process that involves jumps (spikes) and diffusion.

JUMP DIFFUSION

The **jump diffusion** process is a stochastic process that involves jumps (spikes) and diffusion.

Now let's consider the stochastic differential equation (SDE):

$$dS_t = \mu S_t dt + \sigma S_t dW_t \tag{2.1}$$

Where $S_t = S(t)$ denotes the spot price

$S_0 = S(0)$ denotes the spot price at time $t = 0$

μ denotes the *drift rate* of S_t

σ denotes the volatility (standard deviation) of S_t

$W_t = W(t)$ denotes a Brownian motion

The *stochastic drift* represents the annualized average return of the spot price.

The *drift rate* is denoted by the parameter μ. It is the expected return or rate at which the average spot price changes (Figure 2.4).

Brownian motion is the random movement of particles suspended in a liquid or gas, caused by collisions of molecules of the surrounding medium. This random movement is named after its identifier, Scottish botanist Robert Brown (1773–1858).

In mathematics, Brownian motion is described by the *Wiener process*, which is a continuous-time random process named in honor of Norbert Wiener. The Wiener process W_t has the following three key properties, which are utilized in developing some financial models:

1. $W_0 = W(0) = 0$
2. W_t is almost everywhere continuous.
3. Over finite increments of time t_{i-1} to t_i, $W(t_i) - W(t_{i-1})$ is normally distributed with mean zero and variance $t_i - t_{i-1}$.

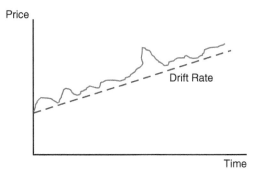

FIGURE 2.4 Drift Rate

The electricity spot price model (2.1) is a random walk jump-diffusion SDE, adopted from Merton (1976). It has a deterministic and a random component:

$$dS_t = \underbrace{\mu S_t}_{\text{Deterministic}} dt + \underbrace{\sigma S_t}_{\text{Random}} dW_t$$

Please note that a *random walk* is a mathematical formalization of a path that consists of a succession of random steps (Figure 2.5).

RANDOM WALK

A **random walk** is a mathematical formalization of a path that consists of a succession of random steps.

Via stochastic integration, which is discussed in Chapter 5 of *Paul Wilmott Introduces Quantitative Finance* (2007), the integral form of this Merton SDE is

$$S(t) = S(0)e^{\left(\mu - \frac{1}{2}\sigma^2\right)t + \sigma(W(t) - W(0))} \tag{2.2}$$

Due to the exponential nature of the solution to this random walk jump-diffusion SDE model, the electricity spot price can never get below

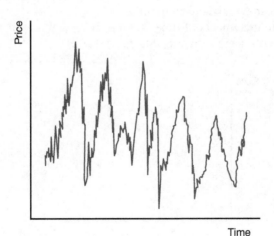

FIGURE 2.5   Random Walk Example

zero. The limitation of this SDE model is that it ignores the mean-reverting behavior of electricity spot prices (Kaminski 1997).

2.1.2   Mean Reversion: Ornstein-Uhlenbeck Process

Let's consider the stochastic differential equation (SDE):

$$dS_t = \alpha(\mu - S_t)dt + \sigma dW_t \tag{2.3}$$

Where $S_t = S(t)$ denotes the spot price

$S_0 = S(0)$ denotes the spot price at time $t = 0$

μ denotes the drift rate (expected return) of S_t

σ denotes the volatility (standard deviation) of S_t

$\alpha > 0$ denotes the *speed of mean reversion* and characterizes the velocity at which such trajectories will regroup around μ in time

$W_t = W(t)$ denotes a Brownian motion

This SDE (2.3) is the Ornstein-Uhlenbeck (OU) process—also referred to as the *Vasicek* process. It is a random process that models the velocity of a Brownian particle under the influence of friction. Over time, this process tends to drift toward its long-term mean (Figure 2.6). Hence, it is said to be *mean-reverting* (Ornstein and Uhlenbeck 1930; Vasicek, 1977).

The SDE (2.3) incorporates the tendency of electricity prices to gravitate toward a "normal" equilibrium price level that is usually governed by the cost of production and level of demand. Mean-reverting processes such as the SDE (2.3) embody the economic argument that when electricity prices are

- ■ "Too high," demand will decrease, and supply may increase, producing a counterbalancing effect.
- ■ "Too low," the opposite will occur, again pushing prices back toward some kind of long-term mean.
- ■ Please note that the electricity demand may not always decrease significantly even though the price is high. In addition, please note that the supply can increase if peaker power plants ("peakers") are brought online. Peakers are power plants that generally run only when there is a high demand, known as peak demand, for electricity.

A limitation of the application of the Ornstein-Uhlenbeck process to model electricity spot prices is that there is nothing that prevents S_t from becoming negative.

The SDE (2.3) has the following solution:

$$S_t = S_0 e^{-\alpha t} + \mu(1 - e^{-\alpha t}) + \int_0^t \sigma e^{\alpha(z-t)} dW_z \qquad (2.4)$$

A limitation of the application of the Ornstein-Uhlenbeck process to model electricity spot prices is that there is nothing that prevents S_t from becoming negative. Please note that we will discuss negative electricity prices in section 2.1.6. In addition, negative electricity prices are discussed in a wind energy case study presented in Chapter 9.

Some sample paths of different OU processes with $\alpha = 1$, $\mu = 1.2$, and $\sigma = 0.3$ may be found in Figure 2.6:

top curve: initial value $t_0 = 2$

middle curve: initial value normally distributed so that the process has invariant measure

lower curve: initial value $t_0 = 0$

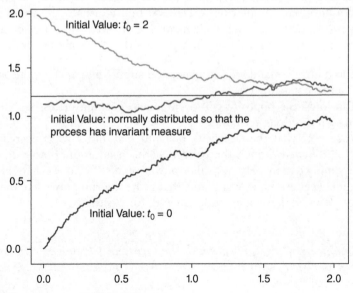

FIGURE 2.6 Ornstein-Uhlenbeck Process

2.1.3 Mean Reversion: Schwartz Type 1 Stochastic Process

Let's consider the stochastic differential equation (SDE:)

$$dS_t = \alpha(\mu_L - \ln(S_t))S_t dt + \sigma_L S_t dW_t \qquad (2.5)$$

Where $S_t = S(t)$ denotes the spot price

$S_0 = S(0)$ denotes the spot price at time $t = 0$

μ_L denotes the long-term average value of $\ln(S_t)$

σ denotes the volatility (standard deviation) of S_t

α denotes the *speed of mean reversion* and characterizes the velocity at which such trajectories will regroup around μ_L in time

$W_t = W(t)$ denotes a Brownian motion

The Schwartz type 1 model (equation 2.5) is a log price Ornstein-Uhlenbeck stochastic process. In this case, the mean reversion process is used to model the log of the electricity spot price. Hence, a log-spot less than zero still corresponds to a spot price greater than zero.

The SDE (2.5) has the following solution, as derived in Equation 2.6 (Huang 2012):

$$S(t) = \exp\left\{\ln(S_0)e^{-\alpha t} + \left(\mu_L - \frac{\sigma^2}{2\alpha}\right)[1 - e^{-\alpha t}] + \int_0^t e^{\alpha(x-t)}\sigma dW(x)\right\} \qquad (2.6)$$

This process is often utilized in electricity spot price modeling. However, it is normally *tweaked* to handle spikes in electricity prices, blackouts, seasonality, geographical regions of the national power grid, and so forth (Clewlow and Strickland 2000).

Example: During peak demand hours, the price of electricity can be very high. Conversely, during low consumption hours—late night for example—the price of electricity may be low. There can be huge variations in prices between peak hours and off-peak hours. To account for this variation, models may be tweaked to reach an adjusted normalized or time-diffused forecasted value.

2.1.4 Mean Reversion with Jumps

Let's consider the following stochastic differential equation (SDE):

$$dS_t = \underbrace{\alpha(\mu_L - \Phi\kappa_m - \ln(S_t))S_t\, dt}_{\substack{\text{Path of } S_t \text{ as a Mean-reverting} \\ \text{Process}}} + \underbrace{\sigma S_t dW_t}_{\substack{\text{Perturbations Induced} \\ \text{by Diffusion}}} + \underbrace{\kappa S_t dq_t(\lambda)}_{\text{Spikes (Jumps)}} \qquad (2.7)$$

Where $S_t = S(t)$ denotes the spot price

$S_0 = S(0)$ denotes the spot price at time $t = 0$

μ_L denotes the long-term average value of ln (S_t) (the logarithm of the spot price at time t)

σ denotes the volatility (standard deviation) of S_t

α denotes the *speed of mean reversion* and characterizes the velocity at which such trajectories will regroup around μ_L in time

$W_t = W(t)$ denotes a Brownian motion

$dq_t = dq(t)$ denotes a Poisson process with intensity λ that describes the jump occurrence

κ denotes a jump with log-normal distribution

κ_m denotes the mean jump size

γ denotes the jump volatility

$\Phi\kappa_m$ denotes the compensation term required to take into account the jump effect

In addition, the following relationship holds:

$$\ln(1+\kappa) \sim N\left[\ln(1+\kappa_m) - \frac{\gamma^2}{2}, \gamma^2\right]$$

The SDE (2.7) addresses key characteristics of spot price dynamics, namely mean-reversion and spikes. It takes into consideration the perturbations induced by the diffusion and the spikes with respect to the deterministic trend. The inclusion of jumps into this SDE leads to the loss of a closed-form mathematical solution, that is, a simple formula for its mathematical solution. Hence, computer algorithms are utilized to obtain numerical solutions to the SDE (2.7) (Clewlow and Strickland 2000).

2.1.5 Two-Factor Model

A two-factor model for electricity spot prices is discussed in (Birge, Ning, and Kou 2010). It is implemented to model the peak demand as a two-factor mean-reverting jump-diffusion process. This process attempts to describe two different mean-reverting features related to the normal peak and abnormal spikes in the demand.

The two-factor model was designed to capture some intrinsic features of electricity prices.

The two-factor model was designed to capture some intrinsic features of electricity prices, such as mean reversion, spikes, and seasonality. Numerical examples in (Birge et al. 2010) suggest that their two-factor model yields more reasonable results than the one-factor models. This two-factor model also incorporates the oligopolic feature of electricity spot markets.

2.1.6 Negative Prices

Thus far we have discussed stochastic models for which the electricity spot price can never get below zero. Some interesting points about negative prices for electricity are as follows:

- Have been observed for some time now in the United States, Australia, and Canada.
- Are a recent development in European power markets.
- Have been permitted at Germany's European Energy Exchange (EEX) spot market since autumn 2008.
- Are discussed in a wind energy case study presented in Chapter 9.

The primary cause of negative prices is the inability of certain generation units to ramp down power generation when there is no demand to consume all the power generated. The excess power can be consumed by artificial loads at a charge to ensure the reliability of the grid. Usually negative prices are not observed for more than five to six hours a day.

Negative prices pose a problem for some of the previously discussed stochastic models. A few suggestions for handling negative prices are as follows:

- The negative price issue is sometimes addressed with modeling by using daily average prices (which are mostly positive), or by adjusting the sample by removing some outliers.
- Schneider (2011/2012) presents a modeling approach based on the integration of the area of the hyperbolic sine transformation into stochastic price models. He suggests this transformation might be more appropriate for power spot prices than the previously discussed logarithmic transformation. This model is applied to spot modeling of the German EEX and the West Texas market of the Electric Reliability Council of Texas (ERCOT). An example of the valuation of an option is carried out.
- An empirical analysis of negative prices is presented in "Wind Power Integration, Negative Prices and Power System Flexibility" (Nicolosi 2010).

2.2   FORWARD PRICES

The *forward price* is a predetermined delivery price for an underlying commodity, currency, or financial asset decided upon by the buyer and the seller to be paid at a predetermined date in the future. At the inception of a forward contract, the forward price makes the value of the contract zero.

> *At the inception of a forward contract, the forward price makes the value of the contract zero.*

If a forward contract is settled before its maturity date, it is a *financial forward contract* since no electricity is physically delivered. A forward contract is a physical contract if the electricity is delivered physically. *Physical forward contracts* may be traded on an exchange or in a bilateral manner through over-the-counter (OTC) transactions.

The *forward price* can be determined by the following formula:

$$F(t,T) = e^{r(T-t)}S(t)$$

For *storable energy assets*, the forward price can be determined by the following formula:

$$F(t,T) = e^{(r+s-y)(T-t)}S(t)$$

Where r represents the risk-free interest rate

$S(t)$ represents the spot price of the underlying asset

$F(t,T)$ represents the forward price of the underlying asset at time t with maturity at T

y represents the convenience yield (benefit of holding the asset)

s represents the storage cost

2.2.1   Forward and Futures Markets

As previously discussed, forward contracts are similar to futures contracts (Figure 2.7):

- Futures contracts trade over exchanges. The details of a futures contract are listed below.
- Forward contracts trade in the OTC market (Figure 2.8).

FIGURE 2.7   Futures and Forward Contracts

The *futures market* is regulated and the forwards market is unregulated:

Unregulated versus Regulated Market

Unregulated	Regulated
Trading in the unregulated forward market is done by individual parties outside the purview of the exchanges. This is known as the *over-the-counter (OTC) market*.	Trading in the regulated futures market is done through designated commodity futures exchanges.

Note

The OTC market consists primarily of large commercial participants (e.g., airlines and oil companies) who use this market solely for hedging purposes.

A *futures contract* is a highly standardized financial instrument in which two parties enter into an agreement to exchange an underlying security (such as soybeans, crude oil, and ethanol) at a mutually agreed-upon price at a specific time in the future. Both the buyer and the seller have the right and the obligation to fulfill the contract's terms.

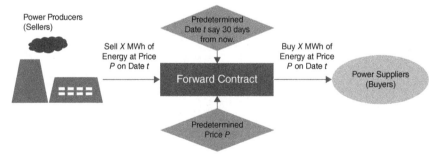

FIGURE 2.8   Forward Contract

The key details of a futures contract are as follows:

- Underlying asset: What asset does the contract represent?
- Quantity: How much of the asset is bought or sold?
- What is the last trading day of the futures contract?
- How is the futures contract quoted?
- What is the symbol for the contract?
- What exchange does the contract trade on?

Agricultural futures have traded since the 1860s. The first contract originated on the Chicago Board of Trade in 1865. *Energy futures* were not introduced until the 1970s. Futures contracts in the U.S. are mainly traded on the New York Mercantile Exchange (NYMEX), Chicago Mercantile Exchange (CME), and Intercontinental Exchange (ICE). Information on global exchanges can be found in Chapter 3.

2.2.2   Contango and Backwardation

When the forward price exceeds the spot price, the market is said to be in *contango*. Contango occurs when market participants anticipate any decrease in supply or increase in demand of the energy asset. To hedge against potential increase in prices in the future, market participants drive up the future prices and future prices would become more than the expected spot price (Figure 2.9).

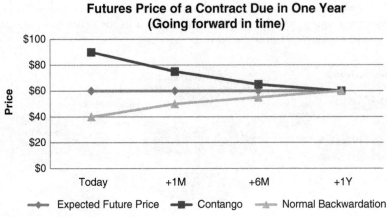

FIGURE 2.9   Contango and Backwardation

> *When the forward price exceeds the spot price, the market is said to be in **contango**.*

Just the opposite occurs in the case of *backwardation*. A backwardation market is when the spot price exceeds the forward price. When price declines are anticipated by the market participants, they drive the future prices further down to hedge against decreasing prices.

The futures market is in *contango* if $F(t,T) > e^{r(T-t)}S(t)$

The futures market is in *backwardation* if $F(t,T) < e^{r(T-t)}S(t)$

2.3 CHAPTER WRAP-UP

In this chapter we examined two common approaches to modeling electricity price dynamics:

1. The movements of the forward curve and the behavior of forward prices.
2. Spot price dynamics and derivation of forward prices from the model.

Either approach may be employed. Properly calibrated, one can transform one method into the other.

REFERENCES

Birge, J., C. Ning, and S. Kou. 2010. "A Two-Factor Model for Electricity Spot and Futures Prices." Texas Quantitative Finance Festival. http://www2.mccombs.utexas.edu/conferences/tqff/TQFF_Program.pdf.

Clewlow, L., and C. Strickland. 2000. *Energy Derivatives, Pricing and Risk Management.* London: Lacima.

Huang, A. 2012. "Remarks on Mean Reverting Processes." PG&E Quant Group. http://207.67.203.54/elibsql05_P40007_Documents/QUANT%20DOCS/MeanRevertHedgeB_pge_ts.pdf.

Kaminski, Vincent. 1997. "The U.S. Power Market." In *The Challenge of Pricing and Risk Managing Electricity Derivatives*, 149–171. London: Risk Publications.

Merton, Robert. 1976. "Option Pricing When Underlying Stock Returns Are Discontinuous." *Journal of Financial Economics* 3:125–44.

Nicolosi, Marco. 2010 (March). "Wind Power Integration, Negative Prices and Power System Flexibility—An Empirical Analysis of Extreme Events in

Germany." EWI Working Paper, No. 10/01, EWI Institute of Energy Economics at the University of Cologne. www.ewi.uni-koeln.de/fileadmin/user_upload/Publikationen/Working_Paper/EWI_WP_10-01_Wind-Power-Integration.pdf.

Ornstein, L. S., and G. E. Uhlenbeck. 1930. "On the Theory of the Brownian Motion." *Physical Review* 36(5): 823. doi:10.1103/PhysRev.36.823.

Riedhauser, Chuck. 2003 (January 3). "A Forward Curve Model Tutorial." PG&E PEC-Energy Procurement-Quantitative Analysis Group. http://pge.com/quant.

Schneider, Stefan. 2011/2012. "Power Spot Price Models with Negative Prices." *Journal of Energy Markets* 4 (Winter): 77–102. www.risk.net/digital_assets/6064/jem_schneider_web.pdf.

Vasicek, O. 1977. "An Equilibrium Characterization of the Term Structure." *Journal of Financial Economics* 5(2): 177–88, doi:10.1016/0304-405X(77)90016-2.

Wilmott, P. 2007. *Paul Wilmott Introduces Quantitative Finance*, 2nd ed. Chichester, England: Wiley Global Finance.

CHAPTER 3

Plain Vanilla Energy Derivatives

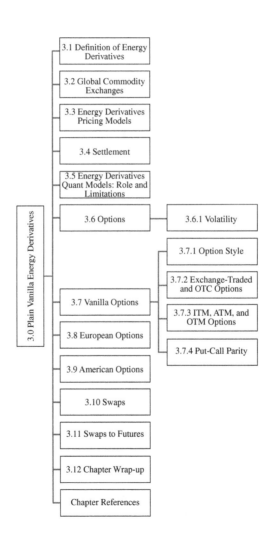

The term *derivative* has been tossed around quite a bit recently. If we've made any progress during the ongoing, seemingly endless financial crisis, it's that people now recognize the word derivatives. So what are derivatives? Why are they important in the energy markets?

In Chapters 3 and 4, we define, illustrate, and discuss various types of energy derivatives—plain vanilla and exotics. Then in subsequent chapters we examine the primary applications of these energy derivatives to

- Hedge or manage price risk
- Speculate or "gamble"

Energy generators wish to hedge their output to protect themselves against falling prices. End users wish to hedge against price increases for purchases of energy products. Financial institutions are essentially uninvolved in the physical energy markets. However, many large banks are active in the over-the-counter (OTC) and exchange-traded derivatives markets.

3.1   DEFINITION OF ENERGY DERIVATIVES

What are energy derivatives? Let's take a look at three different definitions. The first two definitions are more technical in nature. The third definition is from a regulator's perspective.

1. *Investor Words* defines an energy derivative as a derivative whose underlying asset is some type of energy product, such as oil, natural gas, or electricity. Energy derivatives may be options, futures, or swap agreements. They are used by speculators and by organizations that desire a hedge against fluctuations in energy prices.
2. The *Cambridge Dictionary* defines energy derivatives as financial products, such as options (i.e., the right to buy or sell something in the future), whose values are based on an energy product, for example, gas or electricity.
3. The *Markets in Financial Instruments Directive* (MiFID) defines energy derivatives specifically:

   MiFID Annex 1 Section C
   (5) *Options, futures, swaps, forward rate agreements and any other derivative contracts relating to commodities that must be settled in cash or may be settled in cash at the option of one of the parties (otherwise than by reason of a default or other termination event);*
   (6) *Options, futures, swaps, and any other derivative contract relating to commodities that can be physically settled provided that*

they are traded on a regulated market and/or an MTF (Multi-lateral Trading Facility);

(7) Options, futures, swaps, forwards and any other derivative contracts relating to commodities, that can be physically settled not otherwise mentioned in C.6 and not being for commercial purposes, which have the characteristics of other derivative financial instruments, having regard to whether, inter alia, they are cleared and settled through recognized clearing houses or are subject to regular margin calls. (Wasenden 2012)

ENERGY DERIVATIVE

An energy derivative is a derivative whose underlying asset is some type of energy product, such as oil, natural gas, or electricity. Energy derivatives include options, futures, and swap agreements.

3.2 GLOBAL COMMODITY EXCHANGES

Many energy derivatives are traded on global commodity exchanges. These exchanges—summarized by products—are listed in Table 3.1.

TABLE 3.1 Commodity Exchanges

Exchange	Products
New York Mercantile Exchange (NYMEX)	Coal, Crude Oil, Electricity, Natural Gas, Refined Products (www.cmegroup.com/trading/energy/) Please note that NYMEX was acquired by the CME GROUP.
Chicago Board of Trade (CBOT)	Ethanol (www.cmegroup.com/trading/energy/)
Intercontinental Exchange (ICE)	Coal, Crude Oil, Electricity, Emissions, Liquefied Natural Gas, Natural Gas, Refined Products (https://www.theice.com/products.jhtml)
NASDAQ OMX Commodities	Carbon, Power, Natural Gas (www.nasdaqomx.com/commodities/markets/products/)
International Commodity Exchanges (complete list)	www.commodityonline.com/commodity-exchanges/global-futures-trading-exchanges-and-website-address/

3.3   ENERGY DERIVATIVES PRICING MODELS

In the previous chapters we introduced two types of *plain vanilla* energy derivatives: futures and forwards. This chapter will be devoted to the definition and illustration of other plain vanilla energy derivatives products listed in Table 3.2. The *exotic* energy derivatives products listed in this table will be defined and discussed in Chapter 4.

> *A vanilla derivative has an expiration date and a straightforward strike price. The expiration date is the day beyond which a derivatives contract becomes void.*

TABLE 3.2   Commodity Derivatives

Plain Vanilla	Exotic
Futures	American Cash or Nothing Options
Forwards	Perpetual American Options
Swaps	Asian Options ■ Fixed Strike Asian Call Options ■ Average Price Options
European Options	Swing Options
American Options	Barrier Options
	Digital Options
	Swaptions
	Refineries as Real Options
	Multiasset Options ■ Compound Options ■ Baskets ■ Best-of ■ Worst-of ■ Spread Options
	Types of Spread Options ■ Spark Spreads ■ Crack Spreads ■ Basis Spreads ■ Natural Gas Transportation as a Locational Spread ■ Generation Assets as Strips of Spark Spreads ■ Natural Gas Storage as a Basket of Calendar Spreads
	Load Following
	Tolling

Note:

- An *exotic derivative* is one of a broad category of derivatives that may include complex financial structures.
- A *plain vanilla derivative* is any derivative that is not exotic. A vanilla derivative has an expiration date and a straightforward strike price. The date on which one has a right to exercise a derivative, if chosen to do so, is the *expiration date* or expiry.

3.4 SETTLEMENT

Exchanges would always prefer cash settled over physical delivery because it is much easier… Physical delivery requires a tremendous amount of work. . . . It's a real nightmare.

Rick Thachuk
President of Worldlink Futures Inc.
(McMahon 2006)

SETTLEMENT

Settlement is the act of fulfilling a derivatives contract. It can be done in one of two ways, as specified per type of contract: (1) physical delivery and (2) cash settlement.

Settlement is the act of fulfilling a derivatives contract, and can be done in one of two ways, as specified per type of contract: (1) physical delivery and (2) cash settlement.

1. **Physical Delivery**
   A derivatives contract is physically settled if the underlying asset is to be physically delivered in exchange for a specified payment.
   The processes to be followed by a depositor and a buyer while dealing with physical commodities through an exchange delivery process with the accredited warehouses and other service providers may be found in the NCDEX *Physical Delivery Guide* (2012).
2. **Cash Settlement**
   With cash settlement, the underlying asset is not physically delivered. Instead, the derivatives contract is settled for an amount of money equal to what the derivative's market value would be at expiration if it were a physically settled derivative.

> *Physical delivery of an underlying asset is common with commodities and bonds. However, in practice, it occurs only on a small percentage of contracts.*

In practice, physical delivery of an underlying asset occurs only on a small percentage of commodity contracts. The vast majority of contracts never go to physical delivery (MarketsWiki 2012; McMahon 2006; NASDAQ 2012).

As illustrated in Figure 3.1, most derivatives contracts are settled by purchasing a covering position, that is

- Buying a contract to cancel out an earlier sale (covering a short).
- Selling a contract to liquidate an earlier purchase (covering a long).

3.5 ENERGY DERIVATIVES QUANT MODELS: ROLE AND LIMITATIONS

The derivatives markets have exploded in the past few decades, transforming the financial and energy markets into a viral network of derivatives contracts. According to various sources, including the *Bank for International Settlements* (BIS) in Switzerland, the size of the global derivatives markets is estimated to be between 1.2 and 1.5 *quadrillion* dollars! (BIS 2012; Cohan 2010)

A large number of energy derivatives trade outside exchanges in the OTC market. Trading energy derivatives in the OTC market is not transparent

> According to various sources, including the Bank for International Settlements (BIS) in Switzerland, the size of the global derivatives markets is estimated to be between 1.2 and 1.5 quadrillion dollars!

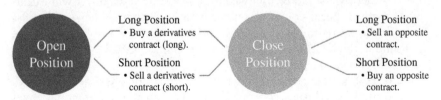

FIGURE 3.1   Derivatives Contract Closing

because these derivatives markets are not regulated. Hence, it is difficult to estimate the size of the OTC markets.

> *Trading in the over-the-counter (OTC) energy derivatives markets is not very transparent and these derivatives markets are not regulated. Hence, it is difficult to estimate the size of the OTC markets.*

BIS publishes data on global OTC derivatives trading volume for broad groupings of commodities. This BIS data may be used as a proxy for trends in the trading volume of OTC energy derivatives. Outstanding energy derivatives contracts were valued at approximately $3.1 trillion in 2011 (D'Ecclesia 2012).

A study of energy derivatives quant models would be incomplete without mentioning how Enron and other energy market participants utilized derivatives for purposes other than risk management. For example, Enron is on record for employing energy derivatives to misreport earnings, and hide debt—among other things.

When Enron imploded in 2001, some energy derivatives models made their way into mainstream news headlines, court cases, bankruptcy proceedings, and even Hollywood movies about Enron's collapse. There are several case studies and articles detailing Enron's use of derivatives and why they may have led to Enron's demise. The U.S. Energy Information Administration (EIA 2002) and McLean and Elkind (2004) have published some details as to how Enron and other energy traders utilized energy derivatives to misreport earnings and hide debt.

As the implosion of Enron illustrated, the applications of some quantitative models have fallen short in providing useful representations of energy problems. I became intimately familiar with the limitations of some of the derivatives models used by energy traders during my employment at Enron. I was exposed to limitations of quantitative models used to trade electricity, oil, gas, credit, and weather derivatives. Some of these model limitations were discussed in the previous chapter, and will be discussed further in this chapter.

Mathematical modeling involves "a heroic simplification of a problem using the minimum possible number of basic variables in order to come to grips with the essentials" (Wisniewski 1992). Ideally one wishes to develop an energy model framework that

- Enables abstraction based on logical formulations using mathematics.
- Is simple enough to allow data collection and analysis.
- Is practical and tractable in the sense that it serves as an aid to implement an energy application.

- Enables better visualization of the main elements of an energy problem.
- Forms a basis for communication, decreasing ambiguity and improving the chances of agreement on results.

3.6 OPTIONS

An option is a derivatives instrument whose price is derived from other assets, such as stocks, stock indexes, exchange-traded funds (ETFs), government securities, foreign currencies, commodities, gas, oil, electricity, and so forth. Options can provide trading and investment flexibility, such as tools for leveraging and risk management.

An energy option is a derivatives instrument whose underlying asset is some type of energy product, such as oil, natural gas, or electricity. It represents a contract sold by one party (options writer) to another party (options holder). The contract offers the buyer the right, but not the obligation, to buy or sell energy at an agreed-upon price (the *strike* or *exercise* price) during a certain period of time or on a specific date (*exercise date*).

ENERGY OPTION

An energy option is a derivative whose underlying asset is some type of energy product, such as oil, natural gas, or electricity. It represents a contract sold by one party (options writer) to another party (options holder).

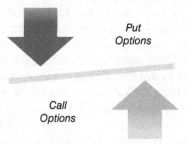

There are two basic types of options—puts and calls—defined as follows:

1. **Put Options:** The buyer of *put options* (*floors*) pays a premium for the right, but not the obligation, to sell energy at a specified price (the *strike* or *exercise* price) at a specified point in time.
2. **Call Options:** End users utilize *call options* (*caps*) to establish a maximum ceiling price (relative to an indexed price) that they will pay for energy at a specified point in time.

The following terms are key to understanding options. Additional key terms will be presented on an as needed basis (CBOE 2012; Risk Glossary 2012).

- **Strike Price:** The *strike price (exercise price)* is the stated price for which the underlying asset may be purchased (in the case of a call) or sold (in the case of a put) by the option holder upon exercise of the option contract.
- **Premium:** The option seller normally receives an *option premium* at the origination of the options contract. The *premium* is the price of an option contract, determined in the competitive marketplace, which the buyer of the option pays to the option writer for the rights conveyed by the option contract.

STRIKE PRICE

The strike price (exercise price) is the stated price for which the underlying asset may be purchased (in the case of a call) or sold (in the case of a put) by the option holder upon exercise of the option contract.

- **Underlying Asset:** Options are derivatives because their value is derived from the value of an underlying asset. This asset is subject to being purchased or sold upon exercise of the option contract.

  Examples of underlying assets are stocks, stock indexes, ETFs, government securities, foreign currencies, commodities, gas, oil, electricity, and so forth.
- **Payoff:** A payoff diagram is a graphical representation of the potential outcomes of an options strategy, as is illustrated in Figure 3.2. Profit or loss is graphed on the vertical axis, and various prices of the underlying asset are graphed on the horizontal axis. Results may be depicted at any point in time, although the graph usually depicts the results at expiration of the options involved in the strategy.
- **Volatility:** The volatility is a measure of the fluctuation in the market price of the underlying asset.

The **payoff** of a cash-settled option where the underlying asset is a commodity is the same as any other cash-settled call option.

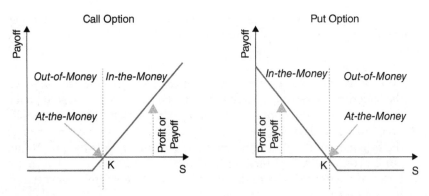

FIGURE 3.2 In-the-Money (ITM), Out-of-the-Money (OTM), and At-the-Money (ATM)

3.6.1 Volatility

Correct pricing of energy derivatives requires market participants to know what volatility is going to be. Energy prices have historically been more volatile than other commodity and financial asset prices. The main causes of these large price variations are disturbances in demand or supply.

The following factors impact supply and demand and contribute to energy price volatility.

- **Extreme weather conditions:** Extreme hot or cold temperatures will increase energy demand, driving costs up. Likewise, extreme weather conditions such as hurricanes can disrupt supply and also elevate costs.
- **Economic conditions:** Growing economies with increased infrastructure demands drive up energy demand and costs. Poorly performing economies often result in reduced demand and lower costs.
- **Availability of supply:** When there is a shortage of fossil fuels, other more expensive forms of energy generation will need to be used resulting in higher energy prices.

Various volatilities, as proxies, are used to estimate price volatilities:

- Actual
- Implied
- Forward
- Historical/Realized/Statistical

Actual volatility (AV) is the measure of the amount of randomness in an asset at any particular time. The AV is supposed to be an input into all option pricing models. It is a quantity that exists at each instant, that is, there is no *timescale* associated with AV.

Example: The AV is now 15 percent. . . . Now it is 20 percent. . . . Now it is 18 percent.

Implied volatility (IV) of an option is the volatility that, when used in the Black-Scholes option pricing model, yields the theoretical value equal to the current market price of that option. An important difference of modeling energy and commodity prices from stocks or asset spot prices generally is that the commodity spot is not tradable. This information needs to be incorporated when modeling IV.

Forward volatility (FV) is the volatility over a time period, or a future instant.

Historical volatility (HV) is the standard deviation of historical daily price changes (i.e., daily returns) over a specified deviation. Hence, the HV is a backward-looking measure of the amount of randomness over some time period in the past. One may estimate the HV by two different procedures:

1. Standard procedure
2. Zero-mean procedure

Some commonly utilized models for approximating volatility are

- *Constant Elasticity of Variance* (CEV) model
- *Generalized Autoregressive Conditional Heteroskedasticity* (GARCH)
- *Stochastic Alpha, Beta, Rho* (SABR)

These volatility models are based on the assumption that the volatility of the underlying asset is stochastic. The CEV model is especially utilized for modeling commodities. More details on volatility models may be found in

- "On Implied Volatility Reconstruction for Energy Markets" (Deryabin 2010)
- "Volatility Models for Commodity Markets" (Fackler and Tian 1999)
- "Forecasting Volatility in Commodity Markets" (Kroner, Kneafsey, and Claessens 1993)
- "Implied Volatility in Crude Oil and Natural Gas Markets" (Le 2009)

3.7 VANILLA OPTIONS

A *vanilla option* is a call or put option that has standardized terms and no special or unusual features. Vanilla options are generally traded on exchanges, such as those listed in Table 3.1. As we discuss in subsequent sections, vanilla options have well-known pricing models. *Exotic options* have more complex features and are generally traded over the counter.

VANILLA OPTION

A **vanilla option** is a call or put option that has standardized terms and no special or unusual features. Vanilla options are generally traded on exchanges.

3.7.1 Option Style

An *option style* refers to whether or not an option contract can be exercised before the expiration date or not. There are two styles of options:

- **European Options:** A *European-style option* may be exercised only at the expiration date, that is, at a single predefined point in time.
- **American Options:** An *American-style option* may be exercised at any time before the expiration date.

OPTION STYLE

An **option style** refers to whether or not an option contract can be exercised before the expiration date or not.

3.7.2 Exchange-Traded and Over-the-Counter Options

Options may be traded in two ways:

1. **Exchange-traded products on the commodity exchanges (listed in Table 3.1):** Holders of exchange-traded options may receive one of the following on exercise:
   - A cash settlement
   - A futures contract that can be cash settled
2. **Over-the-counter (OTC) products:** With OTC options, market participants may choose the characteristics of the options traded.

3.7.3   In-the-Money, At-the-Money, and Out-of-the-Money Options

The *intrinsic value* is the amount by which an option is in-the-money.

- The *intrinsic value of a call option* is the difference between the underlying asset price and the strike price.
- The *intrinsic value of a put option* is the difference between the strike price and the underlying asset's price.
- In the case of both puts and calls, if the respective difference value is negative, the intrinsic value is given as zero.

Suppose we denote $S_t = S(t)$ as the price of the underlying commodity at time t. Then in-the-money (ITM) is a term describing any option that has intrinsic value.

- A *call option is in-the-money* if the price of the underlying asset (S_T) is higher than the strike price (K) of the call, that is, $S_T > K$.
- A *put option is in-the-money* if the price of the underlying asset (S_T) is below the strike price (K), that is, $S_T < K$.

ITM, ATM, OTM

- **In-the-money** (ITM) is a term describing any option that has intrinsic value.
- An option is **at-the-money** (ATM) if the strike price of the option is equal to the market price of the underlying security.
- **Out-of-the-money** (OTM) is a term describing an option that has no intrinsic value.

An option is *at-the-money* (ATM) if the strike price (K) of the option is equal to the price of the underlying asset (S_T), that is, $S_T = K$. This term describes the *moneyness* of an option.

Out-of-the-money (OTM) is a term describing an option that has no intrinsic value.

- A *call option is OTM* if the price of the underlying asset (S_T) is less than the strike price (K) of the call, that is, $S_T < K$.
- A *put option is OTM* if the price of the underlying asset (S_T) is greater than the strike price (K), that is, $S_T > K$.

3.7.4 Put-Call Parity

Parity describes an ITM option trading for its intrinsic value; that is, an option trading at parity with the underlying asset. Also used as a point of reference, an option is sometimes said to be trading at a half-point over parity or at a quarter-point under parity. An option trading under parity is a discount option.

The *payoff* (Figure 3.3) of a cash-settled option where the underlying asset is a commodity is the same as any other cash-settled call option (Burger, Graeber, Schindlmayr 2007; Eydeland and Wolyniec 2003). More specifically, the *payoff for cash-settled options* is calculated as follows:

$$Parity_{\text{call option}} = Payoff_{\text{call option}} = \max\,[S_T - K, 0]$$
$$Parity_{\text{put option}} = Payoff_{\text{put option}} = \max\,[K - S_T, 0]$$

Where $S_t = S(t)$ denotes the price of the underlying commodity at time t
         T = the expiration date
         K = the strike (exercise) price

Note: Once the method of modeling the price S is chosen, the payoff of the physically settled option is the same as for the financially settled option (Eydeland and Wolyniec 2003).

Put-call parity defines a relationship between the price of a European call option and European put option—both with identical strike price, expiration date, and underlying asset. If the call option is ITM, then the put option is OTM, and vice versa:

$$C(t) = P(t) + S(t) - K \cdot B(t,T)$$

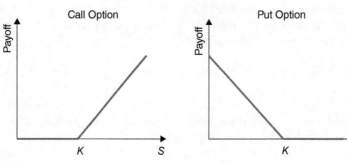

FIGURE 3.3   Payoff

Where $C(t)$ is the value of the call at time t

$P(t)$ is the value of the put at time t, that has the same expiration date as that of the call

$S(t)$ is the price of the underlying asset at time t

K is the strike price

$B(t,T)$ is the present value at time t of a zero-coupon bond that matures to \$1 at time T. This is the present value factor for K.

3.8   EUROPEAN OPTIONS

European options provide the foundation and framework from which other derivatives may be priced. Much has already been written about the derivation and the solutions to these types of options (Edyeland 2003). Hence, in this book we focus on illustrating how European options are applied in the energy markets.

The following are the five inputs to the European options pricing model —Equation (3.1) below:

1. Price of the underlying asset
2. Exercise (strike) price
3. Expiration date
4. Volatility of the underlying asset
5. Risk-free interest rate

$$C = \eta(SN(\eta d_1)e^{-qt} - Ke^{-rt}N(\eta d_2)) \qquad (3.1)$$

Where $$d_1 = \frac{\ln\frac{S}{K} + \left((r-q) + \frac{1}{2}\sigma^2\right)t}{\sigma\sqrt{t}}$$

$$d_2 = d_1 - \sigma\sqrt{t}$$

$$N'(x) = \frac{1}{\sqrt{2\pi}}e^{-\frac{1}{2}x^2}$$

$N'(x)$ is the normal density function

$$N(x) = \int N'(y) \cdot dy$$

$N(x)$ is the cumulative normal distribution function

C is the current value of option

S is the price of underlying asset

K is the exercise price

t is the time of expiration in years

σ is the annual volatility of the asset in percent

r is the risk-free interest rate

q is the continuous dividend yield

$\eta = 1$ for call options

$\eta = -1$ for put options

Equation (3.1) is the *Black-Scholes model* for pricing European options (Black and Scholes 1973). It is a *closed-form solution* for pricing European options. This pricing model can be expressed in terms of a finite number of certain well-known mathematical functions. The Black-Scholes model can be easily programmed and implemented on a trading floor.

Another famous closed-form solution for pricing European options is the *Black model*. It is a variant of the Black-Scholes model (Black 1976).

$$c = e^{-rT}\left[FN(d_1) - KN(d_2)\right]$$

Where C is the current value of option

           F is the futures price

           K is the exercise price

           T is the maturity of contract

           T' is the delivery date

           σ is the annual volatility on the asset in percent

           r is risk-free interest rate

           $N(\cdot)$ is cumulative normal distribution function

$$d_1 = \frac{\ln(F/K) - \left(\dfrac{\sigma^2}{2}\right)T}{\sigma\sqrt{T}}$$

$$d_2 = \frac{\ln(F/K) - \left(\dfrac{\sigma^2}{2}\right)T}{\sigma\sqrt{T}} = d_1 - \sigma\sqrt{T}$$

The corresponding put price is

$$p = e^{-rT} \left[KN\left(-d_2\right) - FN(-d_1) \right]$$

Some of the modeling assumptions and limitations of the Black-Scholes formula are listed in Table 3.3. It is often asked how one can rely on a mathematical formula such as the Black-Scholes with all its limitations as listed in Table 3.3. It is a formula "with a series of variables that are provably inaccurate and based on a flawed assumption, exponentially inaccurate variables, and outdated models about the nature of options." In spite of all the changes and advances in quantitative finance, the Black-Scholes model is still used by many as the benchmark for options pricing (Thomsett 2012).

> *In spite of all the changes and advances in quantitative finance, the Black-Scholes model is still used by many as the benchmark for options pricing. (Thomsett 2012)*

TABLE 3.3 Modeling Assumptions and Limitations of Black-Scholes Formula

Dividends	The underlying asset pays a constant dividend yield.
Exercise	The European option can only be exercised on the expiration date.
Interest	The risk-free interest rate is constant.
Margins	There are no margins.
Price	The price movements of the underlying asset follow a lognormal distribution.
Taxes	There are no taxes.
Trading	Trading in the underlying asset is continuous and has no price gaps.
Transactions	There are no transaction costs.
Volatility	The volatility of the underlying asset is constant.

3.9 AMERICAN OPTIONS

As indicated in Table 3.2, another group of options classified as vanilla options are *American options*. These are the most commonly traded options in the market. The exchange-traded energy options on the International Petroleum Exchange (IPE) and NYMEX are American options.

In Table 3.4 we summarize various models for pricing American options. With the exception of a few special cases discussed in Table 3.4, the derivatives pricing models for American options will not have closed-form solutions as we saw in the case of the models for European options. They will instead have *numerical solutions*, which are approximations that can be evaluated in a finite number of standard operations (Risk Glossary 2012).

TABLE 3.4   American Options Pricing Models

Type of American Option	Description of American Pricing Model
American Calls with No Dividends	One may utilize a mathematical model to price American calls without dividends. This is because it is never beneficial to exercise such options prior to expiry. The attribute of no early exercise means that such American options may be priced via the Black-Scholes option formula, where dividends are forced to zero.
American Calls with a Single Dividend (Roll-Geske-Whaley method)	American call options with a single dividend may be priced with the Roll-Geske-Whaley closed-form solution (Roll 1977).
American Options Approximation (Barone-Adesi and Whaley method)	This pricing model for American options is essentially a European option adjusted for an early exercise premium (Barone-Adesi and Whaley 1987).
American Options Approximation (Bjerksund-Stensland model)	There is evidence that the numerical approximation of American options by this pricing method is more accurate in pricing long dated options than the Barone-Adesi and Whaley (1987) method.
American Put Option Approximation (Geske-Johnson method)	This pricing model breaks down the problem so that the exercise of the American option can happen at three points in time over the life of the option and hence may be evaluated as three different options: (1) At expiration, utilizing the Black-Scholes model. (2) Halfway through the life of the option and at expiry. (3) One-third or two-thirds or at expiry during the life of the option. The weighted average of (1), (2), and (3) is the value of an American put option (Geske and Johnson 1984).

TABLE 3.4 (*continued*)

Type of American Option	Description of American Pricing Model
American Option Approximation (Ju-Zhong method)	Ju and Zhong developed an iterative model to improve on the models of MacMillan (1986) and Barone-Adesi (1987) for very short or very long dated option maturities (Ju and Zhong 1999).
Binomial Trees (Cox-Ross-Rubinstein formula; Rendleman and Bartter model)	In the Binomial Trees method, a tree lattice is constructed to represent the movements of the stock under geometric Brownian motion. The option is priced relative to the stock price through means of backward induction (Cox, Ross, and Rubinstein 1979; Rendleman and Bartter 1979).
Accelerated Binomial Tree (Breen)	Breen's model lies somewhere in between the CRR binomial tree and the Geske-Johnson put approximation method (Breen 1991).
Trinomial Tree (Boyle)	The Trinomial Tree methodology is similar to the binomial method. This method also employs a lattice-type method for pricing options by using a three-pronged path compared to the two-pronged path used with Binomial Trees. This enables the trinomial method to converge to accurate values faster than its binomial counterpart.
Jump-Diffusion (Merton)	In Merton (1976), a European option pricing formula is derived when the underlying asset returns are generated by a combination of continuous and jump processes. Several authors have suggested ways to price American-style options with jumps (d'Halluin, Forsyth, and Labahn 2004).
Monte Carlo Simulation	Several authors have developed models that utilize quasi-Monte Carlo simulation to price American options: Broadie and Detemple (1996); Caflisch (1998); Caflisch, Morokoff, and Owen (1997); and Longstaff and Schwartz (2001).
Finite Differences Method (Brennan and Schwartz)	Numerical algorithms, such as finite difference methods, may be applied to price American options. By incorporating an early exercise "test" within a numerical algorithm, one can determine the value of an American option as given by a stochastic partial differential equation and its initial and boundary conditions using Crank-Nicolson numerical methods (Brennan and Schwartz 1978).
Other Computational Methods	It is quite difficult to find closed-form analytical solutions to price American options. Hence, quite a bit of research has gone into developing numerical approximations to the price of American options (Broadie and Detemple 1996; Caporale and Cerrato 2005; Carr and Faguet 1996; Figlewski, Gao, and Ahn 1999; Johnson 1983).

3.10   SWAPS

A *swap* is a derivative contract in which counterparties exchange an asset (or liability) for a similar asset (or liability) for two purposes:

1. Lengthening (or shortening) maturities
2. Raising (or lowering) coupon rates to maximize revenue or minimize financing costs

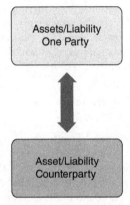

SWAP

A swap is a derivatives contract in which counterparties exchange an asset (or liability) for a similar asset (or liability).

Swaps are not exchange-traded instruments. They are customized contracts that are traded in the OTC market between private parties. Because swaps occur on the OTC market, there is risk that one of the counterparties may default on the swap.

Example: A *financial swap* is a derivative contract in which counterparties exchange cash flows of one party's financial instrument for those of the other party's financial instrument.

FINANCIAL SWAP

A financial swap is a derivative contract in which counterparties exchange cash flows of one party's financial instrument for those of the other party's financial instrument.

Swaps are also referred to as

- Contracts for differences
- Fixed for floating contracts

Note that the differences may be settled in cash for specific periods: monthly, quarterly, bi-annually, or annually.

A *plain vanilla energy swap* is very similar to a financial swap. It is a derivatives contract in which counterparties exchange a floating price for a fixed price over a specified period of time. In addition, the plain vanilla energy swap is an off-balance sheet contract that involves no transfer of the energy commodity; it is financially settled (Figure 3.4).

PLAIN VANILLA ENERGY SWAP

A **plain vanilla energy swap** is a derivatives contract in which counterparties exchange a floating price for a fixed price over a specified period of time.

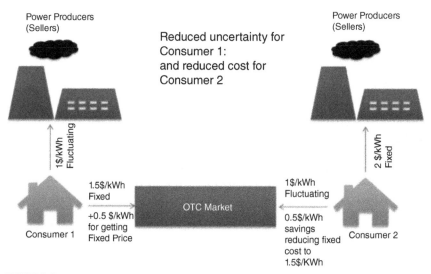

FIGURE 3.4 Plain Vanilla Energy Swap

Key components of a plain vanilla swap contract

- Duration
- Fixed price
- Floating price
- Volume

3.11 SWAPS TO FUTURES

Energy swaps have traded on the Intercontinental Exchange (ICE) trading platform for more than a decade. However, due to the Dodd-Frank Wall Street Reform and Consumer Protection Act, ICE converted its cleared energy swap contracts to economically equivalent futures contracts in October 2012. These products will continue to be listed and traded in the same manner on the ICE platform and cleared at ICE Clear Europe (ICE 2011, 2012).

3.12 CHAPTER WRAP-UP

In this chapter we defined, illustrated, and discussed various types of plain vanilla energy derivatives, as listed in Table 3.2. Also, we listed the global commodities exchanges where some of these energy derivatives are traded. Finally, in subsequent chapters we will examine applications of these energy derivatives to

- Hedge or manage energy price risk
- Speculate or gamble in the energy markets

REFERENCES

Bank for International Settlements (BIS). 2012. "Exchange Traded Derivatives Statistics." www.bis.org/statistics/extderiv.htm.

Barone-Adesi, G., and R. Whaley. 1987. "Efficient Analytic Approximation of American Option Values." *Journal of Finance* 42(2): 301–320.

Black, Fischer, and Myron Scholes. 1973. "The Pricing of Options and Corporate Liabilities." *Journal of Political Economy* 81(3): 637–654. https://www.cs.princeton.edu/courses/archive/fall02/cs323/links/blackscholes.pdf.

Black, Fischer. 1976. "The Pricing of Commodity Contracts." *Journal of Financial Economics* 3: 167–179. http://ideas.repec.org/a/eee/jfinec/v3y1976i1-2p167-179.html.

Breen, R. 1991. "The Accelerated Binomial Option Pricing Model." *Journal of Financial and Quantitative Analysis* 26: 153–64.

Brennan, M., and E. Schwartz. 1978. "Finite Difference Methods and Jump Processes Arising in the Pricing of Contingent Claims." *Journal of Finance and Quantitative Analysis* 13:462–74.

Broadie, M., and J. Detemple. 1996. "American Option Valuation: New Bounds, Approximations, and a Comparison of Existing Methods." *Review of Financial Studies* 9(4): 1211–50.

Burger, M., B. Graeber, and G. Schindlmayr. 2007. *Managing Energy Risk*. Chichester, England: Wiley Finance.

Caflisch, R. 1998. "Monte Carlo and Quasi-Monte Carlo Methods." *Acta Numerica*: 1–49.

Caflisch, R., W. Morokoff, and A. B. Owen. 1997. "Valuation of Mortgage-Backed Securities Using Brownian Bridges to Reduce Effective Dimension." *Journal of Computational Finance* 1: 27–46.

Caporale, G., and M. Cerrato. 2005 (February). "Valuing American Put Options Using Chebyshev Polynomial Approximation." London Metropolitan University Working Paper.

Carr, P., and D. Faguet. 1996. "Fast Accurate Valuation of American Options." Working Paper, Cornell University, Ithaca, NY.

Chicago Board Options Exchange (CBOE). 2012. "Options Dictionary." www.cboe.com/LearnCenter/Glossary.aspx.

Cohan, Peter. 2010. "Big Risk: $1.2 Quadrillion Derivatives Markets Dwarfs World GDP." www.dailyfinance.com/2010/06/09/risk-quadrillion-derivatives-market-gdp/.

Cox, J., S. Ross, and M. Rubinstein. 1979. "Option Pricing: A Simplified Approach." *Journal of Financial Economics* 7 (September): 229–263.

D'Ecclesia, Rita. 2012. "Commodities and Commodity Derivatives: Energy Markets." www.ems.bbk.ac.uk/for_students/msc_finance/comm1_emec054p/energy_12.pdf.

d'Halluin, Y., P. A. Forsyth, and G. Labahn. 2004. "A Penalty Method for American Options with Jump Diffusion Processes." *Numerische Mathematik* 97(2): 321–352.

Deryabin, Mikhail. 2010. "On Implied Volatility Reconstruction for Energy Markets." *International Journal of Human and Social Sciences* 5:13. www.waset.org/journals/ijhss/v5/v5-13-128.pdf.

Eydeland, A., and K. Wolyniec. 2003. *Energy and Power: Risk Management*. Hoboken, NJ: Wiley Finance.

Fackler, P. L., and Y. Tian. 1999. "Volatility Models for Commodity Markets." Proceedings of the NCR-134 Conference on Applied Commodity Price Analysis, Forecasting, and Market Risk Management. Chicago, IL. www.farmdoc.illinois.edu/nccc134/conf_1999/pdf/confp16-99.pdf.

Figlewski S., B. Gao, and D. H. Ahn. 1999. "Pricing Discrete Barrier Options with an Adaptive Mesh Model." Journal of Derivatives 6(4): 33–43.

Geske, R., and H. E. Johnson. 1984. "The American Put Option Valued Analytically." *Journal of Finance* 39: 1511–1524.

Intercontinental Exchange (ICE). 2011. "Delisting of Cleared Only Swaps." https://www.theice.com/publicdocs/futures_us/exchange_notices/ExNotDelistingSwaps.pdf.

———. 2012. "Swaps to Futures." https://www.theice.com/s2f_products.jhtml.

Johnson, H. 1983. "An Analytical Approximation for the American Put Price." *Journal of Financial & Quantitative Analysis* 18: 141–48.

Ju, N., and R. Zhong. 1999. "An Approximate Formula for Pricing American Options." *Journal of Derivatives* 7(2): 31–40.

Kroner, Kenneth F., Devin P. Kneafsey, and Stijn Claessens. 1993. "Forecasting Volatility in Commodity Markets." Research Working Paper WPS 1226, *The World Bank*. http://econ.worldbank.org/external/default/main?pagePK=641 65259&theSitePK=469072&piPK=64165421&menuPK=64166322&entit yID=000009265_3961005141748.

Le, Duong. 2009. "Implied Volatility in Crude Oil and Natural Gas Markets." *ResearchGate*. www.researchgate.net/publication/228425050_Implied_Volatility_in_Crude_Oil_and_Natural_Gas_Markets.

Longstaff, F. A., and E. S. Schwartz. 2001. "Valuing American Options by Simulation: A Simple Least-Squares Approach." *Review of Financial Studies* 14(1): 113–147.

MacMillan, W. 1986. "Analytic Approximation for the American Put Option." *Advances in Futures and Options Research* 1:119–139.

MarketsWiki. 2012. "Physical Delivery." www.marketswiki.com/mwiki/Physical_delivery#cite_note-0.

McLean, Bethany, and Peter Elkind. 2004. *The Smartest Guys in the Room: The Amazing Rise and Scandalous Fall of Enron.* New York: Penguin Books.

McMahon, Chris. 2006. "Financial Settlement vs. Physical Delivery." *Futures.* www.futuresmag.com/2006/07/25/financial-settlement-vs-physical-delivery.

Merton, R. 1976. "Option Pricing When Underlying Stock Returns are Discontinuous." *Journal of Financial Economics* 3: 125–144.

NCDEX. 2012. *Physical Delivery Guide*, v 1.1. www.ncdex.com/Downloads/ClearingServices/PDF/Physical_delivery_Guide_15022012.pdf.

Rendleman, R., and B. Bartter. 1979. "Two-State Option Pricing." *Journal of Finance* 34: 1093–1110.

Roll, R.. 1977., "An Analytic Valuation Formula for Unprotected American Call Options on Stocks with Known Dividends." *Journal of Financial Economics* 5:, 251–258, 1977.

Thomsett, Michael., 2012. "Black-Scholes—The Wrong Assumptions Make This Model Fatally Flawed—Updated." *Thomsett Options.*, http://thomsettoptions.com/black-scholes-the-wrong-assumptions-make-this-model-fatally-flawed-updated/, 2012.

U.S. Energy Information Administration (EIA). 2002. "Derivatives and Risk Management in the Petroleum, Natural Gas, and Electricity Industries." www.eia.gov/oiaf/servicerpt/derivative/chapter3.html.

Wasenden, Odd-Harald, 2012. "Supervision and Regulation of Energy Derivatives Trading: An Introduction to the Main Legislation and Some of the Challenges in Practice.," *Florence School of Regulation*, Brussels, May 23, 2012. http://www.florence-school.eu/portal/page/portal/FSR_HOME/ENERGY/Policy_Events/Workshops/2012/EU%20Energy%20Law%20%20Policy/120523_Wasenden_Odd-Harald.pdf.

Wisniewski, D., 1992. "Mathematical Models and Measurement.," *Rasch Measurement Transactions*, 5(:4): p. 184, 1992.

CHAPTER 4

Exotic Energy Derivatives

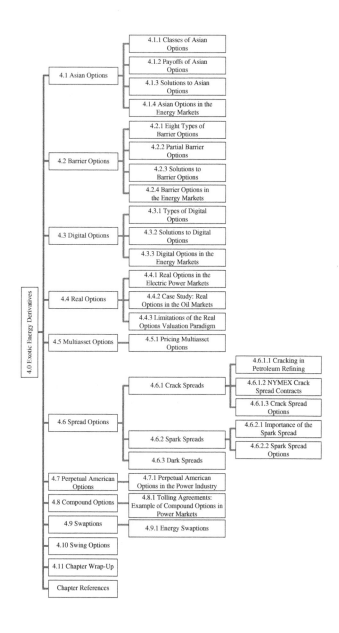

In the previous chapter we discussed plain vanilla energy derivatives. In this chapter we will discuss the various types of exotic energy derivatives listed in Table 3.2. Recall that an *exotic derivative* was defined to be any of a broad category of derivatives that may include complex financial structures. A more detailed definition of exotic derivatives—from Section C (10) of Annex 1 to the Markets in Financial Instruments Directive (MiFID)—is as follows:

> *Options, futures, swaps, forward rate agreements and any other derivative contracts relating to climatic variables, freight rates, emission allowances or inflation rates or other official economic statistics that must be settled in cash or may be settled in cash at the option of one of the parties (otherwise than by reason of a default or other termination event), as well as any other derivative contracts relating to assets, rights, obligations, indices and measures not otherwise mentioned in this Section, which have the characteristics of other derivative financial instruments, having regard to whether, inter alia, they are traded on a regulated market or a multilateral trading facility (MTF), are cleared and settled through recognized clearing houses or are subject to regular margin call. (Pointon 2006; Wasenden 2012)*

Exotic derivatives have more complex features than commonly traded plain vanilla derivatives, normally relating to determination of payoff. As we see from the MiFID definition, exotics may also include derivatives with a nonstandard underlying, structured for a particular client or a particular market. Other characteristics of exotic derivatives are the following:

- In most cases the pricing of an exotic derivative is not trivial.
- Some exotic derivatives are modeled utilizing numerical simulation or lattice-based methodologies.
- Some exotic derivatives may be structured from plain vanilla derivatives. This approach may allow for a benchmark against which the exotic derivatives may be calibrated.
- Hedging is often more complicated for exotics than for plain vanilla derivatives, as we will discuss in Chapters 5, 6, and 9.
- Trading of exotic derivatives in secondary markets is illiquid or nonexistent.

4.1 ASIAN OPTIONS

Asian options were first introduced in Tokyo, Japan, in 1987. David Spaughton and Mark Standish—employees of Bankers Trust—were in Tokyo on business when they developed the first commercially used pricing formula for options linked to the average price of crude oil. Because they were in Asia at the time, they called the options "Asian options" (Falloon and Turner 1999; Palmer 2010).

The terminal value of Asian options depends upon the value of the underlying asset, not only on the expiration date, but also at points in time prior to expiry. Hence, Asian options are *path-dependent options*. Path-dependent options are options in which the payoff depends on the average of a sequence of the prices of the underlying asset over some predetermined period of time. This sequence or pattern is the path that determines the value of the option dependent on it (Figure 4.1).

PATH-DEPENDENT OPTIONS

Path-dependent options are options in which the payoff depends on the average of a sequence of the prices of the underlying asset over some predetermined period of time. This sequence or pattern is the path that determines the value of the option dependent on it.

4.1.1 Classes of Asian Options

Asian options are also known as

- Average value options
- Average rate options
- Average price options

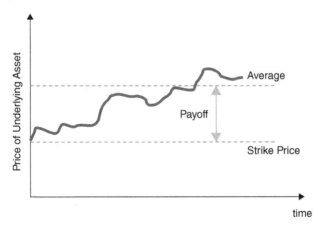

FIGURE 4.1 Asian Call Option

There are two main classes of Asian options:

1. *Floating-strike* Asian options pay the difference between the average price of the underlying energy asset and the spot price of the underlying asset.
2. *Fixed-strike* Asian options pay the difference between the average price of the underlying energy asset and the prespecified strike price.

Asian options may also be classified as follows:

- *Discrete Asian options*—the average is calculated from the underlying asset's prices at discrete times.
- *Continuous Asian options*—all the underlying asset's prices on the real line are used in the calculation of the average.
- *Forward-start Asian options*—A forward-start option is the advance purchase of a put or call option with a strike price that will be determined at a later date, typically when the option becomes active. Although a forward-start option becomes active at a specified date in the future, the premium is paid in advance. In addition, the time to expiration and the underlying asset are established at the time the forward-start option is purchased. Two features are combined in forward-start Asian options: averaging the underlying price and postponing the starting date to the future. Forward-start Asian options are sometimes utilized in energy markets. (Eydeland and Wolyniec, 2003)

4.1.2   Payoffs of Asian Options

The payoffs of Asian options depend on

- The path taken by the underlying asset on a specific set of dates during the life of the option
- A weighted combination (arithmetic or geometric averages; weighted arithmetic or weighted geometric averages) of events through a certain period of time

A discrete fixed-strike Asian call option with fixing dates $T_1, T_2, \ldots T_n$ may have the following payoff at time $T \geq T_n$

$$\text{Payoff} = \max \left[m(T) - K, 0 \right],$$

Where K = strike price

$m(T)$ is the arithmetic mean of the spot prices of the underlying energy asset

$$m(T) = \frac{1}{n} \sum_{i=1}^{n} S(T_i)$$

4.1.3 Solutions to Asian Options

Exact closed-form analytical solutions do not exist for Asian options. This is primarily due to the fact that the weighted average of a set of lognormal random variables has a distribution that is largely intractable. Some analytic and numerical approximations of solutions to Asian options are discussed in Burger, Graeber, and Schindlmayr (2007); Curran (1992); Eydeland and Wolyniec (2003); Haug (2006a); Kemna and Vorst (1990); Klassen (2001); Levy (1992); Riedhauser (2001b, 2004); Shu (2006); Taleb (1997); Thoren (2005); Turnbull and Wakeman (1991); and Vorst (1992).

4.1.4 Asian Options in the Energy Markets

Advantages of Asian options in the energy markets include the following:

- They are popular in hedging periodic cash flows because they cost less than plain vanilla options on the same underlying assets.
- Asian options are cheaper than plain vanilla options because the arithmetic mean has a lower volatility compared to the underlying asset at a single point in time.
- Asian options can mitigate the possibility of spot price manipulations or spikes in the underlying prices at settlement.
- Floating-strike Asian options allow the option holder to make daily decisions about buying or selling spot gas or power at a strike price determined at the beginning of the month as a settled value of the monthly index.
- Floating-strike Asian options are used very often in the energy markets, because they may be used to manage price risks on a daily basis.
- Energy is normally delivered over a period of time, requiring that price risk be hedged over this specified time period. Asian options are commonly utilized for such hedging in energy markets.
- We present an application of Asian options in a renewable energy case study in Chapter 9.

4.2 BARRIER OPTIONS

BARRIER OPTION

A barrier option is also path-dependent. Its value changes if the underlying asset reaches or surpasses a specified price.

TABLE 4.1   Barrier Options

	Knockout Barrier Options	Knock-In Barrier Options
Price ⬇	*Down-and-out* puts and calls These options give the holder the right but not the obligation to buy or sell an underlying asset at a pre-determined strike price so long as the price of that asset did not go below a pre-determined barrier during the option lifetime. More specifically, once the price of the underlying asset falls below the barrier, the option is knocked-out and no longer carries any value.	*Down-and-in* puts and calls These options are the opposite of down-and-out barrier options. They only have value if the price of the underlying asset falls below the barrier during the options lifetime. If the barrier is crossed the holder of the down-and-in option has the right to buy or sell an underlying asset at the predetermined strike price on the expiration date.
Price ⬆	*Up-and-out* puts and calls These options are similar to down-and-out barrier options. Up-and-out options are knocked out if the price of the underlying asset rises *above* the predetermined barrier.	*Up-and-in* puts and calls These options are similar to down-and-in options. The barrier is placed above the current price of the underlying asset and the option will only be valid if the price of the underlying asset reaches the barrier before expiration.

Where S is the price of the underlying asset, and
B is a barrier.

A ***barrier option*** is also path-dependent. Its value changes if the underlying asset reaches or surpasses a specified price. The option's value at expiration depends upon both the value of the underlying asset at expiration and on whether past values of the underlying asset has hit a barrier.

Barrier options have the following two features—as detailed in Table 4.1:

1. *Knockout*—a feature that causes the option to immediately terminate if the underlying asset reaches a certain barrier level.
2. *Knock-in*—a feature that causes the option to become effective only if the underlying asset first reaches a certain barrier level.

4.2.1   Eight Types of Barrier Options

There are eight types of barrier options. Four of these options knock-in (or knockout) when they are in-the-money. The eight types of barrier options—defined in Table 4.1—are available in the over-the-counter (OTC) energy

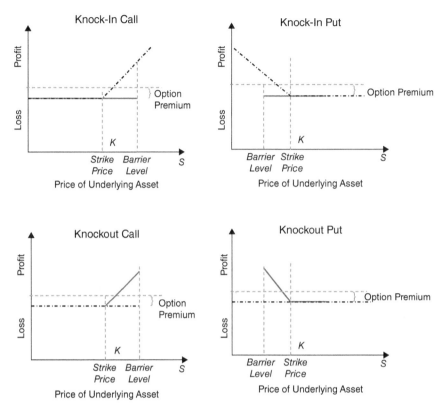

FIGURE 4.2 Payoff Diagrams for Four Types of Barrier Options

markets. The payoffs for four of these barrier options are illustrated in Figure 4.2. (James 2007).

4.2.2 Partial Barrier Options

A *partial barrier option* is a barrier option where the barrier is active for only part of the option life. Some examples of partial barrier options are:

- Type A partial barrier option: A single barrier that is currently active but ends at some time prior to option expiration. From that point until expiration, there is no barrier, and hence the option is vanilla.
- Type B partial barrier option: There is currently no barrier but a single barrier becomes active at some time prior to expiration. The barrier lasts through option expiration.
- Barriers that repeatedly turn on and off.

PARTIAL BARRIER OPTION

A **partial barrier option** is a barrier option where the barrier is active for only part of the option life.

4.2.3   Solutions to Barrier Options

Some analytical and numerical approximations of solutions to barrier options are discussed in the literature. See Merton's "Theory of Rational Option Pricing" (1973), Reiner and Rubenstein's "Breaking Down the Barriers" (1990), Riedhauser's "Green Function Solution for Barrier Options" (1997a), and Zhang's "Exotic Options Bundled with Interruptible Electricity Contracts" (2005).

4.2.4   Barrier Options in the Energy Markets

Barrier options may be utilized by energy producers for risk management purposes. An *interruptible electricity contract* (IEC) is a type of a power contract bundled with electricity options that can be used in demand-side management. A portfolio comprised of electricity options integrated with an IEC is the same as an exotic option composed of several barrier call options (Zhang 2005).

4.3   DIGITAL OPTIONS

A digital option provides an energy market participant with a fixed payout profile. More specifically, the digital options buyer receives the same payout irrespective of how far in-the-money (ITM) the option closes. The value of the payout of these types of options is determined at the onset of the contract and doesn't depend on the magnitude by which the price of the underlying asset moves. So, for example, whether an energy trader is ITM by $10,000 or $50,000, the amount that she receives will be the same.

DIGITAL OPTION

A digital option is an option whose payout is fixed after the underlying asset exceeds a predetermined threshold or strike price. The value of the payout of these types of options is determined at the onset of the contract and doesn't depend on the magnitude by which the price of the underlying asset moves.

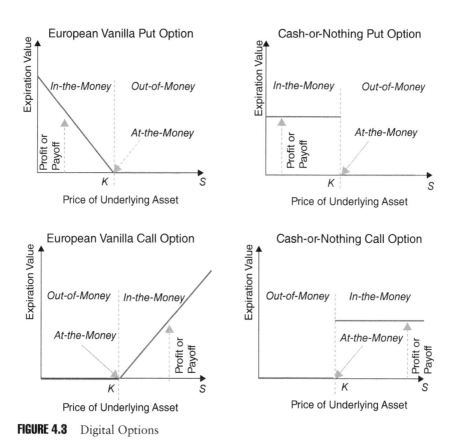

FIGURE 4.3 Digital Options

Example: Illustrations of discontinuous payoffs of digital options may be found in Figure 4.3.

4.3.1 Types of Digital Options

A digital option has various synonyms:

- Binary option
- All-or-nothing option
- Cash-or-nothing option
- Asset-or-nothing option

Each of these forms of digital options can be European or American. They may also be structured as a put or call.

A *cash-or-nothing (CON)* option can be viewed as a "pure bet" on an underlying asset.

A *European CON call* option pays a fixed amount of money if it expires in-the-money and nothing otherwise, that is:

- If $S > K$ at expiry, the option holder is paid a fixed amount of cash.
- If $S \leq K$ at expiry, the option holder receives nothing.

A *European CON put* option pays a fixed amount of money if it expires out-of-the-money and nothing otherwise, that is:

- If $S < K$ at expiry, the option holder is paid a fixed amount of cash.
- If $S \geq K$ at expiry, the option holder receives nothing.

Example: In Figure 4.3 we compare the payoff of a European vanilla call with that of a European CON call option.

> A *cash-or-nothing (CON) option can be viewed as a "pure bet" on an underlying asset.*

Example: An *American CON* option—illustrated in Figure 4.4—is issued out-of-the-money and makes a fixed payment if $S = K$. This fixed payment may be made immediately or deferred until the option's expiration date. Since the amount of cash paid is fixed there is no benefit in continuing to hold the American CON once the strike has been exceeded. As soon as the strike is hit, this digital option should be exercised.

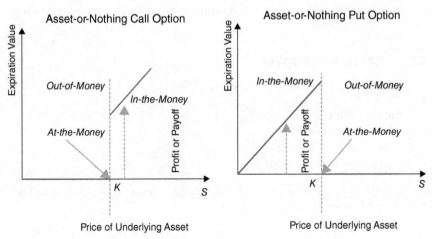

FIGURE 4.4 Asset-or-Nothing Options

The following conditions hold for an *asset-or-nothing* (AON) call option:

- If $S > K$ at expiry, the option holder is paid the value equal to one unit of the underlying asset for each option held.
- If $S \leq K$ at expiry, the option holder receives nothing

In addition, the following conditions hold for an asset-or-nothing (AON) put option:

- If $S < K$ at expiry, the option holder is paid the value equal to one unit of the underlying asset for each option held.
- If $S \geq K$ at expiry, the option holder receives nothing.

4.3.2 Solutions to Digital Options

Some pricing methods for digital options are discussed in the literature. See Eydeland and Wolyniec (2003), Huang and Yang (2007), Margrabe (1978), Reiner and Rubenstein (1990), Riedhauser (1997a, 2001a), and Zhang (1998).

4.3.3 Digital Options in the Energy Markets

> *Digital options are implicit in payoff functions of certain underlying energy assets.*

Digital options are implicit in payoff functions of certain underlying energy assets. In the energy markets one may encounter *spread digital options*:

- *Spread CON:* If the spread exceeds the strike price at expiry, the option holder will receive a fixed amount of money.
- *Spread AON:* If the spread exceeds the strike price at expiry, the option holder will receive the underlying spread or the underlying asset (Figure 4.5).

William Margrabe initially introduced exchange options in his seminal 1978 paper. These types of options allow an option holder to exchange one asset for another. They are often utilized in foreign exchange markets, bond markets, and stock markets, among others. Exchange options have since found many applications in the energy and commodity markets (Margrabe 1978).

In Huang and Yang (2007), the authors consider a special exchange option, where the option is triggered when value of asset A is greater than that of asset B, while the payoff is given in one of the assets. In energy

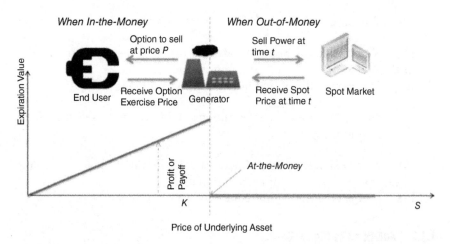

FIGURE 4.5   Application of Digital Options in the Energy Markets

market, this type of option is embedded in forward contracts that allow delivery of a different commodity.

Examples

> **Example 1.** Natural gas producer A is under contract to provide natu-
> ral gas to counterparty B at delivery point C at a fixed price. Gas
> producer A may also wish to have the flexibility to stop delivering
> gas to counterparty B, pay a small fee, and instead to sell gas at
> market price at delivery point D.
>
> **Example 2.** In electricity markets there exist contracts that specify de-
> livery termination if, for example, North Platte (NP) 15 price is
> higher than California-Oregon Border (COB) price and COB price
> is greater than contract price.
>
> **Example 3.** This type of digital option may also be useful to hedge risks
> of some illiquid energy assets.
>
> **Example 4.** Variations of these digital options can also be seen in En-
> ergy Demand Response (DR) programs. In DR programs, partici-
> pants are required to reduce load (energy consumption) when called
> upon. The call can be triggered by
>
> - System load conditions (system reserve margin)
> - Market heat rate
> - Temperature

The holder of the DR right may decide not to trigger the response if it is determined not to be economical.

4.4   REAL OPTIONS

Real options valuation (ROV) applies option valuation techniques to capital budgeting decisions. A *real option* is the right—but not the obligation—to undertake certain business initiatives, such as those listed in the figure below.

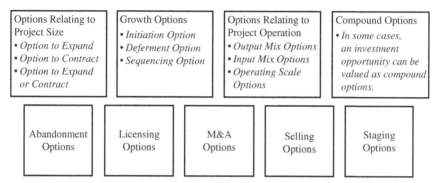

Options Relating to Project Size • *Option to Expand* • *Option to Contract* • *Option to Expand or Contract*	Growth Options • *Initiation Option* • *Deferment Option* • *Sequencing Option*	Options Relating to Project Operation • *Output Mix Options* • *Input Mix Options* • *Operating Scale Options*	Compound Options • *In some cases, an investment opportunity can be valued as compound options.*
Abandonment Options	Licensing Options	M&A Options	Selling Options	Staging Options

Technically, real options are not derivatives instruments, but are actual options (in the sense of "choice") that may be gained by undertaking certain endeavors. Real options are generally distinguished from financial options in that they are not traded as securities.

REAL OPTION

A real option is the right—but not the obligation—to undertake certain business initiatives.

4.4.1   Real Options in the Electric Power Markets

Investments in electricity generation are typically very large, involving substantial sunk costs.

Investments in electricity generation are typically very large, involving substantial sunk costs. These investments also involve a great deal of uncertainty, such as:

- Demand
- Price

- Construction costs
- Production costs
- Regulations

Example: An electric utility may have the option to switch between various fuel sources to generate power. Hence a flexible plant, although more expensive may actually be more valuable. This is an example of an input mix real option.

Example: The opportunity to

- Invest in the expansion of a power plant is a *real call option.*
- Sell the plant is a *real put option.*

Power utilities can implement a *discounted cash flow* (DCF) approach to try to value large investment projects having predictable cash flows. Recall that the DCF method is a valuation method used to estimate the attractiveness of an investment opportunity. If the value arrived at through DCF analysis is higher than the current cost of the investment, the opportunity may be a good one.

$$DCF = \frac{CF_1}{(1+r)^1} + \frac{CF_2}{(1+r)^2} + \cdots + \frac{CF_n}{(1+r)^n}$$

Where $\{CF_i\}_{1 \leq i \leq n}$ are cash flows, and

r is the discount rate (weighted average cost of capital, that is, the WACC).

However the DCF method is not capable of evaluating investments in electricity generation characterized by a large degree of uncertainty and managerial and operational flexibility. If taken into consideration, real options may greatly affect the valuation of potential investments. Alternative investment valuation methods, such as DCF, may not include the benefits that real options provide. In the 1990s and 2000s the real options (RO) framework became quite popular in the power industry as a tool for evaluating investment projects. Real options were rarely applied to the electricity sector prior to the 1990s because this energy sector was monopolized and highly regulated. While operating in monopolized markets, electric utilities did not have an incentive to fully address the issue of total investment costs because all risks and costs could be passed on to consumers (Brajkovic 2010).

4.4.2 Case Study: Real Options in the Oil Markets

Imai and Nakajima utilize a real options (RO) framework to evaluate an oil refinery project when the prices of the output products are uncertain and

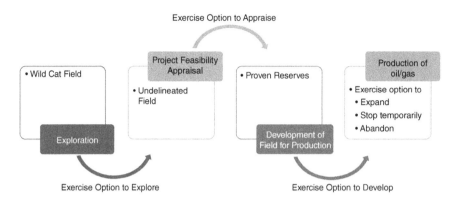

FIGURE 4.6 Applications of Real Options in the Oil Industry

management has some flexibility to switch operating process—as illustrated in (Figure 4.6). The authors develop a multinomial lattice model and provide numerical examples that are based on a detailed case study, analyzing how a lattice-based RO approach is useful in practice. They evaluate the project including the value of flexibility, and specify the value of each process unit. The authors also discuss the optimal construction and switching strategy and demonstrate it under a sample price fluctuation. Their main conclusion is that the flexibility of the project is so profitable that management should not ignore the value of flexibility in evaluating a project (Imai and Nakajima 2000).

Please note that a more detailed case study of ROV in the energy markets is presented in Chapter 9.

4.4.3 Limitations of the Real Options Valuation Paradigm

Some of the RO literature is based on different combinations of unrealistic assumptions, such as:

- *Perfect correlation*: Most underlying projects are not perfectly correlated to any tradable assets in the financial markets. Hence the no-arbitrage pricing approach loses its foundation in RO valuation.
- *Choice of a stochastic process for the underlying asset price*: In the Black-Scholes framework, the underlying asset price is assumed to follow a continuous stochastic process. However, for real assets, this assumption may be violated. For example, jumps may occur in prices. Hence a geometric Brownian motion may not be a good approximation for the underlying real asset. One can overcome this problem by utilizing

models that account for the nonstandard price distributions, such as jump-diffusion models (He 2007).

- *Exercise property*: The exercise of a real option may involve the need to build a power plant or to drill oil wells, for example. Such actions may take years to be completed. Hence the lifetime of some real options may be less than the stated life of the project (He 2007).
- *Infinite time horizon*: Some investment may be decades long, but many strategic investments involve much shorter time periods.
- *Absence of competition*: For the most part, competition erodes the value of flexibility.

Other pricing methods and resources for ROV may be found at www .real-options.org.

4.5   MULTIASSET OPTIONS

A *multiasset (multifactor) option* is an option whose payoff depends upon the performance of two or more underlying assets. There are three types of multiasset options:

1. *Basket options* are options on a portfolio or "basket" of underlying assets.
2. *Quantos* are derivatives that have an underlying asset denominated in one currency, but settled in another currency without exposure to currency fluctuations.
3. *Rainbow options* are multifactor options other than basket options or quantos.

4.5.1   Pricing Multiasset Options

To price options on multiple assets, Han (2011) derived the following stochastic differential equation:

$$\frac{\partial V}{\partial t} + \frac{1}{2}\sum_{i,j=1}^{n}\alpha_{ij}S_iS_j\frac{\partial^2 V}{\partial S_i \partial S_j} + \sum_{i=1}^{n}(r - q_i)S_i\frac{\partial V}{\partial S_i} - rV = 0 \qquad (4.1)$$

Where $\{S_i\}_{1 \leq i \leq n}$ are the prices of the underlying assets

$$dS_i = S_i\mu_i dt + S_i\sum_{j=1}^{m}\sigma_{ij}dW_j \ (1 \leq i \leq n)$$

$V(S_1,\ldots,S_n,t)$ is an option derived from the underlying assets

dW_i $(1 \leq i \leq n)$ are one-dimensional Brownian motions

$E(dW_i) = 0$

$Var(dW_i) = dt$

$Cov(dW_i, dW_j) = \rho_{ij}dt$ is the covariance $(i \neq j)$

ρ_{ij} is the correlation coefficient between the ith and jth assets.

$$\alpha_{ij} = \sum_{k=1}^{m} \sigma_{ik}\sigma_{jk} \ (i, j = 1,\dots,n)$$

r = the interest rate

q_i = the dividend rate of asset S_i $(1 \leq i \leq n)$

Modeling multiasset options are complex because their premiums rely on multidimensional joint probability distribution of prices. Numerical approximations to Equation (4.1) for the case of two risky assets are presented in Han (2011). Further discussions of multiasset models are presented in Burger et al. (2007), Clewlow and Strickland (1999), and Hikspoors (2008).

4.6 SPREAD OPTIONS

In the energy industry, producers are often concerned with the difference between the *inputs* and *outputs* of energy processes, rather than the level of these prices.

Example: Oil refiners' profits are tied directly to the spread between the price of crude oil and the prices of refined products.

In this section we will take a look at inter-commodity spreads and spread options. These are very important tools and products in the energy markets.

An *intercommodity spread* in the commodities market is a spread consisting of a long position and a short position in different, but related, commodities.

Examples of intercommodity spreads in the energy markets are listed in Table 4.2. In Chapter 5 we will introduce other types of energy spreads: locational, time, calendar, and so forth.

INTERCOMMODITY SPREAD

*An **intercommodity spread** in the commodities market is a spread consisting of a long position and a short position in different, but related, commodities.*

TABLE 4.2 Intercommodity Spreads in the Energy Markets

	Input	Output	Intercommodity Spread
Crack Spread	Crude Oil	Refined Petroleum Products	Price of Refined Petroleum Products – Price of crude oil
Heat Spread	Crude Oil	No. 2 Heating Oil	Price of No. 2 heating oil – Price of crude oil
Gasoline Spread	Crude Oil	Unleaded Gasoline	Price of unleaded gasoline – Price of crude oil
Resid Spread	Crude Oil	No. 6 Fuel Oil	Price of No. 6 fuel oil – Price of crude oil
Frac Spread	Natural Gas	Gas Liquids	Price of gas liquids – Price of natural gas
Spark Spread	Natural Gas	Electricity	Price of electricity – Price of natural gas burned to generate electricity
Dark Spread	Coal	Electricity	Price of electricity – Price of coal used to generate electricity

Energy Asset #1 • Input	Energy Process Associated with the Intercommodity Spread	Energy Assets • Outputs (one or more refined energy products)

A *spread option* is an option that derives its value from the difference between the prices of two underlying assets, that is, from inter-commodity spreads.

Spread options can be written on equities, bonds, currencies, commodities, and so forth. These types of derivatives can be purchased on exchanges, but are primarily traded in the OTC market.

4.6.1 Crack Spreads

An oil refiner is caught between two markets:

1. The raw materials to be purchased
2. The finished products to be sold

Prices of raw materials and finished products are subject to variables of supply and demand. Such price uncertainty can put refiners at risk when crude prices rise, while finished products' prices remain static or decline.

In the crack spread process petroleum refiners

- Buy crude oil
- Process and refine it via the cracking process as illustrated in Figure 4.7
- Sell heating oil and gasoline products

Crude Oil	Refiner	Heating Oil, Gasoline Products
• Buy	• Cracking Process	• Sell

4.6.1.1 Cracking in Petroleum Refining

CRACKING IN PETROLEUM REFINING

Cracking in petroleum refining is the process by which heavy hydrocarbon molecules are broken up into lighter molecules by means of heat and usually pressure and sometimes catalysts.

The term *crack* refers to the technological process used in petroleum refineries:

Cracking in petroleum refining is the process by which heavy hydrocarbon molecules are broken up into lighter molecules by means of heat and usually pressure and sometimes catalysts. Cracking is the most important process for the commercial production of gasoline and diesel fuel.

The *crack spread* is the differential between the price of crude oil and petroleum extracted from it. It is the profit margin that an oil refiner can expect to make by "cracking" crude oil.

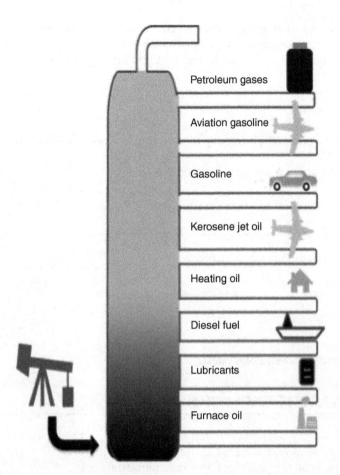

FIGURE 4.7   Cracking in Petroleum Refining

4.6.1.2 New York Mercantile Exchange Crack Spread Contracts

Petroleum refiners are more concerned about the difference (spread) between their input and output prices than about price levels. Refiners' prices are directly tied to the spread between the price of crude oil (input) and the prices of refined products (output). Refiners can reliably predict all costs, except for that of crude oil. The crack spread is the major uncertainty. To help manage this uncertainty, in 1994 New York Mercantile Exchange (NYMEX) launched the *crack spread contract*.

Crack spread contracts take general market risks out of a commodity trade by switching to a more specific price risk. The focus shifts from a guess about general states of energy prices to specific price differences between the *raw material* (crude oil) and the *product* (heating oil, gasoline), and so forth.

Example:
Purchase

- 3 crude oil futures (30,000 barrels)

Sell (one month later)

- 2 unleaded gasoline futures (20,000 barrels)
- 1 heating oil future (10,000 barrels)

This 3-2-1 ratio approximates the ratio of refinery output: 3 barrels of crude oil producing 2 barrels of unleaded gasoline and 1 barrel of heating oil. Buyers and sellers of crack spread contracts are only concerned with the margin requirements for the crack spread contract. They do not deal with individual margins for the underlying trades.

Example: Following is a more detailed illustration of a 3-2-1 crack spread (see Table 4.3).

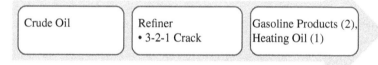

Suppose we consider energy assets with the following prices:

Input: Crude oil is $25 per barrel
Outputs:

- Gas is 80¢ per gallon
- Heating oil is 70¢ per gallon

TABLE 4.3   3-2-1 Crack Spread

Crude Oil (Barrel)	Gas (Gallon)	Heating Oil (Gallon)	Gas (Barrel)	Heating Oil (Barrel)	Buy Oil	Sell Gas	Sell Heating Oil	Gross Crack Margin	Crack Spread
25	0.8	0.7	33.6	29.4	75	67.2	29.4	21.6	7.2

Using a ratio of 3 crude oil to 2 gasoline plus 1 heating oil, the 3:2:1 gross cracking margin is calculated as follows to obtain the 3:2:1 crack spread:

(80¢ per gal × 42 gal/barrel = $33.60 per barrel of gas) × 2 = $67.20

70¢ per gal × 42 gal/barrel = $29.40 per barrel of heating oil

The sum of the revenues from the refined products is: $96.60

3 barrels of crude ($25 × 3) = $75

Gross cracking margin = $96.6 − $75 = $21.60

3:2:1 crack spread is $21.60/3 barrels = $7.20 per barrel (margin)

4.6.1.3 Crack Spread Options

Crack spread options are puts and calls on the one-to-one ratio between the New York Harbor heating oil futures or New York Harbor unleaded gasoline futures contract and the Exchange's light, sweet crude oil futures contract. The underlying spread and options price is expressed as dollars and cents per barrel (NYMEX 2000).

CRACK SPREAD OPTIONS

Crack spread options are puts and calls on the one-to-one ratio between the New York Harbor heating oil futures or New York Harbor unleaded gasoline futures contract and the Exchange's light, sweet crude oil futures contract.

Example:

Suppose

- June gasoline is priced at 60.30¢ per gallon ($25.33 per barrel).
- June crude oil is priced at $19.66 per barrel.

Then the June gasoline crack spread is $5.67 ($25.33 − $19.66). The equation is the same for heating oil.

NYMEX crack spread options protect against the growth or shrinkage in the *difference* between prices. If a refiner thinks that a currently profitable spread will disappear, it can buy a *crack spread put option.*

If a large consumer of refined products thinks the spread will grow while the price of crude oil is stable, it can buy a *crack spread call option* to compensate for potentially large increases in petroleum product prices when refinery margins grow.

The payoffs of crack spread put and call options may be found in Table 4.4.

TABLE 4.4   Payoffs of Crack Spread Options

	Payoffs of Crack Spread Options
Crack Spread Call Option	$\max(F_1(T,s_1) - F_2(T,s_2) - K, 0)$
Crack Spread Put Option	$\max(K - F_1(T,s_1) + F_2(T,s_2), 0)$

Where, $F_1(T,s_1)$ = price of an s_1-maturity futures contract on commodity 1
$F_2(T,s_2)$ = price of an s_2-maturity futures contract on commodity 2
T = maturity, and
K = strike price on the spread between these 2 contracts

As discussed in section 4.5, multiasset options have payoffs that depend on the prices of two or more underlying instruments. Modeling such options may be a bit complicated, as the premiums depend on multidimensional joint probability distribution of prices. Two methods for pricing crack spread options are as follows:

Method 1
■ Treat the spread as traded separately from two underlying commodities.
■ Offer options on this new commodity.
■ Pricing of these options is complicated by the fact that the spread can have negative values.
■ Black-Scholes formula can't be used. It's based on the assumption of a lognormal distribution of prices at the horizon defined only for positive values.
■ We may assume the spread has a normal distribution and use the pricing formula developed by Brennan (1979) and Wilcox (1991).
■ *Shortcoming of this method*: The distribution of the spread is not necessarily normal or even symmetric.
■ *Advantage of this method*: Ease of implementation on computers, because it produces a formula for option valuation.

Method 2
■ Assume two prices defining the spread follow a joint lognormal distribution of the two forward prices.
■ Price the option as the discounted, expected value of the payoff in a risk-neutral world.
■ Let $P(t,T)$ denote discounting the future cash flows back to today.
■ Then the value of the option at time t can be written as:

$$\text{Crack\_Spread } (t; K, F_1, F_2, s_1, s_2)$$
$$= P(t,T) \times E_t[\max(0, F_1(T, s_1) - F_2(T, s_2) - K)]$$

- The options prices are computed via Monte Carlo simulation.
- To simulate the joint behavior of energy prices on which the portfolio depends, one must compute the volatility functions of the two commodities from the covariance matrix of all relevant forward prices.

More on crack spread options and their pricing methods are discussed in Burger et al. (2007), Eydeland and Wolyniec (2003), EIA (2002), He (2007), NYMEX (2000), Riedhauser (2002), and Taleb (1997).

4.6.2 Spark Spreads

The *spark spread* is similar to the crack spread. It was developed in the electricity markets as an intermarket spread for electricity and natural gas (NYMEX 2000).

SPARK SPREAD

Spark spread is the difference between the market price of electricity and its cost of production.

Spark Spread

= Output price − Input price

= (Price of power) − (Price of fuel burned to generate power)

= (Electricity price − Gas price)/(Power plant efficiency)

= Price of Electricity − [(Cost of Gas) * (Heat Rate)]

= \$/MWh − [(\$/MMBtu) * (MMBtu/MWh)]

The spark spread is the difference between the market price of electricity and its cost of production. It is also a trading strategy based on the differences in the price of electricity and its cost of production. Traders can profit from changes in the spark spread through OTC trading in electricity contracts. The spark spread is expressed in dollars per megawatt-hour (\$/Mwh).

HEAT RATE

Heat rate is a measure of the thermal efficiency of a power generating unit.

Spark spreads are often quoted using a convention based on the assumption of a heat rate of 10,000. The *heat rate* is a measure of the thermal efficiency of a power generating unit.

$$K_H = \text{Heat rate} = \frac{\text{Btu content of fuel consumed in power production}}{\text{KWh generation of facility}}$$

Typical measures of heat rate:	
Average unit	10,000 Btu/KWh
Efficient unit	7,500 Btu/KWh
Inefficient unit	15,000 Btu/KWh

4.6.2.1 Importance of the Spark Spread

Why the spark spread is so important!

- It reflects the costs of producing power from a specific facility.
- It is a tool for managing the risk of owning a power plant.
- It is the primary metric for investors to track earnings of generating companies.
- It helps utilities determine their bottom lines.

If the spark spread is positive, the utility makes money.

If the spark spread is negative, the utility loses money.

- The value of a strip of spark-spread options gives the value of the power plant over a given time period.
- The value of this strip of spark spreads will be higher than that obtained using discounted cash flow (DCF) because the embedded real options (RO) valuation incorporates the additional value of being able to shut the plant down in times with unfavorable prices.

All other costs (operation and maintenance, capital, and other financial costs) must be covered from the spark spread. If the spark spread is small on a given day, electricity generation may be delayed until a more profitable spread arises.

Example:
Suppose the prices of natural gas and power are as follows:

> Price of natural gas = $2.00/MMBtu
> Price of power = $25/MWh

Also, suppose the heat rate is 10,000 Btu/kWh
Then the spark spread is computed as follows:

> Spark spread = Price of Electricity − [(Cost of Gas) * (Heat Rate)]
> = $25/MWh − ($2.00/MMBtu)*(10,000Btu/kWh)
> = $0.005/kWh

This spark spread compares the cost of generating power at a certain heating efficiency with the cost of buying power from the grid.

- Spark spread > 0: It is more economical to buy gas.
- Spark spread < 0: It is more economical to buy power from the grid.

Spark spreads look at a very simple world:

- A world where the turbine sits next to the switchyard.
- Both sit on top a natural gas pipeline.
- There are no transaction costs, no transmission costs, no transportation costs.
- In this example, it's assumed that the power plant is natural gas-fired.

4.6.2.2 Spark Spread Options

> *A **spark spread option** gives the buyer the right but not the obligation to buy the price difference between electricity and natural gas adjusted for power plant efficiency.*

A *spark spread option* gives the buyer the right but not the obligation to buy the price difference between electricity and natural gas adjusted for power plant efficiency.

The holder of a *European spark spread call option* written on fuel G at a fixed heat rate K_H has the right, but not the obligation, to pay at the option's maturity K_H times the fuel price at maturity time T and receive the price of one unit of electricity. If the value of this option at time t is $C(S_E^T, S_G^T, K_H, t)$ then the payoff at time T is

$$C(S_E^T, S_G^T K_H, T) = \max(S_E^T - K_H S_G^T, 0)$$

Where S_E^T is the spot price of electricity at time T

S_G^T is the spot price of fuel G at time T

Pricing spark-spread options requires stochastic process models for the electricity price and the gas price, as well as the correlation between the two. In Maribu, Galli, and Armstrong (2007) spark-spread options are priced by utilizing mean-reverting models (with a seasonal trend) to model both electricity and gas. More on spark spread options and their pricing methods are discussed in Burger et al. (2007), Deng and Oren (2006), Eydeland and Wolyniec (2003), He (2007), Hsu (1998), Maribu et al. (2007), NYMEX (2000), Riedhauser (2000), and Siclari and Castellacci (2011).

4.6.3   Dark Spreads

> A *clean dark spread* represents the difference between the prices of electricity and the price of coal used to generate that electricity, corrected for the energy output of the coal plant.

A *dark spread* is comparable to the spark spread. In the case of a dark spread the power plant is fired with coal instead of gas.

Dark Spread = Price of Electricity − (Price of Coal Used to Generate Electricity)

The CO_2 impact is not included in the dark spread calculation. Hence, this is considered the "dirty" dark spread.

A *clean dark spread* represents the difference between the prices of electricity and the price of coal used to generate that electricity, corrected for the energy output of the coal plant.

Clean Dark Spread = Dirty Dark Spread − (Carbon Price × Coal CO_2 Emissions Factor)

As in the case of the spark spread, the clean dark spread is important because it reflects the costs of producing power from a coal-fired facility.

If the clean dark spread is positive, it is profitable
to generate electricity on a baseload basis for
the period in question.

If the clean dark spread is negative, generation
would be a loss-making activity.

More on dark spreads, dark spread options and the related pricing methods may be found in "The Valuation of Clean Spread Options" (Carmona, Coulon, and Schwarz 2012).

4.7 PERPETUAL AMERICAN OPTIONS

A *perpetual American option* is an option that has no maturity date. It is infinitely lived. These options are also referred to as *nonexpiring options* or *expirationless options*. Their valuation is independent of time (Haug 2006b; McKean 1965; Merton 1973).

PERPETUAL AMERICAN OPTION

A perpetual American option is an option that has no maturity date.

A closed form analytical *solution for a perpetual American call option* on a stock is given by

$$C = \frac{K}{h_1 - 1}\left(\frac{h_1 - 1}{h_1}\frac{S}{K}\right)^{h_1}$$

Where $h_1 = \frac{1}{2} - \frac{b}{\sigma^2} + \sqrt{\left(\frac{b}{\sigma^2} - \frac{1}{2}\right)^2 + \frac{2}{\sigma^2}}$

S = current price of the underlying financial asset

K = strike price

b = cost of carry rate (cost of interest plus any additional costs)

σ = volatility of the underlying asset

A closed form analytical solution for a perpetual American put option on a stock is given by

$$P = \frac{K}{1-h_2}\left(\frac{h_2-1}{h_2}\frac{S}{K}\right)^{h_2}$$

Where $\quad h_2 = \frac{1}{2} - \frac{b}{\sigma^2} - \sqrt{\left(\frac{b}{\sigma^2} - \frac{1}{2}\right)^2 + \frac{2}{\sigma^2}}$

Pricing methods for perpetual American options are discussed in Boyarchenko and Levendorskii (2002), Huang (2008), and Yu and Hom (2004). In particular, in Huang (2008) we find solutions to perpetual American calls and puts. He also presents solutions to perpetual barrier options and perpetual digital options, among others.

4.7.1 Perpetual American Options in the Power Industry

Brajkovic (2010) utilizes an RO framework to analyze a base load coal-fired power plant. The following assumptions are made in his analysis:

- The real option to invest is a perpetual American option.
- The profitability of the power plant depends upon the value of the dark spread.

This research has two objectives:

1. Determine the most appropriate stochastic process to model the evolution of dark spread prices.
2. Assess how the choice of the stochastic process affects investment decisions within the RO framework.

4.8 COMPOUND OPTIONS

A *compound option* is an option on another derivative. At some time in the future, the holder has the right to enter into another derivative (call, put, swap, etc.), which expires at a still later time. Examples of compound options include:

- Call on call
- Call on put
- Put on call
- Put on put
- Swaptions
- Call-on-toll
- Options on forward acquisitions

Note: A *call-on-toll* will be discussed at the end of this section. *Swaptions*—options on swaps—will be discussed in Section 4.9.

Let us consider a call on a call, that is, a call option whose underlying asset is another call option. The holder of this compound option has the right, but not the obligation, at time T_C to pay the strike price K_C for a call with expiration T_U and strike price K_U.

The payoff function of this compound option at T_C is

$$max[C(T_C, S_{T_C}; T_U, K_U) - K_C; 0]$$

Where K_C = strike price for the call option on the option

K_U = strike price for the underlying option

T_C = time to maturity for the call option on the option

T_U = time to maturity for the underlying option

$C(T_C, S_{T_C}; T_U, K_U)$ is the Black-Scholes call option formula with strike K_U and time to maturity T_U

$S_t = S(t)$ is the price at time t of the underlying asset of the call option

Hence, at time T_C the compound option will be exercised if the value of the underlying call option at that time is greater than the strike price K_C of the compound option. In the case of a European compound call option, the value at time t is

$$C_{call-on-call} = S_t N(b_1 + \sigma\sqrt{T_c - t}, \; b_2 + \sigma\sqrt{T_U - t}; \; \sqrt{(T_C - t)/(T_U - t)})$$
$$- K_U e^{-r(T_U - t)} N(b_1, b_2; \sqrt{(T_c - t)/(T_U - t)}) - e^{-r(T_c - t)} K_C N(b_1)$$

Where $b_1 = \dfrac{\ln(S_t / S^*) + (r - \sigma^2/2)(T_C - t)}{\sigma\sqrt{T_C - t}}$

$b_2 = \dfrac{\ln(S_t / K_U) + (r - \sigma^2/2)(T_U - t)}{\sigma\sqrt{T_U - t}}$

$N(x, y; \rho)$ is the standardized bivariate cumulative normal distribution

S^* is the solution to the equation $C(T_C, S^*; T_U, K_U) = K_C$

More on pricing compound options may be found in Edyeland (2003), Geske (1979), Haug (2006b), Hodges and Selby (1987), and Rubinstein (1991). Compound and partial barrier options are considered together in Riedhauser (1997b) because the methods for valuing them are similar.

4.8.1 Tolling Agreements: Example of Compound Options in Power Markets

The option to invest in energy assets can be viewed as a compound option on an option-embedded flexible asset. One is more likely to encounter a *call-on-toll* in the energy markets.

Tolling agreement contracts involve pricing scheduling flexibility of electricity generating facilities (Deng and Oren 2006).

A tolling agreement—illustrated in Figure 4.8—is similar to a common electricity supply contract signed between a buyer and an owner of a power plant but with notable differences:

- For an upfront premium paid to the plant owner, the tolling agreement gives the buyer the right to either operate and control the scheduling of the power plant with the independent system operator (ISO) or simply take the output electricity during prespecified time periods subject to certain constraints.
- There may be other contractual limitations in the contract on how the buyer may operate the power plant or take the output electricity. For example, a tolling contract almost always has a clause on the maximum allowable number of power plant restarts.

A call on a toll is a compound option that allows a holder the right, but not the obligation, to enter into a tolling agreement at some future date T_C in exchange for a payment K_C. That is, the option holder receives a right to operate a power plant for a fixed time horizon in exchange for a fixed payment. During

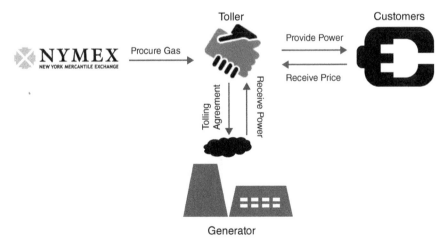

FIGURE 4.8 Tolling Agreement

the life of the contract the renter receives all cash inflows and outflows associated with the power plant. In "Pricing Energy Derivatives by Linear Programming," Ryabchenko and Uryasev (2011) propose a methodology that may be applied to a wide class of tolling agreement contracts. In addition, they present a case study for the pricing of a one-year power tolling agreement contract.

4.9 SWAPTIONS

SWAPTION

A **swaption** is an over-the-counter (OTC) option to enter into a swap — the right, but not the obligation, to enter into a specified type of swap at a specified future date—at a predetermined strike price for fixed payments.

A **swaption** is an OTC option to enter into a swap—the right, but not the obligation, to enter into a specified type of swap at a specified future date—at a predetermined strike price for fixed payments.

Swaptions are specified by the following data:

- Swap fixing dates $T_1, \ldots, T_n$
- Swap type: payer or receiver
- K = strike of the swaption
- The option's maturity date T, where $T < T_1$

The swaption gives the owner the right to buy the swap for zero dollars (i.e., to enter into a long position in the swap at no cost).

Swap	Swaption
At Time 0	At Time 0
−1.1584	Max(−1.1584 − 0,0) = 0
−0.3526	Max(−0.3526 − 0,0) = 0
0.3216	Max(0.3216 − 0,0) = 0.3216
0.9326 Time t at expiry	Max(0.9326 − 0,0) = 0.9326

FIGURE 4.9 Swaption Modeling

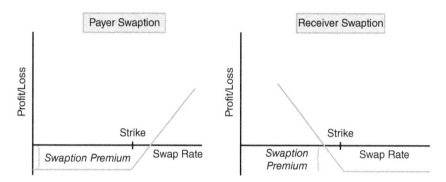

FIGURE 4.10 Swaption

4.9.1 Energy Swaptions

Energy swaptions are options that at maturity give a delivery of an energy swap at the strike price (but not necessarily physical delivery of any energy). The swap can have a financial or physical settlement.

The *energy call swaption formula* is derived in Haug (2006b).

$$c = \frac{\left(1 - \frac{1}{(1+r_j/j)^n}\right)}{r_j} \frac{j}{n} e^{-r_b T_b} [FN(d_1) - KN(d_2)]$$

Where r_j is a swap rate starting at the beginning of the delivery period and ending at the end of the delivery period with j compoundings per year, equal to the number of fixings in the delivery period

r_b is a risk-free continuous compounding zero coupon rate with T_b years to maturity

T_b is the time from now to the beginning of the delivery period

$$d_1 = \frac{\ln(S/X) + \sigma^2 T/2}{\sigma\sqrt{T}}$$

$$d_2 = d_1 - \sigma\sqrt{T}$$

F is the forward swap price observed in the market

j is the number of compoundings per year (number of settlements in a one-year forward contract; in this case it is evenly spread out)

n is the number of settlements in the delivery period for the particular forward contracts

The *energy put swaption formula* is similarly derived in Haug (2006b).

$$p = \frac{\left(1 - \frac{1}{(1+r_i/j)^n}\right)}{r_j} \frac{j}{n} e^{-r_b T_b} [XN(-d_2) - KN(-d_1)]$$

4.10 SWING OPTIONS

Swing options are path-dependent options in the energy markets that allow the option holder to buy a predetermined quantity of energy at a predetermined price while having some flexibility in the amount purchased and the price paid (Figure 4.11).

In the energy markets swing options are also known as:

- Swing contracts
- Take-and-pay contracts
- Variable base-load factor contracts

SWING OPTIONS

Swing options are path-dependent options in the energy markets that allow the option holder to buy a predetermined quantity of energy at a predetermined price while having some flexibility in the amount purchased and the price paid.

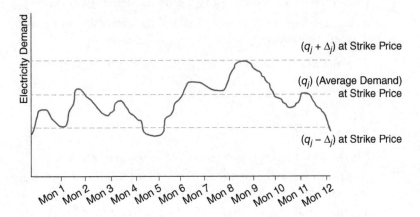

FIGURE 4.11 Swing Options

Energy markets end users can enter into forward contracts in order to hedge against large price fluctuations of energy products. For some market participants this reduction of risk is insufficient because they do not know their exact future need of the energy product. This is an issue for commodities that cannot be stored (such as electricity) or for which storage is very expensive. The swing contract provides some protection against day-to-day price fluctuations from inception to expiration of the contract. Protection is

- *Full* if the strike price is fixed when entering the contract.
- *Partial* if the strike price is linked to the value of the spot price at the beginning of such period.

A swing option guarantees one of two parties periodic delivery of a certain amount of an energy product on certain dates in the future, within a given delivery period:

- Minimum and maximum amount of energy an option holder can buy (or "take") per day and per month.
- How much that energy will cost (strike price).
- How many times during the month the option holder can change (or "swing") the daily quantity of energy purchased.

Swing options have two key components, listed in Table 4.5. In addition, in a typical swing option, there may be further restrictions, as listed in "A Finite-Element Approach for Pricing Swing Options Under Stochastic Volatility" (Wang 2010).

TABLE 4.5 Components of a Swing Options Contract

Set of forward contracts	A base load agreement. The base load agreement is a set of forward contracts with different expiry dates, t_j ($1 \le j \le n$)
	Each forward contract f_j is based on a fixed amount of the commodity q_j.
Fixed number of exercise rights	At each expiry date, the option holder has the right to purchase an excess amount or decrease the base load volume. This means that the amount of the commodity purchased at the strike price by the holder of the swing option can "swing" within a certain range $(q_j + \Delta_j)$.
	If $\Delta_j > 0$, the option exercised by the holder at a suitable time t_j is called *upswing*. An upswing is a buy.
	If $\Delta_j < 0$, the option exercised by the holder at a suitable time t_j is called *downswing*. A downswing is a sell.

There are no analytical closed-form solutions for swing options. Some numerical approximations to swing options may be found in Carmona and Touzi (2008); Dorr (2003); Ibanez (2004); Jaillet, Ronn, and Tompaidis (2004); Kluge (2006); Meinshausen and Hambly (2004); and Wang (2010).

4.11   CHAPTER WRAP-UP

In this chapter we defined, illustrated, and discussed various types of exotic energy derivatives that were listed in Table 3.2. In subsequent chapters we will examine applications of these energy derivatives to

- Hedge or manage energy price risk
- Speculate or gamble in the energy markets

REFERENCES

Boyarchenko, S. I., and S. Z. Levendorskii. 2002. "Perpetual American Options under Levy Processes." *SIAM Journal on Control and Optimization* 40(6): 1663–96. http://epubs.siam.org/doi/abs/10.1137/S0363012900373987?journal Code=sjcodc.

Brajkovic, Jurica. 2010. "Real Options Approach to Investment in Base Load Coal Fired Plant." Energy Institute Hrvoje Pozar. http://papers.ssrn.com/sol3/papers .cfm?abstract_id=1603919.

Brennan, M. J. 1979. "The Pricing of Contingent Claims in Discrete Time Models." *Journal of Finance* 34 (March): 53–68.

Burger, M., B. Graeber, and G. Schindlmayr. 2007. *Managing Energy Risk.* Chichester, England: Wiley Finance.

Carmona, Rene, and Nizar, Touzi. 2008. "Optimal Multiple Stopping and Valuation of Swing Options." *Mathematical Finance* 18(2): 239–68. http://onlinelibrary .wiley.com/doi/10.1111/j.1467-9965.2007.00331.x/abstract.

Carmona, R., M. Coulon, and D. Schwarz. 2012. "The Valuation of Clean Spread Options: Linking Electricity, Emission and Fuels." http://arxiv.org/pdf/1205 .2302.pdf.

Clewlow, L., and C. Strickland. 1999. "A Multi-Factor Model for Energy Derivatives." *Quantitative Finance Research Centre*, University of Technology, Sydney, Australia. http://ideas.repec.org/p/uts/rpaper/28.html.

Curran, Michael. 1992. "Beyond Average Intelligence." *Risk* 5(10): 60.

Deng, S. J., and S. S. Oren. 2006. "Electricity Derivatives and Risk Management." *Energy* 21:940–53. www.ieor.berkeley.edu/~oren/pubs/Deng%20and%20Oren-86.pdf.

Dorr, Uwe. 2003. "Valuation of Swing Options and Examination of Exercise Strategies by Monte Carlo Techniques." PhD thesis, Oxford University, UK. https:// www.maths.ox.ac.uk/system/files/private/active/0/ox_udo_04.pdf.

Eydeland, A., and K. Wolyniec. 2003. *Energy and Power: Risk Management.* Hoboken, NJ: Wiley Finance.

Falloon, William, and David Turner. 1999. "The Evolution of a Market." *Managing Energy Price Risk.* London: Risk Books.

Geske, Robert. 1979. "The Valuation of Compound Options." *Journal of Financial Economics* 7: 63–81.

Han, Jun. 2011. "Pricing Some American Multi-Asset Options." Department of Mathematics, Uppsala University, Sweden. http://uu.diva-portal.org/smash/record.jsf?pid=diva2:302011.

Haug, Espen. 2006a. "Asian Options with Cost of Carry Zero." www.espenhaug.com/AsianFuturesOptions.pdf.

———. 2006b. *The Complete Guide to Option Pricing Formulas,* 2nd ed. New York: McGraw-Hill.

He, Yizhi. 2007. "Real Options in the Energy Markets." Dissertation, University of Twente, The Netherlands. http://doc.utwente.nl/58482/1/thesis_He.pdf.

Hikspoors, Samuel. 2008. "Multi-Factor Energy Price Models and Exotic Derivatives Pricing." PhD thesis, University of Toronto, Canada. www.osti.gov/eprints/topicpages/documents/record/148/2540353.html.

Hodges, S. D., and M. J. P. Selby. 1987. "On the Evaluation of Compound Options." *Management Science* 33(3): 347–355.

Hsu, Michael. 1998. "Spark Spread Options Are Hot." *The Electricity Journal.* www.researchgate.net/publication/223110881_Spark_Spread_Options_Are_Hot!.

Huang, Alex. 2008. "Perpetual American Options." PG&E Quant Group. http://207.67.203.54/elibsql05_P40007_Documents/QUANT%20DOCS/PerpetualOptions_pge_ts.pdf.

Huang, Alex, and Sean Yang. 2007. "Digital Exchange Option." PG&E Quant Group. http://207.67.203.54/elibsql05_P40007_Documents/QUANT%20DOCS/Digital%20Exchange_pge_ts.pdf.

Ibanez, A. 2004. "Valuation by Simulation of Contingent Claims with Multiple Early Exercise Opportunities." *Mathematical Finance* 14(2):223–48.

Imai, Junichi, and Mutsumi Nakajima. 2000. "A Real Option Analysis of an Oil Refinery Project." *Financial Practice and Education* 10(2): 78–91. www.ae.keio.ac.jp/lab/soc/imai/JIMAI/paper/imai_nakajima.pdf.

Jaillet, P., E. Ronn, and St. Tompaidis. 2004. "Valuation of Commodity-Based Swing Options." *Management Science* 50(7): 909–921. http://mansci.journal.informs.org/content/50/7/909.abstract.

James, T. 2007. *Energy Markets: Price Risk Management and Trading.* Hoboken, NJ: Wiley Finance.

Kemna, A. G. Z., and C. F. Vorst. 1990. "A Pricing Method for Options Based on Average Asset Values." *Journal of Banking and Finance* 14: 113–20.

Klassen, T. R. 2001. "Simple, Fast, and Flexible Pricing of Asian Options." *Journal of Computational Finance* 4: 89–124.

Kluge, Tino. 2006. "Pricing Swing Options and Other Electricity Derivatives." PhD thesis, Oxford University, UK. http://eprints.maths.ox.ac.uk/246/1/kluge.pdf.

Levy, Edmond. 1992. "Pricing European Average Rate Currency Options." *Journal of International Money and Finance* 14: 474–491. www.ret.gov.au/energy/Documents/erig/Financial_markets_review_KPMG20070413120316.pdf.

Margrabe, W. 1978. "The Value of an Option to Exchange One Asset for Another." *Journal of Finance* 33: 177–186.

Maribu, K., A. Galli, and M. Armstrong. 2007. "Valuation of Spark-Spread Options with Mean Reversion and Stochastic Volatility." *International Journal of Electronic Business Management* 5(3): 173–181. http://ijebm.ie.nthu.edu.tw/IJEBM_Web/IJEBM_static/Paper-V5_N3/A02.pdf.

McKean, H. P. 1965. "A Free Boundary Problem for the Heat Equation Arising from a Problem in Mathematical Economics." *Industrial Management Review* 6(2): 32–39.

Meinshausen, N., and B. Hambly. 2004. " Monte Carlo Methods for the Valuation of Options with Multiple Exercise Opportunities." *Mathematical Finance* 14(4): 557–83.

Merton, Robert. 1973. "Theory of Rational Option Pricing." *Bell Journal of Economics and Management Science* 4(1): 141–183.

New York Mercantile Exchange (NYMEX). 2000. *Crack Spread Handbook*. http://partners.futuresource.com/marketcenter/pdfs/crack.pdf.

Palmer, Brian. 2010. "Why Do We Call Financial Instruments 'Exotic'?" *Slate*. www.slate.com/articles/news_and_politics/explainer/2010/07/why_do_we_call_financial_instruments_exotic.html.

Pointon, James. 2006. "EU Commodity Markets and Trading: Exotic Derivatives." CALYON Corporate and Investment Bank. www.isda.org/c_and_a/ppt/8-JamesPointon-EU-Commodity-Markets-Trading-Exotic-Derivatives.pdf.

Reiner, Eric, and M. Rubenstein. 1990. "Breaking Down the Barriers." *Risk* 4(8): 28–35.

Riedhauser, Chuck. 1997a. "Green Function Solution for Barrier Options." http://207.67.203.54/elibsql05_P40007_Documents/QUANT%20DOCS/Green_function_pge_ts.pdf.

———. 1997b. "Valuation of Compound and Partial Barrier Options." http://207.67.203.54/elibsql05_P40007_Documents/QUANT%20DOCS/partial_barrier_pge_ts.pdf.

———. 2000. "Fast Spread Option Evaluation." http://207.67.203.54/elibsql05_P40007_Documents/QUANT%20DOCS/fast_spread_pge_ts.pdf.

———. 2001a. "The American Cash-or-Nothing Option." http://207.67.203.54/elibsql05_P40007_Documents/QUANT%20DOCS/Am_CON_pge.pdf.

———. 2001b. "Average Price Options." http://207.67.203.54/elibsql05_P40007_Documents/QUANT%20DOCS/APO_pge_ts.pdf.

———. 2002. "Terminal Correlation in a Spread Option." http://207.67.203.54/elibsql05_P40007_Documents/QUANT%20DOCS/Spread_correlation_pge_ts.pdf.

———. 2004. "Weighted Average Price Options." PG&E PEC-Energy Procurement-Quantitative Analysis Group. January 9. http://207.67.203.54/elibsql05_P40007_Documents/QUANT%20DOCS/Weighted%20average%20price%20options.pdf.

Rubinstein, Mark. 1991. "Double Trouble." *Risk* 5(1): 73.

Ryabchenko, V., and S. Uryasev. 2011. "Pricing Energy Derivatives by Linear Programming: Tolling Agreement Contracts." *Journal of Computational Finance* 14(3): 73–126.www.risk.net/digital_assets/4231/v14n3a3.pdf.

Siclari,M.,andG.Castellacci.2011."BeyondtheSparkSpreadOption—FuelSwitching." *Energy Risk International.* www.olf.com/software/energy-commodities/ articles/energy-risk-beyond-the-spark-spread-option-fuel-switching.pdf.

Shu, Cheng-Hsiung. 2006. "Pricing Asian Options with Fourier Convolution." Thesis, Department of Computer Science and Information Engineering, National Taiwan University. www.csie.ntu.edu.tw/~lyuu/theses/thesis_r93922111.pdf.

Taleb, Nassim. 1997. *Dynamic Hedging: Managing Vanilla and Exotic Options.* New York: John Wiley & Sons.

Thoren, Stefan. 2005. "A Monte Carlo Solver for Financial Problems." Master's thesis, Stockholm Royal Institute of Technology. www.nada.kth.se/utbildning/ grukth/exjobb/rapportlistor/2005/rapporter05/thoren_stefan_05114.pdf.

Turnbull, S. M., and L. Wakeman. 1991. "A Quick Algorithm for Pricing European Average Options." *Journal of Financial and Quantitative Finance* 26: 377–89.

U.S. Energy Information Administration (EIA). 2002. "Derivatives and Risk Management in the Petroleum, Natural Gas, and Electricity Industries." www.eia .gov/oiaf/servicerpt/derivative/chapter3.html.

Vorst, T. 1992. "Prices and Hedge Rations of Average Exchange Rate Options." *International Review of Financial Analysis* 1(3): 179–194.

Wang, Muhu. 2010. "A Finite-Element Approach for Pricing Swing Options Under Stochastic Volatility." PhD thesis, University of Houston, Texas.

Wasenden, Odd-Harald. 2012. "Supervision and Regulation of Energy Derivatives Trading: An Introduction to the Main Legislation and Some of the Challenges in Practice." *Florence School of Regulation*, Brussels, May 23. www.florence-school .eu/portal/page/portal/FSR_HOME/ENERGY/Policy_Events/Workshops/2012/ EU%20Energy%20Law%20Policy/120523_Wasenden_Odd-Harald.pdf.

Wilcox, D. 1991. "Spread Options Enhance Risk Management Choices." *NUMEX Energy in the News* (Autumn): 9–13.

Yu, Carisa, and Hung Hom. 2004. "Pricing American Options without Expiry Date." Hong Kong Polytechnic University. www.soa.org/library/proceedings/ arch/2004/arch04v38n1_7.pdf.

Zhang, P. G. 1998. In *Exotic Options*, 2nd ed. World Scientific.

Zhang, Xian. 2005. "Exotic Options Bundled with Interruptible Electricity Contracts." *The 7th International Power Engineering Conference* (IPEC). http:// ieeexplore.ieee.org/xpl/mostRecentIssue.jsp?punumber=10834.

CHAPTER 5

Risk Management and Hedging Strategies

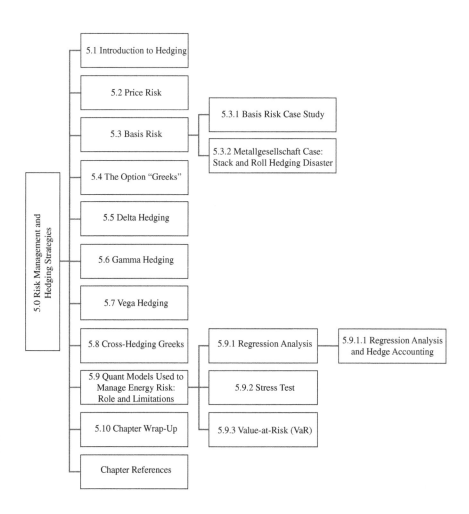

The relationship between risk and return is a fundamental concept in finance. *Risk* includes the possibility that an investor or trader may lose some or all of its original investment. *Risk management* is the process of identification, analysis, and either acceptance or mitigation of uncertainty in investment decision making. In addition, risk management may be viewed as the immunization of a portfolio against risk.

As we will discuss in Section 5.4, the *Greeks* measure the sensitivity of the value of a portfolio to small changes in various parameters. These *Greeks*

- Provide important information for risk management
- Are useful for energy market participants who seek to "hedge" their portfolios from adverse changes in market conditions

Note: We will define a *hedge* in Section 5.1.

Risk management tools may be utilized to insure that a portfolio is not greatly affected by small changes in the price of the underlying energy assets and other key parameters.

Participants in the energy markets perform one or more of the following functions:

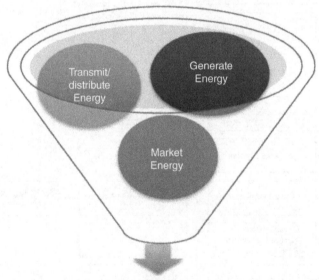

Consume Energy

In Table 5.1 we list five general types of business risks incurred by energy market participants. A more detailed breakdown of these risks may be found in Figure 5.1. In addition, some risks incurred by power market participants may be found in Table 5.2 (EIA 2002).

TABLE 5.1   General Types of Risks Incurred by Energy Market Participants

Risk	Definition
Credit Risk	Risk of loss of principal or loss of a financial reward stemming from a borrower's failure to repay a loan or otherwise meet a contractual obligation. Credit risks are calculated based on the borrowers' overall ability to repay.
Liquidity Risk	The degree to which an asset or security can be bought or sold in the market without affecting the asset's price. Liquidity is characterized by a high level of trading activity. Liquidity risk is also known as "marketability."
Market Risk	The possibility for an investor to experience losses due to factors that affect the overall performance of the financial markets. Market risk, also called "systematic risk," cannot be eliminated through diversification, though it can be hedged against.
Operational Risk	Operational risk is defined in the Basel II regulations as the risk of loss resulting from inadequate or failed internal processes, people and systems, or from external events.
Political Risk	The risk that an investment's returns could suffer as a result of political changes or instability in a country. Instability affecting investment returns could stem from a change in regulations, government, legislative bodies, other foreign policy makers, or military control.

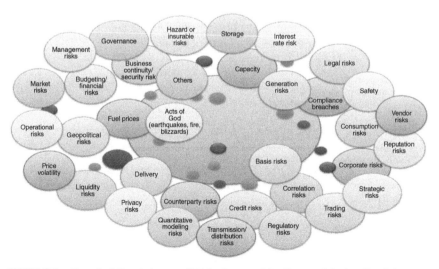

FIGURE 5.1   Detailed Breakdown of Risks Incurred by Energy Market Participants

TABLE 5.2 Risks Incurred by Power Market Participants

Power Market Participant	Risk Exposure	Power Position
Generators	▪ Generators include utilities, federal power authorities, qualifying facilities (small power production and cogeneration facilities), merchant power plants, and on-site industrial plants (FERC, 2012). ▪ These entities own a power plant. Hence, they have a "long" electricity position. ▪ When power prices increase (decrease), the value of the generator increases (decreases).	*Long*
Marketers	▪ Marketers buy and resell power. ▪ A marketer can have either a "long" or "short" position. Marketers that buy (sell) fixed-price power before finding a market for that power have a "long" ("short") position. ▪ *San Diego Gas & Electric* and *Portland General Electric* are examples of utilities that also serve as marketers. Each of these utilities has greater load than generating resources. Hence, they buy power in the wholesale market and resell it at the retail level. Their obligation to serve retail loads gives them a "short" position, since they must buy power in the wholesale markets in order to meet their obligations to customers. ▪ *Enron* was initially a power generator that evolved into a marketer. Jeff Skilling and several other executives decided it was a great idea for Enron to become asset-light and eventually asset-free.	*Long or Short*
End Users	▪ End users may be industrial, commercial, or residential customers. ▪ An electricity end user has a "short" position. Consumers benefit when prices decrease and are hurt when prices increase.	*Short*

5.1 INTRODUCTION TO HEDGING

A *Standard & Poor's Ratings Services* study—based on an analysis of numerous financial reports of various U.S. oil and gas companies—reveals that energy market participants utilize a wide range of financial engineering products and strategies:

▪ Derivatives to manage risks related to various commodity prices.
▪ A variety of financial instruments and hedging practices (S&P 2012).

Hedging strategies generally involve the use of derivatives, such as those introduced in Chapters 2, 3, and 4. Derivatives, when well understood and properly utilized, are beneficial to help energy market participants manage risks through trading and structured hedging strategies. In this chapter we

- Discuss the role of hedging in energy trading and risk management
- Lay the groundwork for the next chapter, where we examine how energy derivatives are utilized in various hedging strategies

HEDGE

A **hedge** is an investment that reduces the risk of adverse price movements in an asset.

Hedging against risk involves the purchasing of financial instruments to offset the risk of adverse price movements.

What is a hedge? What is hedging?

A *hedge* is an investment that reduces the risk of adverse price movements in an asset. Technically, a basic hedge consists of investing in two assets with a negative correlation (statistical measurement of how two assets move in relation to each other).

Hedging against risk involves the purchasing of financial instruments to offset the risk of adverse price movements.

If a market participant employs a hedging strategy it may incur an inevitable tradeoff between risk and return.

One way to grasp the concept of hedging is to think of it as insurance. When energy and financial market participants implement hedging strategies they are insuring themselves against a negative event. Hedging does not prevent a negative event from occurring. If the negative event does occur and the market participant is properly hedged, then any negative impact should be minimized. In financial and energy markets, hedging is more complicated than the payment of insurance premiums.

Regulatory rules may play an important role in hedging strategies (Deng and Oren 2006). In addition, hedging of risk by a corporation is often motivated by the goal of maximizing the firm's value via the reduction of the

- Likelihood of financial distress and its ensuing costs, or
- Variance of taxable incomes and associated present value of future tax liabilities.

If an energy market participant employs a hedging strategy it may incur an inevitable trade-off between risk and return. Hence, a reduction in risk via hedging can mean a reduction in potential profits. More explicitly, if an investment

- *Makes* money, the implementation of a hedge will typically reduce the profit that could have been made.
- *Loses* money, the implementation of a hedge, if successful, will reduce that loss.

5.2 PRICE RISK

Accounting Standards Codification 815 (ASC 815) lays out the requirements and framework for valuing and accounting of derivatives (E&Y 2013). ASC 815 requires that market participants detail the

1. Exposure environment
2. Context for the use of the derivatives
3. Strategy to achieve hedging objectives
4. Derivatives categories according to the liquidity levels

> *Energy market participants are susceptible to market price risk as a consequence of the volatility of energy prices. For example, volatility in natural gas prices over the past decade has resulted in an increased emphasis on risk management activities by energy market participants.*

Energy market participants are susceptible to market price risk as a consequence of the volatility of energy prices. For example, volatility in natural gas prices over the past decade has resulted in an increased emphasis on risk management activities by energy market participants. Since natural gas is also the price-setting fuel in many power markets, the volatility in natural gas prices also has a large impact on retail electricity prices (Graves and Levine 2010).

> *Energy derivatives are not typically designed to mitigate risks associated with daily power price fluctuations.*

Daily fluctuations in electricity prices are the most dramatic manifestation of price volatility. Uncontrolled exposure to price risks can lead to devastating consequences for power market participants. Energy derivatives may be utilized by power market participants to manage, or hedge, price volatility.

Some factors that cause electricity production costs to fluctuate can be found in Table 5.3. Power customers on real-time rates can face prices that may fluctuate by more than 100 percent over several hours. Price volatility alone may not create serious risk. A firm may face significant risks if it has volatile input prices and fixed output prices.

TABLE 5.3 Factors That Cause Fluctuation of Electricity Production Costs

Cause of Fluctuation	Relevant Time Period	Role of Energy Derivatives
Demand	*Daily, Seasonal*	■ Energy derivatives aren't typically used to hedge risks associated with daily price fluctuations. ■ They're used to hedge risks associated with seasonal price fluctuations.
Generation Availability	*Daily, Yearly, Seasonal*	■ A source of cost fluctuation is a function of available generation. ■ Inexpensive hydropower (if there is plentiful rainfall) ■ Wind power (wind power is getting more economical) ■ Fossil plants (with higher operating costs) ■ Derivatives play a useful role in hedging fluctuations associated with generation.
Fuel Cost	*Seasonal and longer*	■ Perhaps the most important source of electricity price volatility is that of the cost of fuel. ■ Fuel cost is affected by seasonality, geopolitical events and changes in global market conditions. ■ Derivatives play a useful role in hedging fluctuations associated with fuel cost.

(continued)

TABLE 5.3   Factors That Cause Fluctuation of Electricity Production Costs (*continued*)

Other Production Costs	*Years to Decades*	▪ Sources of cost fluctuations are changes in the production technology. Technological progress reduces the cost of production. ▪ Production costs may also be affected by environmental and labor costs. ▪ These cost fluctuations may be very important over the life of multiyear contracts, but are generally beyond the time scope of hedging strategies based on energy derivatives.
Transmission Congestion	*Daily, Seasonal and longer*	▪ Congestion occurs when there is not sufficient transmission capacity available to transmit energy from generation location to load location. Transmission congestion is also a major cause of price fluctuations.

Example: Power Marketer's Volatile Input/Fixed Output Price Risks

Suppose a marketer buys power from generators in a spot market and sells power through fixed price contracts, as illustrated in Figure 5.2. The marketer's

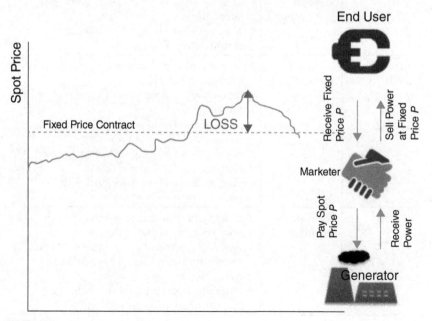

FIGURE 5.2   Marketer's Risks

markup is likely to be small (e.g., less than 10 percent above the spot price). Most of the markup goes towards marketing and overhead cost, leaving only a small profit. If the spot price jumps 25 percent in a given year due to a supply shortage, the marketer could lose several years' worth of profits. This is an unacceptable risk, and the marketer would be interested in hedging it.

Example: Utility's Volatile Input/Fixed Output Price Risks

Suppose an electric utility has more load than generation capabilities. Hence, the utility needs to purchase power in the spot market. The electric utility may encounter price volatility risks if it is under a price-cap regulation or unable to pass costs on to the customers.

Example: Power Generator's Volatile Input/ Fixed Output Price Risks

Generators may encounter price volatility risks if they sell in a market dominated by generation from another fuel. Suppose a generator's fuel cost increases more than the fuel costs of other types of generation. Hence it is likely that spot power prices will not completely cover their increased fuel prices and the generators' profits will suffer.

5.3   BASIS RISK

Basis risk is the primary risk associated with using futures contracts to hedge commodity risks.

- *Basis* is the difference between the futures price and the spot price of the commodity being hedged.
- *Basis risk* is the risk that offsetting investments in hedging strategies will not experience price changes in entirely opposite directions from each other.

> Basis risk is the risk that offsetting investments in a hedging strategy will not experience price changes in entirely opposite directions from each other.

This imperfect correlation between the two investments creates the potential for excess gains or losses in a hedging strategy, thus adding risk to the position, as illustrated in the next short case study.

5.3.1 Basis Risk Case Study

The price of electricity in Denver, Colorado is not likely to be the same as the price at the California-Oregon Border (COB) even though they're all part of the North American Electric Reliability Corporation's (NERC) Western Electricity Coordinating Council (WECC) region. Hence, using a futures contract for the COB may not perfectly hedge price risk in Denver (see Figure 5.3).

As a result of this transaction, the generator receives $25/MWh for his electricity in the spot market.

- He loses $10/MWh on his financial position.
- He ultimately receives only $15/MWh, not $18/MWh for his electricity as initially planned.

The details of this imperfect correlation between the two energy assets, and hence the basis risk, is summarized as follows:

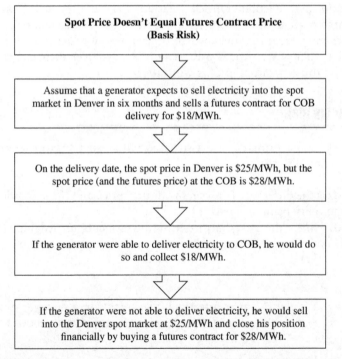

If the electricity price in Denver were perfectly correlated with the price at COB, the generator would be perfectly hedged and could expect to lock in the price at COB less $3/MWh. But if the prices in the two markets are not well correlated, this will undermine the generators' hedge. One way to deal with this risk is to use a basis swap to hedge this basis risk (Stoft et al. 1998).

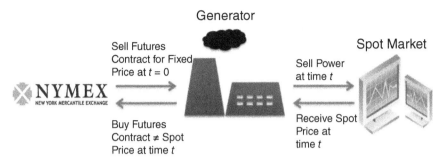

FIGURE 5.3 Spot Price Doesn't Equal Futures Contract Price

5.3.2 Metallgesellchaft Case: Stack and Roll Hedging Disaster

Some other issues that may arise when utilizing futures contracts to hedge commodity risks are as follows:

- The procedures for determining the optimal hedge size are specific and well defined. However, the correlation is an important quantity in the valuation (Eydeland 2003).
- The futures contract commodity might be different from the spot price commodity (i.e., product quality or definition). This could be a problem if the spot market sells electricity on a daily rather than a monthly basis because futures contracts call for delivery over an entire month.
- The generator, end user, or marketer miscalculates the amount of energy to generate or consume.

At Metallgesellchaft (MG) the *Stack and roll* method was used to hedge a long-term physical position with short-term futures contracts. The underlying assets were short positions in long-term forward contracts to deliver oil. A stack and roll hedge was utilized: long positions in short-term futures contracts that were rolled over consecutively (Kuprianov 1995). This hedging strategy depended on:

- Continuation of stable or gently increasing spot oil prices
- Backwardation

Please note that a more detailed discussion on hedging with futures contracts will be presented in Chapter 7. In addition, more on the MG case study will be discussed in Chapters 6 and 9.

5.4　THE OPTION "GREEKS"

An option value may be expressed in terms of the following Taylor series expansion:

$$dV = \underbrace{\frac{\partial V}{\partial S}}_{Delta} dS + \frac{1}{2} \underbrace{\frac{\partial^2 V}{\partial S^2}}_{Gamma} dS^2 + \underbrace{\frac{\partial V}{\partial \sigma}}_{Vega} d\sigma + \underbrace{\frac{\partial V}{\partial \tau}}_{Theta} d\tau + \cdots$$

In Table 5.4 we list first- and second-order *Greeks*. One can derive higher order *Greeks* as well, for example: *Color, Speed, Ultima, Zomma*, and so forth. Some shortcomings of the *Greeks* are discussed in Burger, Graeber, and Schindlmayr (2007); Eydeland (2003); Garner (2012); and Taleb (1997). In addition, Taleb lists ways to tweak the Greeks to deal with various shortcomings.

TABLE 5.4　First- and Second-Order Option "Greeks"

Option Greek	Definition	Mathematical Formulation
Delta	Sensitivity of the derivative price relative to changes in the price of the underlying asset.	$\Delta = \dfrac{\partial V}{\partial S}$
Lambda	Percentage change in the option value per percentage change in the underlying price. Lambda, also known as omega, is a measure of leverage (sometimes called *gearing*).	$\lambda = \dfrac{\partial V}{\partial S} \times \dfrac{S}{V}$
Rho	Rate of change of the option value with respect to changes in the interest rate.	$\rho = \dfrac{\partial V}{\partial r}$
Theta	The "time decay" theta is a measure of the sensitivity of the value of the derivative to the passage of time.	$\theta = -\dfrac{\partial V}{\partial \tau}$
Vega	Sensitivity of the derivative price with respect to volatility.	$\nu = \dfrac{\partial V}{\partial \sigma}$
Charm	The "delta decay" measures the instantaneous rate of change of delta over the passage of time.	$Charm = -\dfrac{\partial \Delta}{\partial \tau} = \dfrac{\partial \theta}{\partial S} = -\dfrac{\partial^2 V}{\partial S \partial \tau}$
Gamma	Rate of change (curvature) in the delta with respect to changes in the price of the underlying asset.	$\Gamma = \dfrac{\partial \Delta}{\partial S} = \dfrac{\partial^2 V}{\partial S^2}$

TABLE 5.4 *(continued)*

Vanna	Sensitivity of the option delta with respect to the change in volatility.	$Vanna = \dfrac{\partial \Delta}{\partial \sigma} = \dfrac{\partial v}{\partial S} = \dfrac{\partial^2 V}{\partial S \partial \sigma}$
Vera	This is a measurement of the rate of change in ρ with respect to volatility.	$Vera = \dfrac{\partial \rho}{\partial \sigma} = \dfrac{\partial^2 V}{\partial \sigma \partial r}$

Where V = the value of the option
           S = price of the underlying asset

5.5   DELTA HEDGING

As previously defined in Table 5.4, delta measures the change in a derivatives' price relative to the price change in the underlying asset. Delta is sometimes referred to as the *hedge ratio*.

Delta for a call option is illustrated in Figure 5.4. In addition, the range of delta for calls and put options are illustrated in Figure 5.5 and discussed in Table 5.5.

DELTA

Delta measures the change in a derivatives' price relative to the price change in the underlying asset. Delta is sometimes referred to as the "hedge ratio."

DELTA HEDGING

Delta hedging is the perfect elimination of risk achieved by exploiting correlation between two financial instruments.

Delta hedging is the perfect elimination of risk achieved by exploiting correlation between two financial instruments. In the case of options, delta hedging is a strategy that aims to reduce the risk associated with price movements in the underlying asset by offsetting long and short positions. That is, it is the partial or complete offset of an underlying energy asset's price risk via holding energy options on the asset.

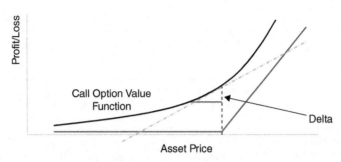

FIGURE 5.4   Delta for a Call Option

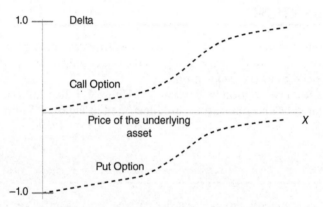

FIGURE 5.5   Delta Range for Call and Put Options

TABLE 5.5   Delta Range

	Delta	Examples
Long Call Position	$0 \leq \Delta \leq 1$	■ If $\Delta = 0.6$, then for every \$1 the underlying price of the energy asset increases, the call option will increase by \$0.60. ■ As an in-the-money (ITM) call option nears expiration, Δ will approach 1.00.
Long Put Position	$-1 \leq \Delta \leq 0$	■ If $\Delta = 0.6$, then for every \$1 the underlying price of the energy asset increases, the put option will decrease by \$0.60. ■ As an ITM put option nears expiration, Δ will approach −1.00.

Note: The sign of a short (sold) option position's delta is opposite that of a long position.

Delta hedging involves the calculation of the number of options necessary to offset the price movement in an underlying position—the *hedge ratio*. Suppose we structure the following portfolio:

$Portfolio_{\Delta\ Hedged}$ = {*Energy Option, Position in the Underlying Energy Asset*}

Delta hedging of this portfolio involves dynamically trading a position in the underlying energy asset in such a manner that over each small interval of time between trades, the change in the option price is offset by an equal and opposite change in the value of the position in the underlying asset.

Example: Suppose we short a European call option (Zhao 2007).

- The delta of this short option is $-\dfrac{\partial V}{\partial S}$.
- In order to delta hedge this position, we should buy $\dfrac{\partial V}{\partial S}$ of the underlying forward contract.
- If P_{value} denotes the value of the hedged portfolio, then

$$P_{value} = -V + \frac{\partial V}{\partial S} S$$

- The change in the hedged portfolio value is zero if the forward price changes by a small amount.

$$\Delta P_{value} = -\Delta V + \frac{\partial V}{\partial S}\Delta S = 0$$

The primary shortcoming of delta hedging is that it requires constant rebalancing of a portfolio. Whenever the price of an underlying asset changes, so does the delta of derivatives based on it. When the delta changes significantly, the composition of any delta hedged portfolio will need to be changed. The amount of rebalancing needed may be minimized by reducing the amount by which the delta changes for a price movement, that is, by reducing the rate of change of gamma—to be discussed in the next section. In addition, further discussion of delta hedging and its applications to energy markets may be found in Chapter 9.

5.6   GAMMA HEDGING

As previously defined in Table 5.4, gamma measures the rate of change (curvature) in the delta with respect to changes in the price of the underlying asset. Gamma for a call option is illustrated in Figure 5.6. It can be described

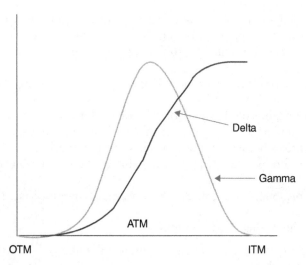

FIGURE 5.6 Gamma Hedging

as the "speed" at which the value of an option changes with respect to changes in the price of the underlying asset.

GAMMA

Gamma measures the curvature of the price curve. It can be described as the "speed" at which the value of an option changes with respect to changes in the price of the underlying asset.

A few key properties to keep in mind regarding gamma is that it is:

- Highest for at-the-money options
- Lowest when an option is deeply in-the-money or completely out-of-the-money
- The same for call and put options
- Negative for both short call and put options positions
- Sensitive for short-term options
- Increasing as the option approaches its maturity
- High when the options delta changes rapidly
- Small when option delta changes relatively little
- Constant and equal to zero for futures

GAMMA HEDGING

Gamma hedging involves the readjustment of a delta hedge. It may be employed to reduce the size of each re-hedge and/or to increase the time between re-hedges, hence reducing costs.

Gamma hedging involves the readjustment of a delta hedge. It may be employed to reduce the size of each rehedge and/or to increase the time between rehedges, hence reducing costs.

5.7 VEGA HEDGING

As previously defined in Table 5.4, vega indicates the sensitivity of the derivative price with respect to volatility. The value of vega is

- Normally maximized at-the-money (ATM).
- Low for deep out-of-the-money (OTM) options (Figure 5.7).

VEGA HEDGING

Vega hedging is utilized to help make a portfolio insensitive to changes in the volatility of the underlying energy asset.

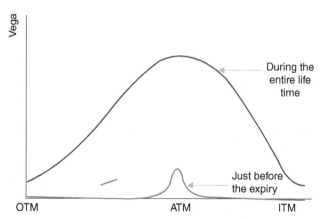

FIGURE 5.7 Vega Hedging

5.8   CROSS-HEDGING GREEKS

Although two energy assets may not be identical, they may be sufficiently correlated to create a hedged position as long as their prices move in the same direction. *Cross hedging* involves hedging a position by investing in two positively correlated securities or securities that have similar price movements.

CROSS HEDGING

Cross hedging involves hedging a position by investing in two positively correlated securities or securities that have similar price movements.

An energy market participant may take opposing positions in each energy asset in an attempt to reduce the risk of holding just one of the assets. The success of cross hedging depends on how strongly correlated the asset being hedged is with the instrument underlying the derivatives contract. When cross hedging, the maturity of the two securities has to be equal. In other words, you cannot hedge a long-term instrument with a short-term security. Both energy assets should have the same maturity.

Example: Suppose the electricity forward market at a power generator's location is not liquidly traded. Then, the electricity forwards from adjacent trading hubs or even forwards on the input fuel, which are liquidly traded, may be utilized to cross hedge the electricity output price (Deng and Oren 2006).

Example: Increased use of alternative fuels and low commodity prices have contributed to the expansion of the ethanol industry. A study in Franken and Parcell (2002) illustrates a cross-hedge relationship between spot ethanol and New York Mercantile Exchange (NYMEX) unleaded gasoline futures.

5.9   QUANT MODELS USED TO MANAGE ENERGY RISK: ROLE AND LIMITATIONS

As is the case for participants in the financial markets, many energy markets participants utilize a host of quantitative models to evaluate risk. Some of the more commonly used risks models are summarized below. I will give a brief overview of the role and limitations of these models in this section.

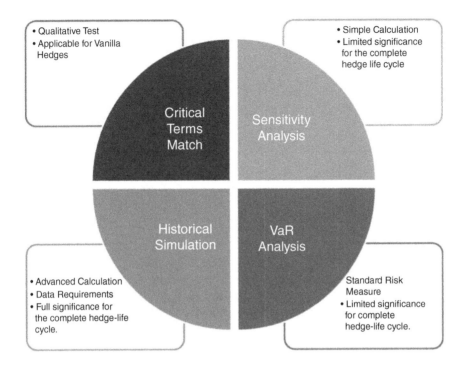

5.9.1 Regression Analysis

The *Financial Accounting Standards Board* (FASB) concluded that market participants may use regression analysis of past changes in fair values or cash flows for assessing hedge effectiveness.

Recall that a regression is a statistical analysis assessing the association between two variables. For example, regression analysis can be utilized to find the relationship between two variables x and y as follows:

$$y = \alpha + \beta x + \varepsilon$$

Where y is the dependent variable—the variable being predicted or explained

α is the intercept point of the regression line and the y-axis

β is the slope of the regression line

x is the independent variable—the variable being used to predict the value of y

ε is the error term—the error in predicting y, given the value of x

TABLE 5.6   Regression Analysis

X_i	Y_i	$X_i - \overline{X}$	$Y_i - \overline{Y}$	$(X_i - \overline{X})(Y_i - \overline{Y})$	$(X_i - \overline{X})^2$
3	23	−7.71	−28.86	222.61	59.51
5	33	−5.71	−18.86	107.76	32.65
7	35	−3.71	−16.86	62.61	13.80
12	56	1.29	4.14	5.33	1.65
13	66	2.29	14.14	32.33	5.22
17	70	6.29	18.14	114.04	39.51
18	80	7.29	28.14	205.04	53.08
Mean $\overline{X} = 10.71$	Mean $\overline{Y} = 51.86$			749.71	205.42

Example of Regression Analysis: The relationship between the variables x and y is illustrated in the following graph. These values for x and y were derived via the regression analysis, which is summarized in Table 5.6.

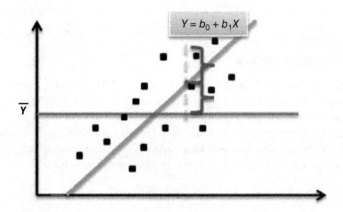

Total sum of squares = Sum of squared residuals + Explained sum of squares

$$\sum_i (Y_i - \overline{Y})^2 = \sum_i (Y_i - Y)^2 + \sum_i (Y_i - \overline{Y})^2$$

To estimate parameters of equation,

$$Y_i = b_o + b_1 X_i + e_i$$

We need to minimize

$$\sum_i e_i^2 = \sum_i (Y_i - b_o - b_1 X_i)^2$$

Where, $\quad b_1 = \dfrac{\sum_i (X_i - \overline{X})(Y_i - \overline{Y})}{\sum_i (X_i - \overline{X})^2} = \dfrac{Cov(X,Y)}{Var(X)}$

$$b_0 = \overline{Y} - b_1 \overline{X}$$

R^2 = Determination (aka R-squared)

$$= \frac{\text{Variances of the Fitted Values}}{\text{Observed Values of the Dependent Values}} = \frac{\sum_i \left(\widehat{Y}_i - \overline{Y}\right)^2}{\sum_i \left(Y_i - \overline{Y}\right)^2}$$

$\widehat{Y}$ = the fitted value

$\overline{X}$ is the mean of $\{X_i\}_{1 \leq i \leq n}$

$\overline{Y}$ is the mean of $\{Y_i\}_{1 \leq i \leq n}$

5.9.1.1 Regression Analysis and Hedge Accounting

The following characteristics are considered guidelines for whether a regression analysis can support the continuation of hedge accounting even when a highly effective dollar offset is not achieved for a particular quarter (E&Y 2013).

- The regression uses appropriate and representative data for the hedge relationship being evaluated and has a minimum of 30 observations of both variables.
- The regression examines the relationship between changes in the value of the derivative and the hedged item.
- The regression evaluates data representative of changes in the value of the variables over a time horizon that coincides with (or is less than) the time horizon of the hedge relationship.
- The user has considered whether the data being regressed should be based on price or value changes of the two variables or on price levels of two variables, and regresses both types of data if considered necessary to avoid distortion of results.
- The user examines the layout of the plotted points—in other words, the distribution of the error terms or residual values. The user considers

whether the problem of autocorrelation is present and makes adjustments to the standard errors of the estimated coefficients as necessary. An unbiased regression equation should have error terms with a constant variance and a random distribution.

- The regression produces an R-squared that exceeds a prespecified level, such as 0.80.
- The hedge ratio of the hedging relationship corresponds with the regression coefficient or beta; that is, the optimal hedge is used.
- The standard error of the estimate is used to determine the reliability (or the statistical significance) of the estimated coefficients, by calculating the t-statistic.
- The t-test is passed for the regression coefficient at a 95 percent confidence level or better, supporting the calculated hedge ratio.
- The y intercept is evaluated to see if it calls into question the usefulness of the regression equation; a high y intercept when small changes in x are expected may be problematic.
- The regression results are appropriately related to the actual hedge relationship being evaluated by the user, and an appropriate dollar offset is projected for the relationship, and evaluated based on the 80 percent to 125 percent standard.

It may be difficult in some situations to meet the standards described in the regression analysis. ASC 815-20-35-2 permits statistical approaches other than regression analysis to be used, such as *stress test* and *value at risk* (VaR).

5.9.2 Stress Test

... Incorporation of stress scenarios into formal risk modeling
would seem to be of first-order importance. However, the
incipient art of stress testing has yet to find formalization and
uniformity across banks and securities dealers. At present,
most banks pick a small number of ad hoc scenarios as their
stress tests...

　　　　　　　　　　　　　　　　　Alan Greenspan (2000)

A *stress test* is an analysis—conducted under unfavorable economic scenarios—that is designed to determine whether a market participant has enough capital to withstand the impact of adverse developments. Stress tests focus on a few key risks, such as credit risk, market risk, and liquidity risk. They are usually computer-generated simulation models that test hypothetical scenarios.

STRESS TEST

Stress test is an analysis—conducted under unfavorable economic scenarios—that is designed to determine whether a market participant has enough capital to withstand the impact of adverse developments.

The *Monte Carlo simulation*—one of the most widely used methods of stress testing—was invented by scientists working on the atomic bomb in the 1940s. It is a computerized mathematical technique that may be utilized to account for risk in quantitative analysis, risk management, and decision making. The term *Monte Carlo simulation* was coined by Metropolis and Ulam (1949) in reference to the casinos in Monte Carlo, Monaco (Thoren 2005).

The core idea of the Monte Carlo simulation is to use random samples of parameters or inputs to explore the behavior of a complex system or process. It shows

- Extreme possibilities: outcomes of going for broke and for the most conservative decision
- Possible consequences for middle-of-the-road decisions

The Monte Carlo simulation (Figure 5.8) is a statistical sampling method because the inputs are randomly generated from probability distributions to

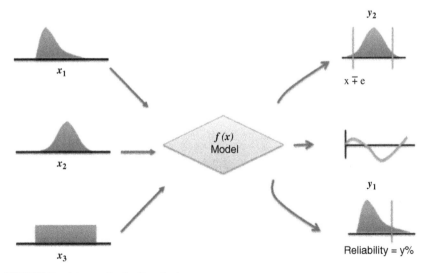

FIGURE 5.8 Monte Carlo Simulation

simulate the process of sampling from an actual population. The data generated from the Monte Carlo simulation can be represented via probability distributions, histograms, and so forth (Wittwer 2004).

The main steps in the Monte Carlo simulation can actually be implemented in Excel. They are as follows:

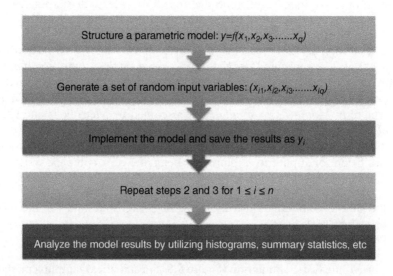

Structure a parametric model: $y = f(x_1, x_2, x_3 \ldots x_q)$

Generate a set of random input variables: $(x_{i1}, x_{i2}, x_{i3} \ldots x_{iq})$

Implement the model and save the results as y_i

Repeat steps 2 and 3 for $1 \leq i \leq n$

Analyze the model results by utilizing histograms, summary statistics, etc

As detailed in Aragones, Blanco, and Dowd (2001), stress tests have some limitations:

- They are subjective because they depend on scenarios chosen by the stress tester.
- The stress testing results depend on the choice of scenarios and skill of the modeler.
- This subjectivity may make it difficult to analyze the results of a stress test objectively.
- This subjectivity may pose problems for senior management, regulators, and other parties trying to assess a firm's stress testing strategy.
- Results of stress tests are difficult to interpret because they give no idea of the probabilities of the events concerned.
- In the absence of this information it is difficult to know how to interpret the stress test results.
- Some stress test strategies are difficult to back test.

Further information on stress testing may be found in Aragones et al. (2001) and Aydin and Kucukozmen (2010).

5.9.3 Value at Risk

Value at risk (VaR) is a statistical technique used to measure and quantify the level of financial risk within a firm or portfolio over a specific time frame at a confidence level. VaR is used by risk managers in order to measure and control the level of risk that the firm undertakes. The risk manager's job is to ensure that risks are not taken beyond the level at which the firm can absorb the losses of a probable worst outcome.

> **VALUE AT RISK**
>
> Value at risk (VaR) is a statistical technique used to measure and quantify the level of financial risk within a firm or portfolio over a specific time frame.

A VaR statistic may be computed via a Monte Carlo simulation. It has three components:

1. Potential loss amount (loss percentage)
2. Confidence level (probability of that loss amount)
3. Time period

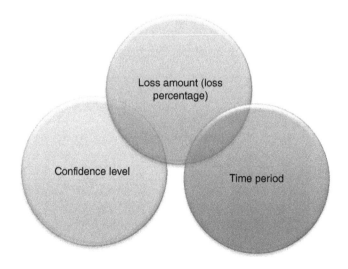

Hence, the VaR statistic may be used to answer questions such as the following:

- With a 95 or 99 percent level of confidence, what is the most I can expect to lose in dollars over the next quarter?
- With a 95 or 99 percent level of confidence, what is the maximum percentage I can expect to lose over the next year?

Example: An oil company determined that it has a 5 percent one-month VaR of $100 million. That is, the oil company has a 5 percent chance that it could lose more than $100 million in any given month. Hence, a $100 million loss should be expected to occur once every 20 months.

Various financial debacles have highlighted the limitations of VaR, such as, the dependency on historical or unrealistic statistical assumptions. Market participants attempt to address these limitations by resorting to stress tests to complement the results of their VaR analyses (Aragones et al. 2001).

5.10 CHAPTER WRAP-UP

In this chapter we defined, illustrated, and discussed various types of risk management and hedging strategies and tools. In subsequent chapters we will examine how energy market participants apply these strategies to manage risk.

REFERENCES

Aragones, J., C. Blanco, and K. Dowd. 2001. "Incorporating Stress Tests into Market Risk Modeling." *Institutional Investor*. www.fea.com/resources/a_stresstest .pdf.

Aydin, N., and C. Kucukozmen. 2010. "Stress Testing of Energy-Related Derivative Instruments Based on Conditional Market Risk Models." Enerji, Piyasa ve Düzenleme (Cilt:1, Sayı:2, Sayfa 121–144), http://epddergi.org/articles/2010-2/ Aydin-Kucukozmen.pdf.

Burger, M., B. Graeber, and G. Schindlmayr. 2007. *Managing Energy Risk*. Chichester, England: Wiley Finance.

Deng, S. J., and S. S. Oren. 2006. "Electricity Derivatives and Risk Management." *Energy* 21: 940–953. www.ieor.berkeley.edu/~oren/pubs/Deng%20and%20 Oren-86.pdf.

Ernst & Young (E&Y). 2013. "Derivative Instruments and Hedging Activities." Ernst & Young Financial Reporting Developments.

Federal Energy Regulatory Commission (FERC). 2012 (July). "Energy Primer: A Handbook of Energy Market Basics." The Division of Energy Market Oversight,

Office of Enforcement, Federal Energy Regulatory Commission. www.ferc.gov/market-oversight/guide/energy-primer.pdf.

Franken, Jason, and Joe Parcell. 2002. "Cash Ethanol Cross-Hedging Opportunities." Working Paper AEWP 2002-9, Department of Agricultural Economics, University of Missouri-Columbia. http://ageconsearch.umn.edu/bitstream/26035/1/aewp0209.pdf.

Garner, Carley. 2012. *Trading Commodities, Commodity Options and Currencies.* Upper Saddle River, NJ: FT Press.

Graves, Frank, and Steven Levine. 2010. "Managing Natural Gas Price Volatility: Principles and Practices across the Industry." The Brattle Group, Inc. www.cleanskies.org/wp-content/uploads/2011/08/ManagingNGPriceVolatility.pdf.

Kuprianov, Anatoli. 1995. "Derivatives Debacles: Case Studies of Large Losses in Derivatives Markets." *FRB Richmond Economic Quarterly* 81(4, Fall): 1–39. http://papers.ssrn.com/sol3/papers.cfm?abstract_id=2129302

Metropolis, N., and S. Ulam. 1949. 1949. "The Monte Carlo Method." *Journal of American Statistical Association* 44: 335–341.

Standard & Poor's (S&P). 2012. "U.S. Oil And Gas Sector Makes Extensive Use Of Commodity Derivatives." Standard & Poor's Ratings Services. www.ratingsdirect.com.

Stoft, S., T. Belden, C. Goldman, and S. Pickle. 1998. "Primer on Electricity Futures and Other Derivatives." Report LBNL-41098, UC-1321, Environmental Energy Technologies Division: Ernest Orlando Lawrence Berkeley National Laboratory. http://eetd.lbl.gov/ea/emp/reports/41098.pdf.

Taleb, Nassim. 1997. *Dynamic Hedging: Managing Vanilla and Exotic Options.* New York: John Wiley & Sons.

Thoren, Stefan. 2005. "A Monte Carlo Solver for Financial Problems." Master's thesis, Stockholm Royal Institute of Technology. www.nada.kth.se/utbildning/grukth/exjobb/rapportlistor/2005/rapporter05/thoren_stefan_05114.pdf.

U.S. Energy Information Administration (EIA). 2002. "Derivatives and Risk Management in the Petroleum, Natural Gas, and Electricity Industries." www.eia.gov/oiaf/servicerpt/derivative/chapter3.html.

Wittwer, J. W. 2004. "Monte Carlo Simulation Basics." Vertex42.com http://www.vertex42.com/ExcelArticles/mc/MonteCarloSimulation.html.

Zhao, Lu. 2007. "Risk Management of Energy Derivatives." Department of Mathematics and Statistics, University of Calgary. www.pptuu.com/show_676745_5.html.

CHAPTER 6

Illustrations of Hedging with Energy Derivatives

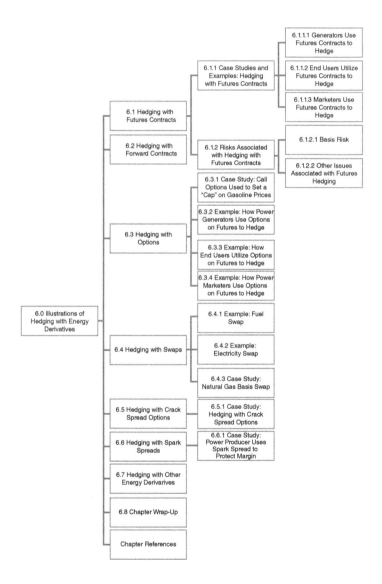

Some of the primary risk management tools available to energy markets participants are the derivatives contracts listed on the exchanges highlighted in Table 3.1. These energy derivatives contracts are beneficial to energy markets participants because they help to

- Reduce exposure to price risk by shifting that risk to market participants with opposite risk profiles or participants who are willing to accept the risk in exchange for profit opportunity.
- Lock in prices and margins.
- Minimize potential for unanticipated loss.
- Provide arbitrage opportunities.
- Improve credit worthiness.
- Increase borrowing capacity.
- Augment financial management and performance capabilities.

> *Some of the primary risk management tools available to energy markets participants are the **derivatives contracts** listed on the exchanges highlighted in Table 3.1.*

In this chapter we present illustrations of various hedging strategies that involve energy derivatives. More specifically, we will present examples and case studies of energy market participants taking positions in energy derivatives that give equal and opposite financial exposure to underlying energy assets, enabling them to protect against large price fluctuations. Hedging strategies are beneficial because they give market participants resources and tools to manage market risk, value deals, and agree on fair pricing of deals.

> ***Hedging strategies** are beneficial because they give market participants resources and tools to manage market risk, value deals, and agree on fair pricing of deals.*

There are two main types of hedging strategies—static and dynamic—summarized in Table 6.1.

- A *static hedge* is a hedge that does not need to be rebalanced as various characteristics (such as volatility) of the price of the energy asset it hedges change.
- This contrasts with a *dynamic hedge* that requires constant rebalancing.

In many cases, the optimal hedge will involve a combination of static and dynamic hedging strategies. More on dynamic and static hedging may

TABLE 6.1 Static versus Dynamic Hedging

Static Hedging	Dynamic Hedging
One-time fixed strategy created to hedge an existing derivative or position. Once the static hedge is structured, it is not adjusted at all.	Structured with a view to having to continually adjust the hedge as the price of the underlying asset that is being hedged changes.
Structured with a view of providing the exact protection up to and including the expiry date of the original position. Hedger will not increase or decrease the size of the hedge over the course of its life as the underlying asset that is being hedged increases or decreases.	Used by derivatives traders to hedge gamma or vega exposures.
Exposes hedger once to "options transactions costs" at every strike.	Exposes hedger to "underlying transactions costs" on every trade.

be found in Black and Scholes (1973), Carr (1999), Haug (2006), Merton (1973), and Taleb (1997).

6.1 HEDGING WITH FUTURES CONTRACTS

Futures contracts have been used as a hedging tool for more than a century in the United States. As discussed in Chapter 5, a hedge involves establishing a position in the derivatives market that is equal and opposite to a position at risk in the physical market.

Example: An energy producer holds 1,000 barrels of crude oil. The producer can hedge by selling one crude oil futures contract. Establishing equal and opposite positions in the cash and futures markets is done to ensure that a loss in one market is offset by a gain in the other market.

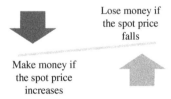

Lose money if the spot price falls

Make money if the spot price increases

HEDGE

A **hedge** involves establishing positions in energy derivatives that give equal and opposite financial exposure to an underlying energy asset.

6.1.1 Case Studies and Examples: Hedging with Futures Contracts

In this section we discuss short case studies and examples to illustrate how the following electricity market participants utilize futures contracts to hedge risk (Stoft et al. 1998).

- Power generators
- End users
- Power marketers

6.1.1.1 Generators Use Futures Contracts to Hedge

A generator expects to sell electricity into the spot market in six months (Figure 6.1). The generator's cost of production = $20/MWh. The current electricity spot price = $20/MWh. The futures price for delivery in six months = $18/MWh. Since the generator is long electricity, it will break even if the spot price remains constant.

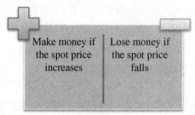

To mitigate this price risk, the generator could sell futures contracts for $18/MWh. In six months, the generator would then sell electricity for the spot price and buy futures contracts to close out its financial position. We have assumed that the futures price converges to the spot price as the delivery date approaches and equals the spot price when the position is closed. In this case, the generator would be perfectly hedged.

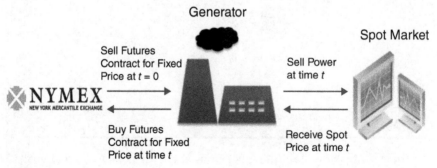

FIGURE 6.1 Generators Use Futures Contracts to Hedge

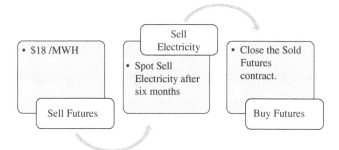

In Table 6.2 we compute the generator's payoff if the spot price increases to $30/MWh and decreases to $10/MWh. In both instances, the generator ultimately receives $18/MWh for delivering electricity and is unaffected by price changes and, therefore, price risk.

The payoff diagram shown in Figure 6.2 illustrates the potential profits and losses associated with the *generator's physical position.*

- If the spot price in six months falls to $10/MWh, the generator would lose $10/MWh because its production costs ($20/MWh) would exceed its payment ($10/MWh).
- But if the spot price rises to $30/MWh, the generators would make $10/MWh.

This payoff diagram in Figure 6.3 illustrates the potential profits and losses associated with the generator's financial position of sold futures contracts.

- If the spot price in six months falls to $10/MWh, the generator would profit by $8/MWh on the sold futures contracts for $18/MWh, but to close out this position, it bought futures contracts for $10/MWh.
- If the spot prices rise to $30/MWh, by contrast, the generator would lose by $12/MWh on the sold futures contract for $18/MWh ($18/MWh − $30/MWh).

TABLE 6.2 Generator's Payoff if Spot Price Fluctuates

Spot Price	↑ $30/MWh	↓ $10/MWh
	Receives $30/MWh for its electricity	Receives $10/MWh for its electricity
	Pays $30/MWh to close out its futures positions	Pays $10/MWh to close out its futures positions
	Receives $18/MWh for its original futures positions	Receives $18/MWh for its original futures positions

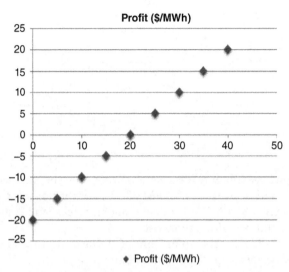

FIGURE 6.2   Generator's Physical Position

The payoff diagram shown in Figure 6.4 illustrates the potential profits and losses associated with the *generator's hedged position.*

- At each spot market price, the hedged profit is the sum of profits from the physical and financial position of sold futures contracts.
- By hedging, the generator has locked in an electricity price of $18/MWh and a loss of $2/MWh.
- Also note that the generator may simply opt to supply the energy as per the contract. It does not necessarily need to buy an opposite futures contract.

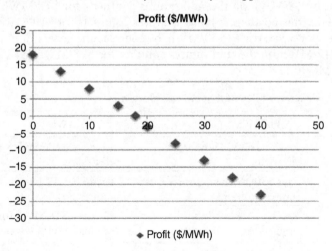

FIGURE 6.3   Generator's Financial Position of Sold Futures Contracts

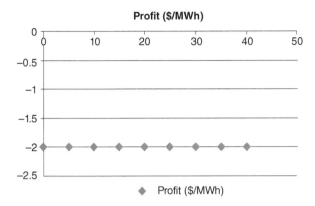

FIGURE 6.4   Generator's Hedged Position

Note: The reader may perhaps be asking the following questions: Why, under any normal circumstances, would a generator be willing to generate at a cost of $20/MWh and be willing to sell into forward markets at $18/MWh? Can't we choose some better numbers? Maybe say perhaps, $26/MWh instead of $18/MWh? We are not trying to give the impression that generation is always a losing business. These hedge strategies can be performed under a variety of scenarios. We chose this set of numbers simply for the sake of illustrating the concept of structuring a hedge from a generator's perspective. A trader or risk manager can simulate a generator's hedge for a variety of scenarios in an excel spreadsheet.

6.1.1.2 End Users Utilize Futures Contracts to Hedge

An end user (e.g., a large manufacturer) anticipates needing electricity in six months (Figure 6.5). Therefore it intends to buy the electricity in the spot market at that time. The current electricity spot price = $20/MWh. The futures price for delivery in six months = $18/MWh.

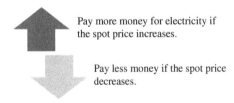

To mitigate this price risk, the end user could buy futures contracts for $18/MWh to lock in electricity prices. In six months, the end user would then buy

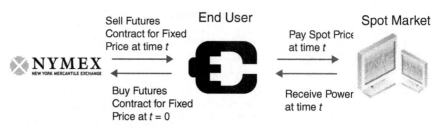

FIGURE 6.5   End Users Utilize Futures Contracts to Hedge

electricity for the spot price and sell futures contracts to close out its financial position. For purposes of this example, it is assumed that the futures price converges to the spot price as the delivery date approaches and equals the spot price when the position is closed. In this case, the end user would be perfectly hedged.

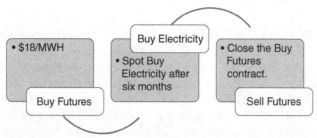

In Table 6.3 we compute the end user's payoff if the spot price increases to $30/MWh and decreases to $10/MWh. In both instances, the end user ultimately pays $18/MWh for purchasing electricity and is unaffected by price changes and, therefore, price risk.

The payoff diagram in Figure 6.6 illustrates the potential profits and losses associated with the *end user's physical position*. We assume that the end user has fixed output prices and can pass on only $20/MWh to its customers.

TABLE 6.3   End User's Payoff if Spot Price Fluctuates

Spot Price	↑ $30/MWh End User	↓ $10/MWh
	Pays $30/MWh for its electricity	Pays $10/MWh for its electricity
	Receives $30/MWh to close out its futures positions	Receives $10/MWh to close out its futures positions
	Pays $18/MWh for its original futures positions	Pays $18/MWh for its original futures positions

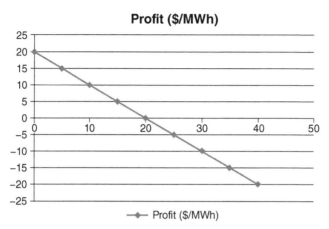

FIGURE 6.6 End User's Physical Position

The payoff diagram shown in Figure 6.7 illustrates the potential profits and losses associated with the *end user's financial position.*

This payoff diagram shown in Figure 6.8 illustrates the potential profits and losses associated with the *end user's hedged position* if the spot price in six months falls to zero or increases to $40/MWh. If the end user locks in a price of $18/MWh and is able to pass on electricity prices of $20/MWh, it stands to make a profit of $2/MWh.

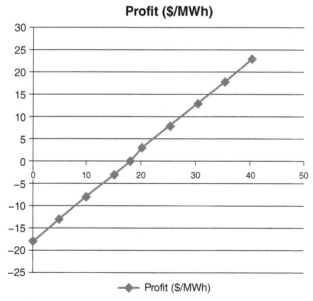

FIGURE 6.7 End User's Financial Position

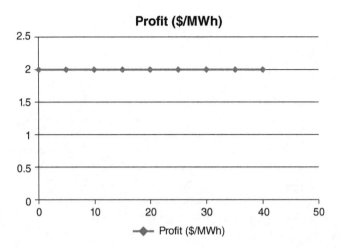

FIGURE 6.8   End User's Hedged Position

- If the spot price converges to the futures price, the end user will be perfectly hedged and unaffected by price changes.
- This is because the gains (losses) in the physical market are offset by the losses (gains) in the financial market.
- The risks associated with hedging for the end user are similar to those faced by the generator.

6.1.1.3 Marketers Use Futures Contracts to Hedge

Marketer's Long Hedge: Assume that a marketer has guaranteed customers that it will deliver electricity to them in six months (Figure 6.9).

> The marketer can buy futures contracts for $18/MWh and sell electricity to the end user for a small markup, say $18.10/MWh.

> Simultaneously, the marketer can close out its futures position by selling futures contracts for $30/MWh (for a gain of $12/MWh over the original purchase price of $18/MWh).

> This transaction guarantees the end-user fixed-price power at $18.10/MWh.

> In addition, if the spot price converges to the futures price, this transaction guarantees the marketer a profit of $0.10/MWh.

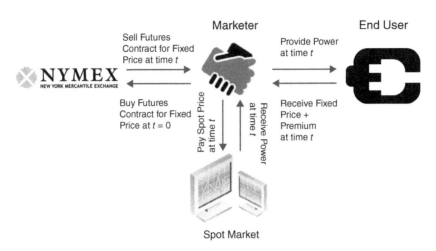

FIGURE 6.9 Marketer's Long Hedge

Marketer's Short Hedge:

Assume that a marketer has agreed to buy electricity from a generator in six months (Figure 6.10).

> The marketer can buy electricity for $17.90/MWh and sell electricity futures for delivery in six months for $18/MWh, thus locking in the fixed price and a profit.

> In six months, if the spot price has increased to $30/MWh, the marketer would pay the generator $17.90/MWh for the power, sell the power on the spot market for $30/MWh, making $12.10/MWh on the physical transaction.

> At the same time, the marketer can close out its futures position by buying futures contracts for $30/MWh, thus losing $12/MWh on its financial position.

> The combined physical and financial positions leave the marketer with a profit of $0.10/MWh.

FIGURE 6.10   Marketer's Short Hedge

6.1.2   Risks Associated with Hedging with Futures Contracts

Some risks associated with hedging with futures contracts are as follows:

- The futures price does not converge to the spot price on the delivery date.
- The monthly futures does not match the daily spot market (i.e., the generator would be hedging daily price risk using a monthly instrument).
- The generator miscalculated and had more (or less) electricity than initially anticipated.

6.1.2.1 Basis Risk

Basis risk is the primary risk associated with using futures contracts to hedge commodity risks (Stoft et al. 1998).

- *Basis* is the difference between the futures price and the spot price of the commodity being hedged.
- *Basis risk* is the risk that offsetting investments in hedging strategies will not experience price changes in entirely opposite directions from each other.

One type of basis risk occurs because of *location-specific factors*:

- Pipeline constraints
- Differences in transportation costs
- Differences in transmission costs

BASIS RISK

Basis risk is the primary risk associated with using futures contracts to hedge commodity risks.

Example: The price of electricity in Denver, Colorado is not likely to be the same as the price at the California-Oregon Border (COB)—even though they're all part of North American Electric Reliability Corporation's (NERC's) Western Electricity Coordinating Council (WECC) region. Hence if an energy market participant uses a futures contract for the COB it may not perfectly hedge price risk in Denver (Figure 6.11).

Assume that a generator expects to sell electricity into the spot market in Denver in six months and sells a futures contract for COB delivery for $18/MWh.

On the delivery date, the spot price in Denver is $25/MWh, but the spot price (and the futures price) at the COB is $28.

If the generator were able to deliver electricity to COB, he would do so and collect $18/MWh.

If the generator were not able to deliver electricity, he would sell into the Denver spot market at $25/MWh and close his position financially by buying a futures contract for $28/MWh.

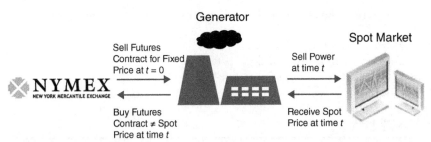

FIGURE 6.11 Spot Price Doesn't Equal Futures Contract Price

As a result of this transaction, the generator

- Receives $25/MWh for his electricity in the spot market.
- Loses $10/MWh on his financial position.
- Ultimately receives only $15/MWh, not $18/MWh for his electricity as initially planned.

If the electricity price in Denver were perfectly correlated with the price at COB, the generator would be perfectly hedged and could expect to lock in the price at COB less $3/MWh. But if the prices in the two markets are not well correlated, this will undermine the generators' hedge. One way to deal with this risk is to use a *basis swap* to hedge this basis risk.

6.1.2.2 Other Issues Associated with Futures Hedging

Some other potential issues that may arise when using futures contracts to hedge commodity risks are as follows:

- The procedures for determining the optimal hedge size are specific and well defined. However, the correlation is an important quantity in the valuation (Eydeland and Wolyniec 2003).
- The futures contract commodity might be different from the spot price commodity (i.e., product quality or definition). This could be a problem if the spot market sells electricity on a daily rather than a monthly basis because futures contracts call for delivery over an entire month.
- The generator, end user, or marketer miscalculates the amount of energy to generate or consume.

Example: Long-Term Hedging via "Stack and Roll"

The *stack and roll* method—introduced in Chapter 5—is used to hedge a long-term physical position with short-term futures contracts. At

Metallgesellschaft (MG), the underlying assets were short positions in long-term forward contracts to deliver oil. A *stack and roll* hedge was utilized: Long positions in short-term futures contracts that were rolled over consecutively. The strategy depended on

- Continuation of stable or gently increasing spot oil prices
- Backwardation

Note: The hedging strategies discussed thus far are theoretically fine. However, in practice some exchange-traded futures markets are not very liquid enough. For example, in many prominent U.S. electricity markets, hedges may be structured by buying a congestion revenue rights (CRR) and financial transmission rights (FTR) option or by utilizing a bilateral forward contract.

More on energy-related hedges with futures contracts may be found in E&Y (2013), Eydeland and Wolyniec (2003), Graves and Levine (2010), New York Mercantile Exchange (NYMEX 2011), and Stoft et al. (1998).

6.2 HEDGING WITH FORWARD CONTRACTS

Recall that a forward contract is an over-the-counter (OTC) agreement between parties to buy (or sell) an energy asset at a specified point of time in the future. The forward price is a predetermined delivery price for an underlying energy asset decided upon by the buyer and the seller to be paid at a predetermined date in the future. At the maturity of a forward contract, the seller will deliver the energy asset and the buyer will pay the purchase price.

If the market price of the energy asset at maturity is

Higher than the price specified in the contract, then the buyer will make a profit.

Lower than the contract price, then the buyer will suffer a loss.

An illustration of a simple forward hedge is as follows:

Example: A marketer plans to buy a certain amount of power in 30 days (Figure 6.12). However, the marketer also wants to eliminate the electricity

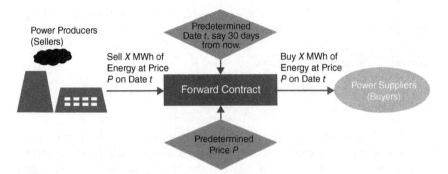

FIGURE 6.12 Forward Hedge

price risk. The marketer can eliminate this risk by taking the buy-side of a forward contract for this power with a maturity of 30 days.

In Bessembinder and Lemmon (2002), a forward hedging strategy is derived in a "closed system," where only producers and retailers (power marketing firms) can take positions (Figure 6.13). This model simplification was made because

- Power cannot be stored (except for hydropower).
- Power marketers must arrange to deliver the power it purchases to retail customers.
- Outside speculators—those who neither produce power nor have delivery contracts with final customers who consume the power—cannot take positions in contracts that require physical power delivery. Outside speculators may participate by taking positions in futures contracts, cash-settled contracts, and so forth.

More information on hedging with forward contracts may be found in Harvey and Hogan (2000), and Woo et al. (2011).

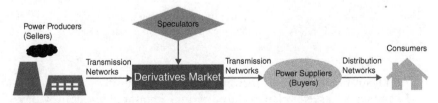

FIGURE 6.13 Hedging in a "Closed" System

6.3   HEDGING WITH OPTIONS

Options on futures offer additional flexibility in hedging risk. These derivatives give hedgers the ability to protect themselves from adverse price moves while participating in favorable price moves. Let's take a look at the following case study to illustrate how energy market participants utilize options on futures to hedge in the natural gas markets (NYMEX 2011).

> *Options on futures offer additional flexibility in hedging risk. These derivatives give hedgers the ability to protect themselves from adverse price moves while participating in favorable price moves.*

6.3.1   Case Study: Call Options Used to Set a "Cap" on Gasoline Prices

April
- A gasoline buyer for a taxi fleet is concerned about a possible increase in gas prices during the summer months.
- Gasoline futures are trading on NYMEX for 65¢.
- The buyer considers purchasing futures contracts to lock in a purchase price of 65¢ for his June supply. The futures contract price does not include taxes.
- The buyer does not want to be significantly above the market if the gas spot prices decline. Therefore he decides to buy a June call option with a strike price of 65¢ for a premium of 4¢.

May 21
- The gasoline buyer purchases spot fuel and liquidates his options position.
- Table 6.4 illustrates two scenarios:
  Scenario I: Gas price increased to 85¢
  The buyer pays 85¢ to his supplier for fuel. The financial offset provided by the 16¢ option profit gives the buyer an effective gasoline cost of 69¢.
  Scenario II: Gas price decreased to 50¢
  The reason the buyer chose to pay the 4¢ call option premium becomes apparent in the second scenario. The buyer pays his supplier 50¢. The 65¢ call is now out of the money. Hence there is a net loss of 4¢—the call options premium paid. This gives the taxi fleet an effective gasoline cost of 54¢. This is 11¢ less than if futures alone were used to hedge.

TABLE 6.4   Options Used to Set a Gas "Cap"

	Scenario I Gas Price Increase	Scenario II Gas Price Decrease
May 21: Gas Spot Price	$0.85	$0.50
May 21: Futures Price	$0.85	$0.50
Cash Market Cost of Gasoline	$0.85	$0.50
Less: Profit/(Loss) on Options		
Sales Price	$0.20	$0
Option Premium	$0.04	$0.04
	$0.16	($0.04)
Effective Cost of Gasoline	$0.69	$0.54

6.3.2   Example: How Power Generators Use Options on Futures to Hedge

In 1996, NYMEX introduced options for electricity. Power generators and end users can use combinations of calls and puts to lock in a particular price range.

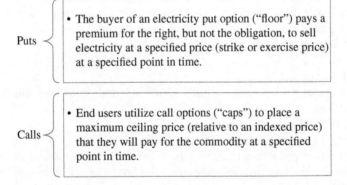

Puts
- The buyer of an electricity put option ("floor") pays a premium for the right, but not the obligation, to sell electricity at a specified price (strike or exercise price) at a specified point in time.

Calls
- End users utilize call options ("caps") to place a maximum ceiling price (relative to an indexed price) that they will pay for the commodity at a specified point in time.

A power generator uses put options to guarantee a minimum price for its electricity in conjunction with the physical sale of electricity. Suppose the electricity futures contract price is $25/MWh. The power generator wishes to receive at least $25/MWh for the physical sale of power. To accomplish this, the power generator purchases a put option for a premium of $1/MWh.

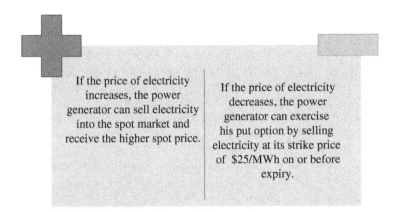

If the price of electricity increases, the power generator can sell electricity into the spot market and receive the higher spot price.

If the price of electricity decreases, the power generator can exercise his put option by selling electricity at its strike price of $25/MWh on or before expiry.

6.3.3 Example: How End Users Utilize Options on Futures to Hedge

A power end user can hedge against price increases by purchasing a call option. Suppose the electricity futures contract price is $25/MWh. The end user wishes to pay no more than $25/MWh. To accomplish this, the end user purchases a call option for a premium of $.75/MWh.

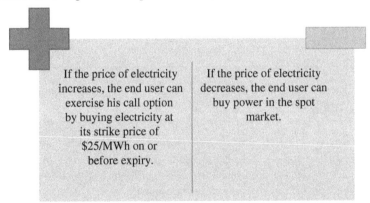

If the price of electricity increases, the end user can exercise his call option by buying electricity at its strike price of $25/MWh on or before expiry.

If the price of electricity decreases, the end user can buy power in the spot market.

6.3.4 Example: How Power Marketers Use Options on Futures to Hedge

Power marketers may

- Exercise put and call options on an exchange or in the OTC market on behalf of power generators and end users.
- Offer puts and calls to generators and end users.

More information on hedging with options may be found in Clewlow and Strickland (2000), E&Y (2013), Eydeland and Wolyniec (2003), Graves and Levine (2010), NYMEX (2011), and Stoft et al. (1998).

6.4 HEDGING WITH SWAPS

As recently reported in *Bloomberg*, more than 50 percent of the $18 trillion in notional daily trading of energy swaps has moved from the OTC market to futures exchanges (Table 6.5). This is in response to the *Dodd-Frank* financial regulations aimed at increasing transparency following the 2008 financial crisis. The U.S. Congress passed the *Dodd-Frank Wall Street Reform and Consumer Protection Act* in 2010 to oversee the unregulated OTC derivatives market (CFTC 2010).

However, even with more swaps business going to the futures markets because of the Dodd-Frank Act, "the swaps market's not going away," Terrence Duffy, executive chairman of CME Group, said. As a result of the *Dodd-Frank* regulations, energy market participants are avoiding higher collateral, capital, and trading expenses to "get the same trades and risk-management benefit" with futures. Under the Dodd-Frank Act, all swap prices and trades will be required to be reported so that regulators can monitor the market (Leising 2013).

> *The U.S. Congress passed the Dodd-Frank Wall Street Reform and Consumer Protection Act in 2010 to oversee the unregulated OTC derivatives market.*

BLOCK TRADE

Some energy market participants who previously traded swaps are now resorting to block trades. A **block trade** is a privately negotiated futures, options, or combination transaction that is permitted to be executed apart from the public auction market.

TABLE 6.5 Energy Swaps Migrating to Futures

Intercontinental Exchange (ICE)	Chicago Mercantile Exchange (CME)
■ 52 percent of *ICE* energy futures volumes during the first half of January 2013 came from contracts that traded as energy swaps prior to October 15, 2012.	■ 90 percent of energy trades on the *CME ClearPort* system are executed as futures as compared with 10 percent before the switch.

Some energy market participants who previously traded swaps are now resorting to block trades. A *block trade* is a privately negotiated futures, options, or combination transaction that is permitted to be executed apart from the public auction market. Participation in block trades is restricted to *eligible contract participants* as that term is defined in the Commodity Exchange Act.

Rule 526 ("Block Trades") governs block trading in Chicago Mercantile Exchange (CME), Chicago Board of Trade (CBOT), NYMEX, and Commodity Exchange (COMEX) products. Block trades are permitted in specified products and are subject to minimum transaction size requirements that vary according to the product, the type of transaction, and the time of execution. Block trades may be executed at any time at a fair and reasonable price (CME Group, 2013a).

Energy swaps are typically used by market participants such as airlines to

- Protect against unforeseen price increases by locking in the price of an energy asset.
- Budget for market uncertainties.
- Reduce reserve.
- Execute longer term hedges.

In the remainder of this section we will present examples and case studies to illustrate how financial and basis swaps may be used by energy market participants to hedge risk. Recall the definition of a financial swap from Chapter 3:

A *financial swap* is a derivative contract in which counterparties exchange cash flows of one party's financial instrument for those of another party's financial instrument.

FINANCIAL SWAP

A **financial swap** is a derivative contract in which counterparties exchange cash flows of one party's financial instrument for those of another party's financial instrument.

A *plain vanilla energy swap* is very similar to a financial swap. It is a derivatives contract in which counterparties exchange a floating price for a fixed price over a specified period of time. In addition, the plain vanilla energy swap is an off-balance sheet contract that involves no transfer of the energy commodity; it is financially settled.

6.4.1 Example: Fuel Swap

A fuel hedge allows a large fuel consuming company to establish a fixed or capped cost, via a commodity swap or option.

A hedger is typically an energy market participant that is a "fixed rate (price) payer" on a swap (Figure 6.14).

The floating index used in energy hedging is normally published in trade publications, such as

- *OPIS: Oil Price Information Service* (www.opisnet.com)
- *Platts Oilgram* (www.platts.com/Products/oilgrampricereport)

The contract settlement may be physical or cash. If it is physically settled, then the hedger may be exposed to extraordinary events or circumstances beyond its control (e.g., war, strikes, riots, crime, etc.).

ELECTRICITY SWAPS

Electricity swaps are utilized to provide short- to long-term hedges against power price uncertainty.

Electricity swaps are utilized to provide short-, medium-, and long-term hedges against power price uncertainty. They are established for a fixed amount of power with reference to a variable spot price at either of two locations:

1. A generator's plant
2. A consumer's premises

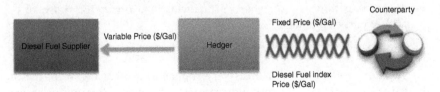

FIGURE 6.14 Fuel Swap

6.4.2 Example: Electricity Swap

Suppose we consider swaps settled against the Dow Jones index of electricity prices at COB (Stoft et al. 1998). COB is part of NERC's WECC region (Figure 6.15).

A schematic overview of a swap transaction from the buyer's perspective is as follows:

Electricity swaps can trade in any size. But they are typically traded in increments of 25 MW on-peaks. Peak hours in COB include:

- 6 A.M. to 10 P.M. (16 hours per day)
- Monday through Saturday (six days a week)

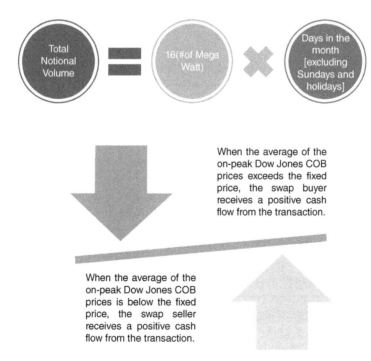

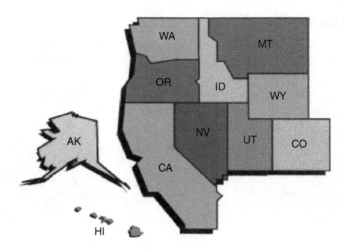

FIGURE 6.15   California-Oregon Border (COB)

6.4.3 Case Study: Natural Gas Basis Swap

A *basis swap* in the energy markets is a swap on the price differential for a product and a major index product (e.g., Brent Crude or Henry Hub gas). These swaps do not eliminate the variability of cash flows; instead, they change the basis or index of variability.

BASIS SWAP

A *basis swap* in the energy markets is a swap on the price differential for a product and a major index product.

A *commodity basis swap* can alter future cash flows to be based off of a regional commodities index rather than a national futures exchange.

This case study illustrates how a natural gas producer can use energy derivatives based on the NYMEX natural gas futures price to hedge its natural gas production in Alberta, Canada. This producer can also use a basis swap to reduce the ineffectiveness in its hedging strategies (ATB Financial 2012).

COMMODITY BASIS SWAP

A **commodity basis swap** can alter future cash flows to be based off of a regional commodities index rather than a national futures exchange.

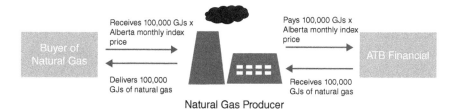

FIGURE 6.16 Natural Gas Basis Swap

Suppose a natural gas producer has a contract to sell 100,000 gigajoules (GJ) each month at the Alberta monthly index price. (Note: 1 GJ ~ 0.947 MMBtu.) The producer wants to guarantee that its revenues from this volume for the next 12 months will not be less than the NYMEX price less $0.75/GJ (Figure 6.16).

Hence, the producer enters into an Alberta basis swap with *Alberta Treasury Branches* (ATB). The natural gas basis swap fixes the difference between NYMEX and the Alberta index price (*Alberta basis*). The seller of an Alberta basis swap

- Receives the future NYMEX price less a negotiated fixed amount of $0.75/GJ multiplied by 100,000 GJ.
- Agrees to pay ATB the future Alberta monthly index price multiplied by 100,000 GJ to the buyer.

This basis swap generally settles five days after the Alberta index is published. However, the settlement day can be negotiated to match the cash flow from the physical sale of the natural gas.

More information on hedging with swaps may be found in ATB Financial (2012), CFTC (2010), CME Group (2013a), EIA (2002), Leising, (2013), and Stoft et al. (1998).

6.5 HEDGING WITH CRACK SPREAD OPTIONS

As discussed in Chapter 4, the *crack spread* is the differential between the price of crude oil and petroleum extracted from it. It is the profit margin that an oil refiner can expect to make by *cracking* crude oil. Crack spreads are often called *paper refineries* (Carmona and Durrelman 2003).

TABLE 6.6   Crack Spreads

1:1 Crack Spread	Buy: 1 crude oil futures Sell: 1 refined product futures
3:2:1 Crack Spread	Buy: 3 crude oil futures contracts Sell: 2 gasoline futures contracts and 1 heating oil futures contract
5:3:2 Crack Spread	Buy: 5 crude oil futures contracts Sell: 5 refined products futures

Some commonly used crack spreads are listed in Table 6.6. Recall, we illustrated the mechanics of a *3:2:1 crack spread* in Chapter 4.

The *crude-to-product ratios* of futures crack spreads listed in Table 6.6 are tailored by energy market participants to best fit their needs. However, crack spread options contracts are standardized exchange-traded derivatives that reflect a one-to-one ratio (NYMEX 2000).

LONG CRACK CALL, OR A SHORT CRACK PUT

A **long crack call, or a short crack put,** is defined as the assignment of futures positions, which at exercise, involve buying an underlying heating oil or gasoline futures contract and selling one underlying crude oil contract.

A *long crack call*, or a *short crack put*, is defined as the assignment of futures positions, which at exercise, involve buying an underlying heating oil or gasoline futures contract and selling one underlying crude oil contract.

Example: A long crack call option may be considered for a petroleum consumer wishing to hedge against a widening of the spread.

A *long crack put*, or a *short crack call*, is defined as the assignment of futures positions, which at exercise, involve selling one underlying heating oil or gasoline futures contract and buying one underlying crude oil futures contract.

Example: A long crack put option may be appropriate for a refiner looking to hedge its profit margin.

Some of the benefits of hedging with crack spread options are listed in Table 6.7.

TABLE 6.7   Benefits of Hedging with Crack Spread Options

Energy market participants have a flexible hedge against variable refining margins in heating oil and gasoline.
Crack puts allow refiners to lock in crude oil cost and product margins without penalty to further market gains.
Crack calls afford product marketers protection during unstable crack spread increases.
Crack spread options furnish traders with a mechanism for hedging the variable relationship between crude oil and refined products.
Crack options allow refiners to generate income by writing options.
A refiner's margin could be hedged by using futures contracts. However, maintaining the futures hedge locks the refiner into a predetermined margin. Crack options give the refiner the right, but not the obligation, to obtain that margin.
Energy marketers and distributors selling gasoline can use options to help maintain their competitive positions in the marketplace.

6.5.1   Case Study: Hedging with Crack Spread Options

Now let's take a look at a short case study to illustrate how to hedge with crack spread options (CME Group 2012). Suppose we have a refiner that

- Buys crude oil for $110.00 per barrel
- Sells gasoline at $3 per gallon ($3/gallon × 42 gallon/barrel = $126 per barrel).

   Then the crack spread = ($126 − $110) per barrel = $16 per barrel

   Of this spread, $6.00 may be fixed and operating costs. This leaves the refiner with a net refining margin of $10.

   Now suppose the refiner buys 50 *April RBOB gasoline crack spread puts* with a strike price of $K = \$16$ per barrel.

   Please note the following:

- RBOB is the acronym for *reformulated blendstock for oxygenate blending* (gasoline production) (CME Group 2009).
- An RBOB gasoline put option traded on an exchange represents an option to assume a short position in the underlying futures contract traded on the exchange (CME Group 2013b).

The underlying assets of the crack spreads options are futures contracts representing 1,000 barrels of crude oil and 42,000 gallons (1,000 barrels) of refined products. Hence by purchasing 50 crack puts, the refiner has effectively hedged the cost of purchasing 50,000 barrels of crude oil and the revenue from the sale of 50,000 barrels of gasoline.

Suppose the crack put is exercised at expiry. This hedge guarantees that neither a rise in crude oil prices nor a fall in gasoline prices can decrease the refining margins below $16. Hence, for the cost of the crack put options premium, a profit margin has been locked in for 50,000 barrels of refined products.

More information on hedging with crack spread options may be found in Alexander and Venkatramanan (2007), CME Group (2012), EIA (2002), and NYMEX (2000, 2011).

6.6   HEDGING WITH SPARK SPREADS

The *spark spread* is similar to the crack spread. As discussed in Chapter 4, it is the difference between the market price of electricity and its cost of production. It is also a trading strategy based on the differences in the price of electricity and its cost of production. The spark spread is sometimes referred to as a *paper plant* (Carmona and Durrelman 2003).

SPARK SPREAD

The **spark spread** is the difference between the market price of electricity and its cost of production.

6.6.1   Case Study: Power Producer Uses Spark Spread to Protect Margin

Now let's take a look at a short case study to illustrate how to hedge with spark spreads (NYMEX, 2011). An independent power producer (IPP) in southeastern United States conducts a market analysis, plant assessment, and an inventory based on the information presented below. As a result, this IPP decides to execute a spark spread to protect electricity margins.

IPP conducts a plant assessment and inventory in April.

- Reviews natural gas acquisition prospects for the summer
- Reviews potential electricity sales for the summer

- Observes electricity prices are strong
- Observes natural gas is an economical buy
- Thinks gas prices may increase as the summer progresses, which could erode the IPP's profit margin for electricity
- Plans a spread strategy that will allow it to lock in a profit margin for its product

IPP conducts market analysis in April (April 25 prices).

- July NYMEX Division Henry Hub natural gas futures is $1.45 per million Btu.
- July Entergy electricity futures is $20 per MWh.
- K_H = Heat Rate = $8,000^{Btu}/_{kWh}$

The natural gas and electricity contracts differ in size. Hence, the appropriate hedge ratio must be calculated to protect the profit margin (Table 6.8). The hedge ratio is determined as follows:

$$\text{Hedge Ratio} = \frac{K_H}{1,000} \times \frac{\text{Size of Electricity Contract in MWh}}{10,000}$$

$$= \frac{8,000\,^{Btu}/_{kWh}}{1,000} \times \frac{736 \times 1,000\,kWh}{10,000} = 588.8\,kWh$$

$$= 0.59\,MWh \text{ (ratio of five to three)}$$

Hedge ratios for various heat rates are listed in Table 6.8. In the case of a hedge ratio equal to 0.59, the IPP executes a 5-to-3 hedge to lock in a margin (Table 6.9).

TABLE 6.8 Hedge Ratios

Heat Rate	Hedge Ratio	Electricity/Natural Gas Contracts
8,000	0.59	5 to 3
10,000	0.74	4 to 3
12,000	0.88	9 to 8
13,500	0.99	1 to 1

TABLE 6.9   IPP Executes a 5-to-3 Hedge to Lock in Margin

April 25	IPP places hedge, sells the spark spread
	Sell 5 Entergy electricity futures
	Buy 3 Henry Hub natural gas futures
	Spark Spread = (Electricity Price − Gas Price)/Electricity Units
	$$= \frac{(5 \cdot 736\,Mwh \cdot \$26\,/\,Mwh) - (3 \cdot 10{,}000\,MMBtu \cdot \$2.45\,/\,MMBtu)}{5 \cdot 736\,/\,Mwh}$$
	= \$6.03 per MWh
July 28	*IPP lifts hedge, buys the spark spread*
	Buy 5 Entergy electricity futures
	Sell 3 Henry Hub natural gas futures
	Spark Spread
	$$= \frac{(5 \cdot 736\,Mwh \cdot \$23\,/\,Mwh) - (3 \cdot 10{,}000\,MMBtu \cdot \$2.45\,/\,MMBtu)}{5 \cdot 736\,/\,Mwh}$$
	= \$1.40 per MWh

Hence, the result of the IPP's hedge—based on the computation in Table 6.9—is as follows:

$$\text{Net Profit: } \$6.03 - \$1.40 = \$4.63 \text{ per MWh}$$

$$(\$4.63 \text{ per MWh}) \times (5 \times 736 \text{ MWh}) = \$17{,}038.40$$

The following additional April market information for natural gas must be factored in when determining the delivered price of electricity:

- Price of natural gas at Henry Hub based on Henry Hub natural gas futures = \$2.45 per million Btu
- Current cost of gas transmission to power plant = \$0.18 per million Btu
- Total projected cost of gas = \$2.63 per million Btu
- Equivalent gas price = \$2.63 × 8 = \$21.04 per million Btu
- Present electric capacity charge = \$2.50 per MWh
- Present electric transmission to Entergy = \$1.50 per MWh
- **Total power cost at Entergy = \$25.04 per MWh**

In July, the IPP must do the following:

- Take delivery of physical gas.
- Sell electricity at the current cash market prices.
- Incur current transportation charges for gas and the capacity.
- Incur transmission charges for electricity.

By July, market conditions have dramatically changed:

- Gas prices spiked up.
- Electricity prices declined due to an abundance of coal-fired power in the region.

When the IPP bought natural gas futures and sold electricity futures in April, it locked in a margin of $6.03 per MWh. In July, the IPP must offset its positions by selling back on the Exchange the gas futures that were purchased and by buying back the electricity futures that were sold. Due to the July market conditions, the IPP is left with a net margin of $4.63 per MWh.

Natural gas and gas transportation also increased the July cash market:

- Gas price = $2.65 per million Btu
- Transportation = $0.20 per million Btu
- Equivalent gas price = $2.85 × 8 = $22.80 per million Btu
- Electric capacity and transmission = $4.00 per MWh
- **Total power cost = $26.80 per MWh**

In closing, hedging was quite beneficial for the IPP. It allowed the IPP to lock in a net margin of $4.63 per MWh.

More information on hedging with crack spreads may be found in Barroll and Oum (2009), Carmona and Durrelman (2003), and NYMEX (2000, 2011).

6.7 HEDGING WITH OTHER ENERGY DERIVATIVES

In the previous sections we covered various hedging strategies that are commonly utilized by energy market participants. In this short section we list references for other types of energy derivatives hedging strategies.

- ***Asian and Barrier Options:*** Bjerstaf and Sodergren (2012), Borovkova and Permana (2010), Carr (1999), Eydeland and Wolyniec (2003), Haug (2006), Linetsky (2004), Taleb (1997), and Weron (2008)
- ***Calendar and Locational Spreads:*** EIA (2002), Graves and Levine (2010), and Soronow (2002)

6.8 CHAPTER WRAP-UP

In this chapter we presented several examples and case studies of how energy market participants utilize energy derivatives to develop hedging strategies. These hedging strategies—if properly structured—are beneficial because they give market participants resources and tools to manage market risk, value deals, and agree on fair pricing of deals.

REFERENCES

Alberta Treasury Branches (ATB) Financial. 2012. "Alberta Natural Gas: Basis Swap." Alberta Treasury Branches. www.atb.com/business/corporate/commodities-and-foreign-exchange/Pages/natural-gas-basis-swap.aspx.

Alexander, C., and A. Venkatramanan. 2007. "Analytic Approximations for Spread Options." ICMA Centre, University of Reading. www.icmacentre.ac.uk/files/pdf/dps/dp_200711.pdf.

Barroll, Daniel, and Yumi Oum. 2009. "Spark Spread Option Deltas Compared to Probability of Operation." http://207.67.203.54/elibsql05_P40007_Documents/QUANT%20DOCS/Delta%20vs%20MWh%20Summary_pge_ts.pdf.

Bessembinder, H., and M. Lemmon. 2002. "Equilibrium Pricing and Optimal Hedging in Electricity Forward Markets." *Journal of Finance* 57(3), 1347-1382. www.tapir.caltech.edu/~arayag/PriHedFws.pdf.

Bjerstaf, Olof, and Juna Sodergren. 2012. "On the Topic of Energy Risk Management." Financial Risk—MSA400. www.math.chalmers.se/~rootzen/finrisk/OlofBjerstafJunaSodergrenEnergyRisk.pdf.

Black, Fischer, and Myron Scholes. 1973. "The Pricing of Options and Corporate Liabilities." *Journal of Political Economy* 81(3): 637–654. https://www.cs.princeton.edu/courses/archive/fall02/cs323/links/blackscholes.pdf.

Borovkova, Svetlana, and Ferry Permana. 2010. "Asian Basket Options and Implied Correlations in Energy Markets." www.feweb.vu.nl/nl/Images/AsianBasketOptions_tcm96-194677.pdf.

Carmona, Rene, and Valdo Durrelman. 2003. "Pricing and Hedging Spread Options." *SIAM Review* 45(4): 627–685. www.cmap.polytechnique.fr/~valdo/papers/siam.pdf.

Carr, Peter. 1999. "Dynamic and Static Hedging of Exotic Equity Options." NationsBanc Montgomery Securities. www.math.columbia.edu/~smirnov/over99.pdf.

Clewlow, L., and C. Strickland. 2000. *Energy Derivatives, Pricing and Risk Management.* London: Lacima.

CME Group. 2009. "RBOB Gasoline Crack Spread Option." NYMEX Rulebook. www.cmegroup.com/rulebook/NYMEX/3/387.pdf.

———. 2012. "Introduction to Crack Spreads." How the World Advances. www.cmegroup.com/trading/energy/files/EN-211_CrackSpreadHandbook_SR.PDF.

———. 2013a. "Block Trades." Trading Practices. www.cmegroup.com/clearing/trading-practices/block-trades.html.

————. 2013b. "RBOB Gasoline Options." Energy Products. www.cmegroup.com/ trading/energy/refined-products/rbob-gasoline_contractSpecs_options.html.

Eydeland, A., and K. Wolyniec. 2003. *Energy and Power: Risk Management*. Hoboken, NJ: Wiley Finance.

Ernst & Young (E&Y). 2013. "Derivative Instruments and Hedging Activities." Ernst & Young Financial Reporting Developments. www.pwc.com/us/en/ cfodirect/publications/accounting-guides/guide-to-accounting-for-derivative-instruments-and-hedging-activities-2013-edition.jhtml.

Graves, Frank, and Steven Levine. 2010. "Managing Natural Gas Price Volatility: Principles and Practices Across the Industry." The Brattle Group, Inc. www .cleanskies.org/wp-content/uploads/2011/08/ManagingNGPriceVolatility.pdf.

Harvey, Scott, and William Hogan. 2000. "California Electricity Prices and Forward Market Hedging." Center for Business and Government, Harvard University, Kennedy School of Government. www.hks.harvard.edu/fs/whogan/mschedge1017.pdf.

Haug, Espen. 2006. *The Complete Guide to Option Pricing Formulas*, 2nd ed. New York: McGraw-Hill.

Leising, Matthew. 2013. "Energy Swaps Migrating to Futures on Dodd-Frank Rules." Bloomberg. www.bloomberg.com/news/2013-01-25/energy-swaps-migrating-to-futures-as-dodd-frank-rules-take-hold.html.

Merton, Robert. 1973. "Theory of Rational Option Pricing." *Bell Journal of Economics and Management Science* 4(1): 141–183.

New York Mercantile Exchange (NYMEX). 2000. *Crack Spread Handbook*. http:// partners.futuresource.com/marketcenter/pdfs/crack.pdf.

————. 2011. "A Guide to Energy Hedging." www.docstoc.com/docs/84385167/ A-GUIDE-TO-ENERGY-HEDGING.

Stoft, S., T. Belden, C. Goldman, and S. Pickle. 1998. "Primer on Electricity Futures and Other Derivatives." Report LBNL-41098, UC-1321, Environmental Energy Technologies Division: Ernest Orlando Lawrence Berkeley National Laboratory. http://eetd.lbl.gov/ea/emp/reports/41098.pdf.

Taleb, Nassim. 1997. *Dynamic Hedging: Managing Vanilla and Exotic Options*. New York: John Wiley.

U.S. Commodities Futures Trading Commission (CFTC). 2010. "Dodd-Frank Wall Street Reform and Consumer Protection Act." U.S. Congress, H.R. 4172. www .cftc.gov/ucm/groups/public/@swaps/documents/file/hr4173_enrolledbill.pdf.

U.S. Energy Information Administration (EIA). 2002. "Derivatives and Risk Management in the Petroleum, Natural Gas, and Electricity Industries." www.eia .gov/oiaf/servicerpt/derivative/chapter3.html.

Woo, Chi-Keung, Ira Horowitz, Arne Olson, Andrew DeBenedictis, David Miller, and Jack Moore. 2011. "Cross Hedging and Forward-Contract Pricing of Electricity in the Pacific Northwest." *Managerial and Decision Economics* 32(4): 265–279. http://onlinelibrary.wiley.com/doi/10.1002/mde.1533/abstract.

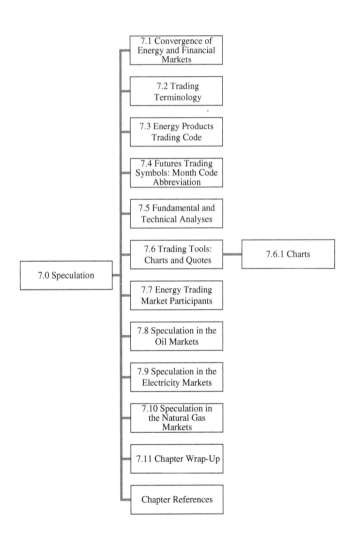

CHAPTER 7

Speculation

In this chapter we will discuss the role speculators play in the energy markets. To accomplish this task we will

- Introduce additional derivatives and trading terminology and notation.
- Present a comparison of speculation and hedging.
- Discuss how traders may incorporate fundamental and technical analysis into their trading strategies to analyze energy markets.
- Define and illustrate trading resources and tools, such as charts and quotes.
- Present illustrations of speculative trading in the oil, natural gas, and electricity markets.

7.1   CONVERGENCE OF ENERGY AND FINANCIAL MARKETS

Various market forces have caused a shift in the balance of power between incumbent energy market participants and new energy trading market entrants (Figure 7.1).

- Price volatility fuels demand for new energy products and services.
- Regulatory changes affect the playing field between banks and energy market participants.
- Risk management tools provide additional insurance to energy market participants.

As a result of these market forces, we are seeing a convergence of financial and energy markets (Carpenter 2007).

Trading is a voluntary exchange of goods and/or services. These exchanges can take place between two parties (*bilateral trade*) or more than two parties (*multilateral trade*). In its original form, trading was a barter deal. Today's traders generally negotiate via exchanges.

Wholesale energy trading is the process of buying and selling in the market to connect supply and demand at realistic price levels. It also provides an efficient means to manage physical and financial risks associated with the supply of commodities (CME Group 2010; EFET 2012).

WHOLESALE ENERGY TRADING

Wholesale Energy Trading is the process of buying and selling in the market to connect supply and demand at realistic price levels.

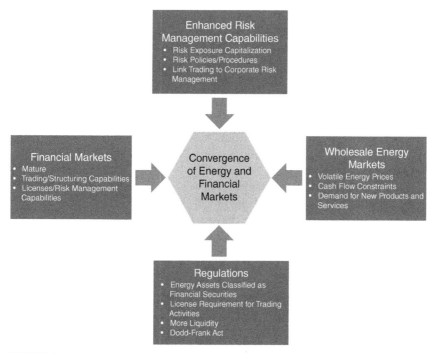

FIGURE 7.1   Convergence of Energy and Financial Markets

Energy traders buy, sell, and/or hold assets for periods of time to make a profit (or prevent a loss) on the difference between the assets' acquisition cost and the market price at time of sale of the assets. Some common trading strategies are

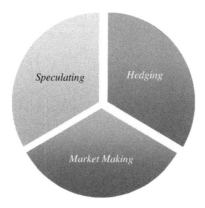

Recall, in the previous two chapters we discussed *hedging*—the act of taking offsetting positions in a derivative in order to balance any gains and losses to the underlying asset. Now we will define *market making* and *speculation*. However, we will focus most of this chapter on the topic of speculation. In addition, throughout this chapter we will introduce several more trading concepts. Please note that a more detailed glossary of energy trading terms may be found in the *Price Waterhouse Coopers* document "Glossary of Terms Used in Trading of Oil and Gas, Utilities and Mining" (PwC 2008).

MARKET MAKER

A market maker is an individual or firm that accepts the risk of holding a certain quantity of a particular security in order to facilitate trading in that security.

A market maker is an individual or firm that accepts the risk of holding a certain quantity of a particular security in order to facilitate trading in that security. In the energy industry a market maker is a trader or energy trading firm that is prepared to buy and sell in the cash or derivatives market to provide a two-sided (bid/ask) market and greater liquidity.

Examples of market makers:

- RWE Supply and Trading GmbH
- EDF Trading Limited
- E.ON Energy Trading SE
- Enron online
- Specialists on exchange floors

SPECULATION

Speculation is a bet on the future direction of price movements of assets. A key motivation to speculate is that the risk of loss is offset by the possibility of a huge gain.

Speculation is a bet on the future direction of price movements of assets. A key motivation to speculate is that the risk of loss is offset by the possibility of a huge gain. Speculation is tantamount to taking a calculated risk—not dependent on pure chance. It is sometimes confused with gambling, which depends on random outcomes or chance.

TABLE 7.1 Speculators

Wholesale Speculators	Locals or inside speculators Members of the exchanges
Scalpers	Trade for their accounts on the floor of the exchange Short-term day traders Help provide liquidity Referred to as market makers
Arbitrageurs	Study relative value of multiple markets Try to take profit from spreads
Day Traders	Typically make one or two trades per day Hold positions only during course of one trading session Close positions before trading session ends
Position Traders	Tend to hold contracts for days, weeks, or months
Retail Speculators	Retail or outside speculators Located off the floor of the exchange Typically position or spread traders

Example: Outright long or short positions in energy assets

A speculator is defined as one who does not produce or use the commodity, but risks his or her own capital trading futures in that commodity in hopes of making a profit on price changes. The goal of a speculator is to make trading profits by being on the "right side" of a price move. Speculators may be classified as shown in Table 7.1.

Speculators have increasingly focused on the energy markets for a number of reasons:

- Wide trading ranges.
- Expanding volatility.
- Increasing liquidity that allows market participants to match their buy and sell orders.
- Energy derivatives may be utilized to profit from the changes in the underlying price of energy products and to amplify those profits through the use of leverage.

Example: If a power generator thought that the spot price of electricity would increase, it can purchase electricity futures (Figure 7.2).

- If the electricity price increased, the generator would receive this higher amount when it sold a futures contract to close out its position and would pay the lower price for the futures contract that it originally bought.

- Conversely, if the generator expected prices to fall, it could sell futures contracts.
- Please note that some arrows in previous schematic diagrams were drawn to illustrate the direction of trade open and trade close. In Figure 7.2 the arrows are in the direction of cash flow. Selling is from Nymex to Generator and buying is from Generator to Nymex. In both the cases Generator would earn/loose the difference between spot and future.

FIGURE 7.2   Generator's Speculative Positions

TABLE 7.2 Speculators versus Hedgers

Speculators	Hedgers
▪ Risk lovers	▪ Risk averse
▪ Seek to profit from price changes	▪ Seek protection against price changes
▪ Create markets	▪ Offset risk associated with market uncertainty
▪ Bet against the movements of the market to try to profit from fluctuations in the market prices	▪ Use markets to lock in today's price for transactions that will occur in the future

Some key distinctions between speculators and hedgers can be found in Table 7.2.

Example: Suppose for the sake of illustration that the power market consisted only of marketers who wished to hedge by buying options. At any given point in time the amount of short hedging in the power options markets can differ from the amount of long hedging. This is where speculators can make a contribution—by providing liquidity to the power market. The speculators

- Can sell options to the marketers, providing them insurance while generating profits.
- Hold no position in the underlying energy asset.
- Increase their risk by being long or short options.
- Are compensated for this increase in risk because hedgers are willing to pay for the insurance that the speculators provide (Stoft et al.1998).

> *At any given point in time, the amount of* **short hedging** *in the power options markets can differ from the amount of* **long hedging**.

Note: In Henn (2013) one can find a list of papers about the impact of commodity speculation. This list is periodically updated and revised. However, it only compiles evidence that supports a negative view of speculation.

7.2 TRADING TERMINOLOGY

Throughout this book we present a wide range of terminology to explain the energy industry, derivatives, risk management, hedging, and trading. In this section we will define a few more terms to help the reader understand energy trading (Table 7.3). However, there are numerous terms that we will omit in this book. For a more detailed glossary of trading terminology, please refer to CME Group's "Glossary" (2013b).

TABLE 7.3 Additional Trading Terminology

Clearing	Procedure through which CME Clearing House becomes the buyer to each seller of a futures contract, and the seller to each buyer, and assumes responsibility for protecting buyers and sellers from financial loss by ensuring buyer and seller performance on each contract. This is affected through the clearing process, in which transactions are matched, confirming that both the buyer's and the seller's trade information are in agreement.
Contract Size	Amount of a commodity represented in a futures or options contract as specified in the contract specifications.
Leverage	Ability to control large dollar amounts of a commodity with a comparatively small amount of capital.
Liquidity	A condition that describes the ability to execute orders of any size quickly and efficiently without a substantial effect on the price.
Margin	Collateral that a holder of a security has to deposit to cover some or all of the credit risk of its counterparty.
	Initial Margin Requirement: percentage of the purchase price of securities (that can be purchased on margin) that must be paid for with cash or marginable securities.
	Maintenance Margin Requirement: amount that must be kept on deposit at all times until a position is closed.
	Spot Assessment: CME Group requires higher margins for energy spot-month positions open on the day prior to the expiration of a futures contract.
Margin Call	A broker's demand on an investor using margin to deposit additional money or securities so that the margin account is brought up to the minimum maintenance margin. Margin calls occur when an account value depresses to a value calculated by the broker's particular formula. This is also known as a *fed call* or *maintenance call*.
Mark-to-Market	To debit or credit on a daily basis a margin account based on the close of that day's trading session. In this way, buyers and sellers are protected against the possibility of contract default.
Open Interest	Total number of futures contracts long or short in a delivery month or market that has been entered into and not yet offset or fulfilled by delivery. Each open transaction has a buyer and a seller, but for calculation of open interest, only one side of the contract is counted. Also known as *Open Contracts* or *Open Commitments*.
Position Limit	The maximum number of speculative futures contracts one can hold as determined by the U.S. Commodity Futures Trading Commission (CFTC) and/or the exchange upon which the contract is traded. Also referred to as *trading limits*.

TABLE 7.3 (*continued*)

Stop Exit Points	Normal or logical stop points used to preserve and protect trading capital: anomaly move, parabolic, percentage of daily change, resistance levels, support levels, system signal, total money objective, and trailing stops.
Tick	Minimum fluctuation in price allowed for a futures or options contract during a trading session as specified by the contract terms in CME Rulebook.
Ticker Symbol	An arrangement of characters representing a particular security listed on an exchange or otherwise traded publicly.
Volume	The number of contracts in futures or options on futures transacted during a specified period of time.

7.3 ENERGY PRODUCTS TRADING CODES

Table 7.4 includes list of codes for some energy products traded on the New York Mercantile Exchange (NYMEX). For more detailed lists of energy products traded please refer to CME Group's "Energy Products" (2013a).

TABLE 7.4 Trading Codes

Product Subgroup	Code	Product Name
Oil	AO	WTI Average Price Options
	CL	Light Sweet Crude Oil Futures
	LO	Crude Oil Options
	QM	E-mini Crude Oil (Financial) Futures are an outright crude oil contract between a buyer and seller. The contract is half the size of the standard Light Sweet Crude contract.
Electricity	B6	PJM Northern Illinois Hub Real-Time Off-Peak Calendar-Month 5 MW Futures
	E4	PJM Western Hub Day-Ahead Off-Peak Calendar-Month 5 MW Futures
	N9	PJM Western Hub Real-Time Off-Peak Calendar-Month 5 MW Futures

(*continued*)

TABLE 7.4   Trading Codes (*Continued*)

Product Subgroup	Code	Product Name
Natural Gas	LN	Natural Gas European Options
	NG	Henry Hub Natural Gas Futures
	NN	Henry Hub Swap Futures
	NP	Henry Hub Penultimate NP Futures
	QG	E-mini Natural Gas Futures are an outright natural gas contract between a buyer and a seller. The contract is about one-quarter the size of the standard Natural Gas futures contract.

7.4   FUTURES TRADING SYMBOLS: MONTH CODE ABBREVIATION

Futures tickers are different from stock symbols.

- Contract months are identified by a month code abbreviation to indicate the month in which a futures contract expires (the *delivery month*). The month code abbreviations for futures contracts can be found in Table 7.5.
- Each futures market has a ticker symbol that is followed by symbols for the contract month and the year.

Example: As denoted in Table 7.4, the natural gas futures have a ticker symbol "NG." The complete ticker symbol for April 2013 natural gas futures is NGJ13.

- "NG" denotes the underlying futures contract.
- "J" denotes an April delivery month.
- "13" denotes the year 2013.

> *Contract months are identified by a month code abbreviation to indicate the month in which a futures contract expires (the delivery month).*

TABLE 7.5   Futures Month Code Abbreviation

Month	Abbreviation (First Year)	Abbreviation (Second Year)
January	F	D
February	G	E
March	H	I
April	J	L
May	K	O
June	M	P
July	N	T
August	Q	R
September	U	B
October	V	C
November	X	W
December	Z	Y

7.5   FUNDAMENTAL AND TECHNICAL ANALYSES

It is essential for energy traders to know how to make reasonable estimates of what will happen to future prices of energy commodities. No trader knows for certain what future prices will be. However, it pays to have an educated guestimate as to whether future energy prices will increase or decrease.

Traders may incorporate fundamental and technical analysis into their trading strategies to analyze energy markets. A technical analyst approaches a security or commodity from charts, while a fundamental analyst starts with related economic, financial, and other qualitative and quantitative factors. Many traders think fundamental analysis is more effective when combined with technical analysis. A trader who utilizes both technical and fundamental analysis is sometimes referred to as a *techno-fundamentalist* (CME Group 2010; Galuschke 2010; Knupp 2011; Mack 1999).

FUNDAMENTAL ANALYSIS

Fundamental analysis is a method of evaluating a security by attempting to measure its intrinsic value via examining related economic, financial, and other qualitative and quantitative factors.

Fundamental analysis utilizes the economics of supply and demand information to determine price expectation. It is a method of evaluating a security by attempting to measure its intrinsic value via examining related economic, financial, and other qualitative and quantitative factors. The goal of performing fundamental analysis is to produce a value that a trader can compare with the asset's current price, with the aim of determining what sort of trading position to take with that asset. When conducting fundamental analysis in the energy markets, a trader may wish to take into consideration physical demand and supply information such as

- Production
- Pipeline and transmission capacity
- Planned and unplanned outages
- Weather
- Economics
- Demographics
- Macro and micro supply and demand
- Arbitrage (transportation changes, dislocations, etc.)
- Seasonality

TECHNICAL ANALYSIS

Technical analysis is a methodology that involves the analysis of charts and market statistics for a security, commodity, or index.

Technical analysis is an approach that involves the analysis of charts and market statistics for a security, commodity, or index (Figure 7.3). Traders may utilize various resources and information to conduct technical analysis: mathematical models, historical data for prices, trading volume, moving averages, maximums and minimums, neural networks, pattern recognition, stochastics, volatility, change indicators, percentage changes, and so forth. A technical analyst may utilize these resources to estimate:

- Price (high, low, and close for each day)
- Volume (number of contracts traded each day)
- Open interest

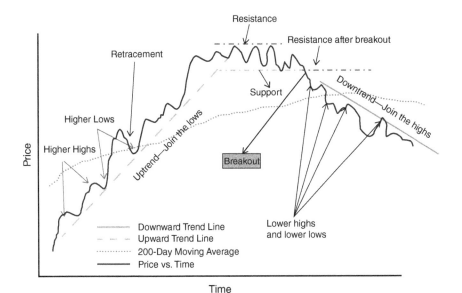

FIGURE 7.3 Technical Analysis Sample

7.6 TRADING TOOLS: CHARTS AND QUOTES

There are some free online resources that traders may use to conduct technical analysis (Table 7.6). Most prices of securities and commodities that are displayed on these free websites are delayed quotes and not real-time quotes (Kowalski 2013).

- A *real-time quote* is the actual price of a security at that moment in time. Most services will charge a fee for real-time quotes.
- *Delayed quotes* are usually 10 to 30 minutes behind real-time market prices.

An energy asset might appear cheap on a short-term basis. However, it might be very expensive on a long-term basis. A short-term trend could be a couple of days to a few weeks for energy assets. A long-term trend could be a few months to a couple of years. One approach to analyze the price of the energy assets is by using *charts*.

> *The **bar chart** is the most popular chart utilized in technical analysis. It shows a picture of what is happening in the market.*

TABLE 7.6 Market Quotes and Charts Resources

Online Trading Resources	Features
http://futures.quote.com	▪ Free quotes on futures and options ▪ Charts with technical studies
http://commoditiesstreetjournal.com	▪ Quotes on commodity and futures markets ▪ Charts on commodity and futures markets ▪ Quotes on futures options for each market
www.barchart.com	▪ Futures quotes organized in single-page format ▪ Commodity and futures quotes separated by categories

The *bar chart* is the most popular chart utilized in technical analysis. It shows a picture of what is happening in the market. The visual representation of price activity over a given period of time may be utilized to spot trends and patterns (Figure 7.4).

- The top of the vertical line of a bar chart indicates the highest price a security traded at during the day.
- The bottom of the vertical line represents the lowest price.
- The closing price is displayed on the right side of the bar.
- The opening price is shown on the left side of the bar.
- A single bar represents one day of trading.

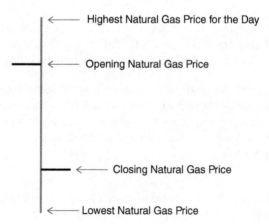

← Highest Natural Gas Price for the Day

← Opening Natural Gas Price

← Closing Natural Gas Price

← Lowest Natural Gas Price

FIGURE 7.4 Bar Chart

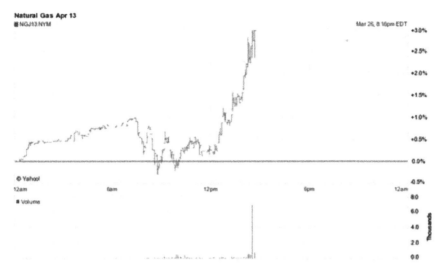

FIGURE 7.5 Natural Gas Price Bar Chart
Source: Yahoo! Finance.

Note: The bar chart is a historical record. It does not show what is going to happen. The technical analyst reads the visual patterns of price movement and attempts to draw conclusions about the likely future direction of the market.

Example: The bar chart in Figure 7.5 displays prices for **Natural Gas Apr 13 (NGJ13.NYM)**—NY Mercantile futures contract. The data in this bar chart was extracted from *Yahoo! Finance*, which is a free online data source.

Natural Gas Apr 13 (NGJ13.NYM)

Open: $3.88

Bid: $3.90

Ask: $3.94

Day's Range: $3.86–$3.99

Volume: 19,350

Candlestick displays the high, low, opening, and closing prices for a security for a single day.

Another type of chart that may be utilized in technical analysis is the *candlestick*. This is a chart that displays the high, low, opening, and closing prices for a security for a single day. The wide part of the candlestick is called the "real body" and tells investors whether the closing price was higher or lower than the opening price (black and red if the asset price closed lower; white and green if the asset price closed higher). The candlestick's shadows show the day's highs and lows and how they compare to the open and close. A candlestick's shape varies based on the relationship between the day's high, low, opening, and closing prices. Candlesticks reflect the impact of traders' emotions on security or commodity prices. They are utilized by technical analysts to determine when to enter and exit trades. Here is an enlarged image of a candlestick. In addition, an example of a candlestick chart for natural gas prices can be found in Figure 7.6. This chart is courtesy of www.Barchart.com, which is listed in Table 7.6.

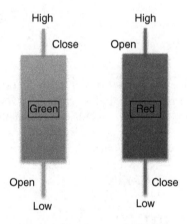

7.7   ENERGY TRADING MARKET PARTICIPANTS

Wholesale energy markets are unique because they involve the trading of network-bound commodities, such as electric power and gas (Figures 7.7, 7.8, and 7.9). These energy commodities cannot be freely traded unless there is equitable third-party access to the transmission grid and gas pipelines respectively. Hence wholesale energy trading cannot be provided on truly competitive terms unless market participants who do not own the relevant essential infrastructure are allowed access on equal terms and conditions to the facilities of those that do (EFET 2012).

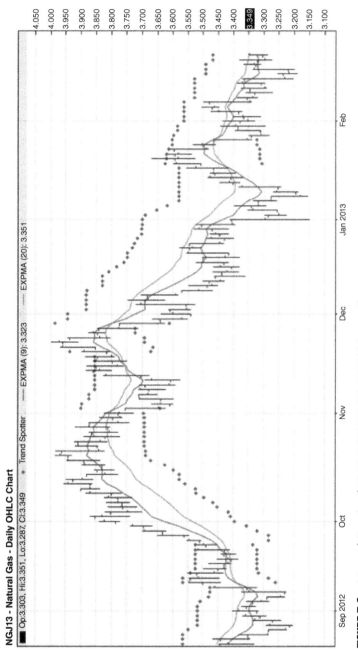

FIGURE 7.6 Natural Gas April 2013 (NGJ13.NYM)-NY Mercantile
© Barchart.com.

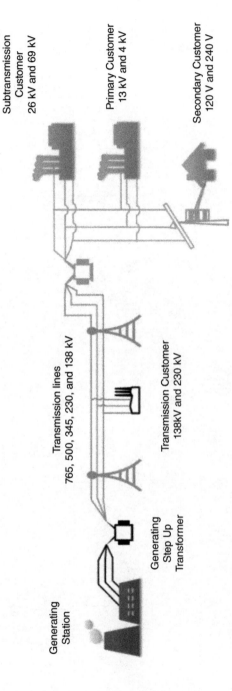

FIGURE 7.7 U.S Electric Transmission Grid

Generating
Station

Generating
Step Up
Transformer

Transmission lines
765, 500, 345, 230, and 138 kV

Transmission Customer
138kV and 230 kV

Subtransmission
Customer
26 kV and 69 kV

Primary Customer
13 kV and 4 kV

Secondary Customer
120 V and 240 V

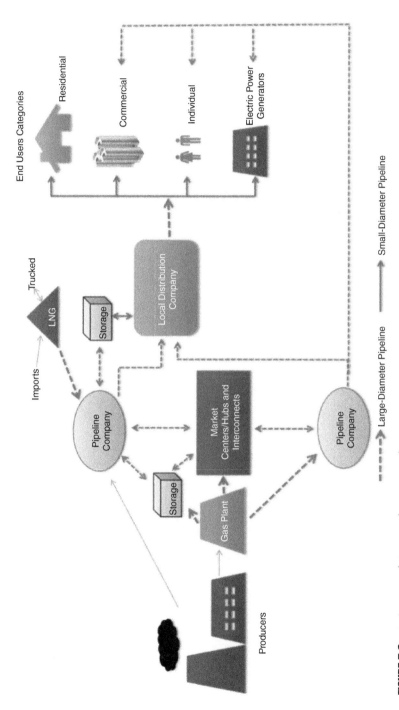

FIGURE 7.8 U.S. Natural Gas Pipeline Network

FIGURE 7.9 An Intricate Web of Interstate and Intrastate Gas Pipelines in the United States
Source: Energy Information Administration, Office of Oil & Gas, Natural Gas Division, Gas Transportation Information System.

FIGURE 7.10 Energy Trading Market Participants

Recall in Chapter 1, we discussed power spot market participants. There are various participants involved in the overall energy trading markets (Figure 7.10).

- Physical players, producers, and marketers: buy or sell physical products or hedge physical supplies and obligations with physical or financial products
- Investors, speculators, hedge funds, and financial institutions: utilize these physical and financial energy products for financial gain (CME 2006).

7.8 SPECULATION IN THE OIL MARKETS

Oil is truly the lifeblood of the global economy.

(Bouchentouf 2011)

Much has been written or said about speculation in the oil markets. A simple web search turns up tens of millions of citations. Even on YouTube one can find thousands of videos on the topic. U.S. Senator Bernie Sanders has gone so far as to say "stop excessive oil speculation now" (Sanders 2012). In addition, Joseph Kennedy II writes that "pure" oil speculators "should be banned from the world's commodity exchanges" (Kennedy 2012).

Some refer to crude oil as the "King of Commodities" (Bouchentouf 2011). Perhaps this is due to the fact that the crude oil is the

- Most-traded nonfinancial commodity in the world
- Supplier of 40 percent of the world's total energy needs
- Base product for many secondary products: *electricity, gasoline, jet fuel, heavy oil, plastics, liquid petroleum gas, diesel fuel, heating oil*
- Base product for petroleum products—the dominant energy resource worldwide

The *Organization of Petroleum Exporting Countries* (OPEC) was founded in 1960. OPEC consists of the world's major oil-exporting nations, including founding members Iran, Iraq, Kuwait, and Venezuela. Approximately 80 percent of the world's proven oil reserves are located in OPEC member countries with 66 percent in the Middle East (Figure 7.11). The OPEC member countries also hold nearly half of the world's natural gas reserves (OPEC 2013).

Approximately 80 percent of the world's proven oil reserves are located in OPEC member countries with 66 percent in the Middle East.

OPEC's key functions are as follows:

- Coordinate the petroleum policies of its members.
- Provide member states with technical and economic aid.
- Manage the supply of oil in an effort to set the price of oil on the world market.
- Avoid oil price fluctuations that might affect the economies of both producing and purchasing countries.

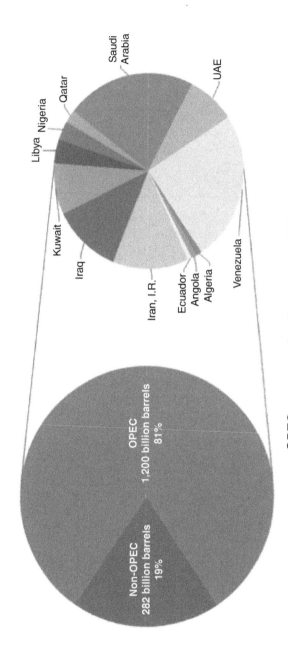

OPEC proven crude oil reserves, end 2011
(billion barrels, OPEC Share)

Venezuela	297.6	24.8%	Iraq	141.4	11.8%	Libya	48.0	4.0%	Algeria	12.2	1.0%
Saudi Arabia	265.4	22.1%	Kuwait	101.5	8.5%	Nigeria	37.2	3.1%	Angola	10.5	0.9%
Iran, I.R.	154.6	12.9%	United Arab Emirates	97.8	8.2%	Qatar	25.4	2.1%	Ecuador	8.2	0.7%

FIGURE 7.11 World Crude Oil Reserves
Source: OPEC Annual Statistical Bulletin 2012.

Crude oil and the products distilled from these oils are traded in over-the-counter (OTC) markets and on exchanges around the world. Recall we listed a few crude oil products in Table 7.4. A more detailed list of products in the oil markets may be found in "Energy Products" by CME Group (2013a) and "Crude Oil Grades and Types" by Intertek (2013). Some global exchanges, such as NYMEX, host trading in futures on crude oil, gasoline, and heating oil. This presents opportunities for trading spreads among these related energy markets (Dash and Skyba 2012).

> *Crude oil and the products distilled from these oils are traded in OTC markets and on exchanges around the world.*

Example: In the previous chapter we presented a case study illustrating how an oil refiner may utilize crack spread options as a hedging tool. In addition, an oil refiner may intentionally or unintentionally speculate.

- *Intentional speculation* in the market in an effort to make a profit: In this case speculation requires that the refiner not have a position in the underlying commodity market.
- *Unintentional speculation:* Suppose, for example, the refiner bought options contracts to hedge its purchase of crude oil in one year. However, one year later, the refiner no longer needs the crude oil.

More information on speculating in the oil markets may be found in CME Group (2011), Engdahl (2008), Fattouh (2012), NYMEX (2000), and Thomson Reuters (2008).

7.9 SPECULATION IN THE ELECTRICITY MARKETS

In the previous chapter we presented a case study illustrating how a power consumer may utilize futures as a hedging tool. Similar to the discussion of speculation in the oil markets, speculation in the electricity markets can be intentional or unintentional. For more information on speculative trading in the power markets please refer to CME Group (2013d), FERC (2012), Saravia (2003), and Stoft et al. (1998).

7.10 SPECULATION IN THE NATURAL GAS MARKETS

> *The Federal Energy Regulatory Commission (FERC) data indicates that natural gas is the second largest primary source of energy consumed in the United States, exceeded only by oil.*

Under the Natural Gas Act (NGA), the Federal Energy Regulatory Commission (FERC) has jurisdiction over U.S. natural gas markets. FERC data indicates that natural gas is the second largest primary source of energy consumed in the United States, exceeded only by oil. Once thought of as a byproduct of oil production, natural gas is sometimes referred to as the *Queen of Commodities*. Some of the largest users of natural gas in North America are listed in Table 7.7. Approximately 25 percent of the U.S. energy consumption comes from natural gas (Bouchentouf 2011; FERC 2012).

The pricing and settlement of natural gas financial products and derivatives are tied to physical natural gas. The value of trading of these products in the financial markets is at least a dozen times greater than the value of physical trading. The map in Figure 7.12 highlights some of the hubs where natural gas for next-day physical delivery is traded on the *Intercontinental Exchange* (ICE).

> *The pricing and settlement of natural gas financial products and derivatives are tied to physical natural gas.*

TABLE 7.7   Largest Users of Natural Gas

Residential	■ Approximately 50 percent of the homes in North America use natural gas for heating, especially during the winter months. ■ Boilers, furnaces, water heaters, outdoor barbeque grills
Industrial	■ Natural gas vehicles (17.4 million worldwide) (NGV 2010) ■ Natural gas used as a source of heat for industrial customers
Electric Power Generation	■ Power plants are the fastest-growing users of natural gas. ■ Approximately one-third of the natural gas consumed in the United States is utilized for the production of electricity.

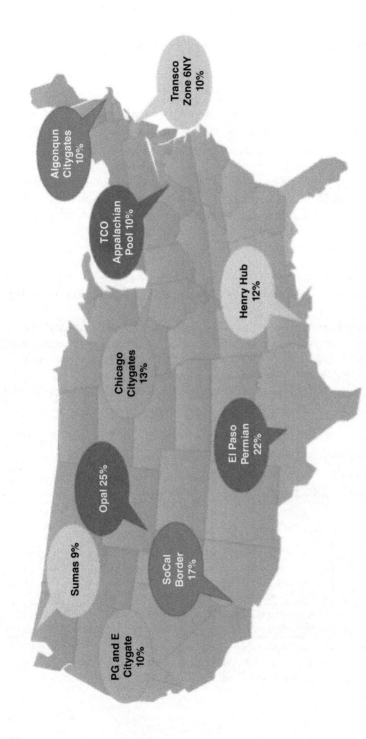

FIGURE 7.12 Natural Gas Hubs in the United States
Source: Energy Information Administration.

A *natural gas hub* is where two or more pipelines connect with each other. The most important hub for natural gas in North America is the *Henry Hub*, located along the U.S. Gulf Coast. This hub is where the benchmark for natural gas prices is determined and traded for delivery on the NYMEX natural gas futures contract.

Example: The *Henry Hub Natural Gas (NG)* futures contract is the third-largest physical commodity futures contract in the world by volume (CME Group 2013c).

Example: An energy trader is bullish (bearish) on natural gas. The trader thinks she can profit from a rise (drop) in natural gas prices by taking up a long (short) position in the natural gas futures market. The trader buys (sells) one or more July NYMEX Division Henry Hub natural gas futures for $1.45 per million Btu.

For more information on speculative trading in the natural gas markets please refer to CME Group (2013c), EIA (2013), and FERC (2012).

7.11   CHAPTER WRAP-UP

In this chapter we discussed the role speculators play in the energy markets. We introduced additional terminology, notation, tools, and analytical techniques: derivatives and trading terminology; fundamental and technical analysis; and charts and quotes. In addition, we compared speculation and hedging. Finally, we presented illustrations of speculative trading in the oil, natural gas, and electricity markets.

REFERENCES

Bouchentouf, Amine. 2011. *Commodities For Dummies*, 2nd ed. Hoboken, NJ: John Wiley & Sons.

Carpenter, Guy. 2007. "Energy Market Convergence: Time to Review Trading Strategies, Risk Management and Operations." Oliver Wyman Group. www .oliverwyman.de/deu-insights/energy_mkt_convergence_ERC_0206.pdf.

CME Group. 2006. "CME Commodity Trading Manual." Chicago Mercantile Exchange. http://gpvec.unl.edu/files/Futures/CME%201%20Commodity%20 Trading%20Manual.pdf.

————. 2010. "Fundamentals of Energy Trading." CME Group Education. www .cmegroup.com/education/interactive/webinars-archived/fundamentals-of-energy-trading.html.

————. 2011. "Light Sweet Crude Oil (WTI) Futures and Options: The World's Most Liquid Crude Oil Benchmark." Energy. www.cmegroup.com/trading/ energy/files/en-153_wti_brochure_sr.pdf.

————. 2013a. "Energy Products." www.cmegroup.com/trading/energy.

————. 2013b. "Glossary." www.cmegroup.com/education/glossary.html.

————. 2013c. "Henry Hub Natural Gas Futures." Energy Products. www
.cmegroup.com/trading/energy/natural-gas/natural-gas.html.

————. 2013d. "Power Industry Terminology." Education. www.cmegroup.com/
education/interactive/webinars-archived/power-industry-terminology.html.

Dash, Stanley, and Erik Skyba. 2012. "Inside the Oil Markets." TradeStation Group.
www.tradestation.com/education/labs/analysis-concepts/inside-the-oil-markets.

European Federation of Energy Traders (EFET). 2012. "Towards a Single European
Energy Market." www.efet.org/Cms_Data/Contents/EFET/Folders/Documents/
Home/~contents/GPC2TV6X8L2STWT8/Highlights-II-Final.pdf.

Engdahl, F. William. 2008. "Perhaps 60% of Today's Oil Price is Pure Speculation." *Oil Economy*. www.engdahl.oilgeopolitics.net/Financial_Tsunami/Oil_
Speculation/oil_speculation.HTM.

Fattouh, Bassam. 2012. "Speculation and Oil Price Formation." *Review of Environment, Energy and Economics*. www.feem.it/userfiles/attach/201253159474Re3-
B.Fattouh-2012902.pdf.

Federal Energy Regulatory Commission (FERC). 2012 (July). "Energy Primer: A
Handbook of Energy Market Basics." The Division of Energy Market Oversight, Office of Enforcement, Federal Energy Regulatory Commission. www
.ferc.gov/market-oversight/guide/energy-primer.pdf.

Galuschke, Holger. 2010. "Technical Analysis Applied on Energy Markets." E.ON
Energy Trading. www.bbv-online.org/downloads/eonpraes.pdf.

Henn, Markus. 2013. "Evidence on the Negative Impact of Commodity Speculation
by Academics, Analysts and Public Institutions." WEED. www2.weed-online
.org/uploads/evidence_on_impact_of_commodity_speculation.pdf.

Intertek. 2013. "Crude Oil Grades and Types." www.intertek.com/petroleum/crude-
oil-types.

Kennedy, Joseph. 2012. "The High Cost of Gambling Oil." *New York Times*. www
.nytimes.com/2012/04/11/opinion/ban-pure-speculators-of-oil-futures.html.

Knupp, Wayne. 2011. "The Importance of Fundamental Analysis." Energy-Koch Trading. http://www.docstoc.com/docs/68419267/The-Importance-of-Fundamental-
Analysis.

Kowalski, Chuck. 2013. "Futures Quote and Chart Websites." About.com Commodities. http://commodities.about.com/od/understandingthebasics/tp/futures-
quotes-charts.htm.

Mack, Iris. 1986. "Block Implicit One-Step Methods for Solving Smooth and Discontinuous Systems of Differential/Algebraic Equations: Applications to Transient Stability of Electrical Power Systems." PhD diss., Harvard University Press.

NGV Communications Group. 2010. "Worldwide NGV Statistics." *NGV Journal*. www
.ngvjournal.dreamhosters.com/en/statistics/item/911-worldwide-ngv-statistics.

New York Mercantile Exchange (NYMEX). 2000. *Crack Spread Handbook*. http://
partners.futuresource.com/marketcenter/pdfs/crack.pdf.

Organization of the Petroleum Exporting Countries (OPEC). 2013. "OPEC Share of
World Crude Oil Reserves 2011." www.opec.org/opec_web/en/data_graphs/330
.htm.

PriceWaterhouse Coopers (PwC). 2008. "Glossary of Terms Used in Trading of Oil and Gas, Utilities and Mining." https://www.pwc.com/gx/en/energy-utilities-mining/pdf/eumcommoditiestradingriskmanagementglossary.pdf.

Sanders, Bernie. 2012. "Stop Excessive Oil Speculation." www.sanders.senate.gov/newsroom/recent-business/stop-excessive-oil-speculation.

Saravia, Celeste. 2003. "Speculative Trading and Market Performance: The Effect of Arbitrageurs on Efficiency and Market Power in the New York Electricity Market." University of California. www.ucei.berkeley.edu/PDF/csemwp121.pdf.

Stoft, S., T. Belden, C. Goldman, and S. Pickle. 1998. "Primer on Electricity Futures and Other Derivatives." Report LBNL-41098, UC-1321, Environmental Energy Technologies Division: Ernest Orlando Lawrence Berkeley National Laboratory. http://eetd.lbl.gov/ea/emp/reports/41098.pdf.

Thomson Reuters. 2008. "Reuters Electronic Trading." Automated Dealing. http://thomsonreuters.com/content/financial/pdf/s_and_t/RET_AutomatedDealing.pd.

U.S. Energy Information Administration (EIA). 2013. "Natural Gas Weekly Update." www.cmegroup.com/education/files/eia-natural-gas-weekly-update-2013-04-17.pdf.

CHAPTER 8

Energy Portfolios

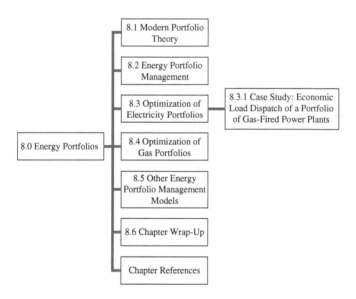

A *portfolio* is a collection of assets held by investors (traders, investment firms, hedge funds, financial institutions, energy market participants, corporations, governments, or individuals).

PORTFOLIO

A portfolio is a collection of assets held by investors (traders, investment firms, hedge funds, financial institutions, and energy market participants).

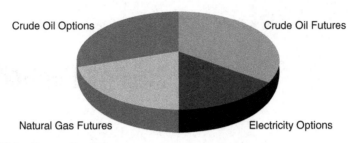

Crude Oil Options

Crude Oil Futures

Natural Gas Futures

Electricity Options

FIGURE 8.1   Energy Portfolio

Example: One can visualize a portfolio as a pie that is partitioned into pieces of varying slices (representing a variety of assets) to achieve an appropriate risk-return portfolio allocation (Figure 8.1).

We talked a bit about portfolios when we introduced multi-asset options in Chapter 4. In this chapter we present some concepts from modern portfolio theory (MPT) and energy portfolio management (EPM). These MPT and EPM concepts are utilized to discuss optimization of electricity and gas portfolios. In addition, we discuss how MATLAB built-in functions may be utilized to optimize a portfolio of gas-fired power plants. This MATLAB case study ties together some of the concepts in this book.

8.1   MODERN PORTFOLIO THEORY

Portfolio diversification is the means by which investors

- Minimize or eliminate risks in a portfolio
- Moderate the effects of individual asset class performance on the portfolio value

Modern portfolio theory (MPT) provides a framework for maximizing portfolio expected returns for a given amount of portfolio risk. It is a mathematical formulation of the concept of diversification in investing, with the aim of selecting a collection of assets that has collectively lower risk than any individual asset. Harry Markowitz was the first to propose a methodology for portfolio selection (Markowitz 1952).

An *efficient frontier* (Figure 8.2 and Table 8.1) is a set of optimal portfolios that offers the

- Highest expected return for a defined level of risk, or
- Lowest risk for a given level of expected return.

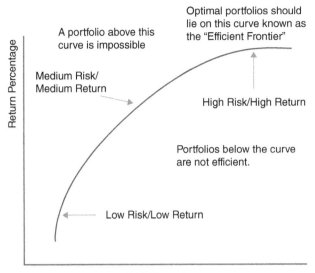

FIGURE 8.2 Efficient Frontier

MODERN PORTFOLIO THEORY (MPT)

Modern portfolio theory (MPT) provides a framework for maximizing portfolio expected returns for a given amount of portfolio risk.

TABLE 8.1 Location of Portfolios with Respect to the Efficient Frontier

Location of Portfolios	Properties
Below	Suboptimal: Don't provide enough return for the level of risk
Cluster to the right	Suboptimal: Have a higher level of risk for the defined rate of return
On the efficient frontier	Optimal: Have the best possible expected level of return for its level of risk

The Markowitz framework is also known as the *mean-variance framework*. The key assumptions in the Markowitz portfolio framework are as follows:

- Investment decisions are based on expected return and risk.
- Expected return is measured via the mean of the asset prices.
- Risk is measured via the variance of the asset prices.
- Investors are only concerned with the utility of their terminal wealth.
- All investors have the same time horizon or terminal time.
- All investors are in agreement with respect to the key parameters in the investment decision-making process: means, variances, correlations of returns on the asset prices.
- Assets are freely exchangeable or replaceable.

MARKOWITZ PORTFOLIO THEORY

The Markowitz portfolio theory is a linear programming problem, which consists of a linear expression for an objective function and linear equality and inequality constraints.

The objective of this Markowitz framework is to maximize the expected return and to minimize the standard deviation of the return.

$$\mu := E[R] = w^T \mu \ \text{(Expected Return)}$$

$$\sigma(R) = \sqrt{w^T \Sigma w} \ \text{(Standard Deviation of the Return)}$$

where $\mu = E[R] = E\left[\sum_{i=1}^{n} w_i R_i\right] = \sum_{i=1}^{n} w_i E[R_i] = \sum_{i=1}^{n} w_i \mu_i = w^T \mu$

$$\sigma^2(R) = E\left[(R - \mu)^2\right] = E\left[\left(\sum_{i=1}^{n} w_i (R_i - \mu_i)\right)^2\right]$$

$$= \sum_{i=1}^{n}\sum_{j=1}^{n} w_i w_j \sigma_{ij} = w^T \mu \ \text{(Variance of the return)}$$

R denotes the return of the portfolio

μ denotes the mean of the portfolio

R_i denotes the return of the ith asset at time t $(1 \leq i \leq n)$

μ_i denotes the mean of the ith asset's return $(1 \leq i \leq n)$

w_i denotes the proportion of the value of the portfolio that asset i makes up $(1 \leq i \leq n)$

$$\sum_{i=1}^{n} w_i = 1$$

σ_{ij} denotes the covariance between the return on asset i and the return on asset j

$\sigma_i^2 = \sigma_{ii}$ denotes the variance of ith asset's return $(1 \leq i \leq n)$

$\Sigma = [\sigma_{ij}]$ denotes the covariance matrix

$w = [w_1, w_2, ..., w_n]^T$

w^T denotes the transpose of vector w

MATLAB

MATLAB (matrix laboratory) is a numerical computing environment and fourth-generation programming language.

With very little computer programming, one can analyze and optimize portfolios of assets in MATLAB by utilizing the *Financial Toolbox*. MATLAB (*matrix lab*oratory) is a numerical computing environment and fourth-generation programming language. Developed by Math-Works, MATLAB allows matrix manipulations, plotting of functions and data, implementation of algorithms, creation of user interfaces, and interfacing with programs written in various languages (MathWorks 2011, 2013). This MATLAB toolbox provides a comprehensive suite of tools to conduct

- Capital allocation
- Asset allocation
- Risk assessment

Despite its theoretical importance, critics of MPT question whether it is an ideal investing strategy, because its model of financial markets does not match the real world in many ways. More on MPT may be found in *Linear Programming 1* (Dantzig and Thapa 1997) and "The Many Facets of Linear Programming" (Todd 2002).

8.2 ENERGY PORTFOLIO MANAGEMENT

Portfolio Management (PM) is the art and science of selecting the right investment policy for investors. This process entails:

- Making decisions about investment policy
- Matching investments to objectives
- Asset valuation and allocation
- Balancing risk against performance
- Maximizing returns
- Portfolio optimization
- Performance measurement

PORTFOLIO MANAGEMENT

Portfolio management (PM) is the art and science of selecting the right investment policy for investors.

The following definitions of PM are utilized in the energy industry (EPA 2006; Steinhurst et al. 2006; Yan 2011):

- *Portfolio management* refers to resource planning that incorporates a variety of energy resources, including supply-side (e.g., traditional and renewable energy sources) and demand-side (e.g., energy efficiency) options.
- The term "portfolio management" has emerged in recent years to describe resource planning and procurement in states that have restructured their electric industry.
- However, the approach can also include the more traditional integrated resource planning (IRP) approaches applied to regulated, vertically integrated utilities.

Energy portfolio management (EPM) is utilized to find an optimal energy solution that can provide useful guidance to energy consumers and policymakers in the selection of optimal energy portfolios with lower cost and less risk. The conceptual framework presents the methodology of EPM, while EPM simulations demonstrate the selection of optimal energy choices, and further, the impacts of social cost on the optimal energy portfolio in the case of United States.

ENERGY PORTFOLIO MANAGEMENT

Energy portfolio management (EPM) is established to find an optimal energy solution that can provide useful guidance to energy consumers and policymakers in the selection of optimal energy portfolios with lower cost and less risk.

EPM models are utilized by energy market participants to obtain an optimal energy consumption solution subject to the constraints such as the following:

Available energy resources	*Diverse technologies*	*Storage constraints*	*Delivery contracts*
Regulations	*Supply contracts*	*Energy social cost structure*	*Volatile fuel prices*
Security of energy resources	*Transmission capacities*	*Consumer energy efficiency programs*	*Public safety*
Peak demand hours consumption reduction programs	*Reliability of energy commodity*	*Public acceptability of generation technologies and fuel sources*	*Environmental standards*

8.3 OPTIMIZATION OF ELECTRICITY PORTFOLIOS

More specific to the electricity markets, a portfolio can include fuel sources for power generation, technology and a set of power contracts for delivery and purchase, including financial contracts (Figure 8.3).

Suppose a power generator has a certain number of generating units online. The *economic load dispatch (ELD) problem* involves finding the optimal allocation of power generation that minimizes the total generating cost while simultaneously satisfying the total required demand.

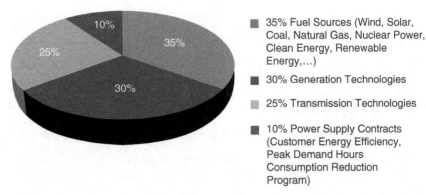

■ 35% Fuel Sources (Wind, Solar, Coal, Natural Gas, Nuclear Power, Clean Energy, Renewable Energy,...)

■ 30% Generation Technologies

■ 25% Transmission Technologies

■ 10% Power Supply Contracts (Customer Energy Efficiency, Peak Demand Hours Consumption Reduction Program)

FIGURE 8.3   Portfolio Diversification for an Electric Power Generator

Objective Function for the ELD Electricity Portfolio optimization:

$$C = \sum_i \left(a_i + b_i P_i + c_i P_i^2 \right)$$

where C = Cost function for a power producer

a_i, b_i, c_i denote the cost coefficients of the ith generator

P_i = Power generated from the ith generator

Constraints for ELD Electricity Portfolio Optimization:

$$D + L = \sum_i P_i \text{ (Power Balance Equation)}$$

$$P_{i,\min} \leq P_i \leq P_{i,\max}$$

where D = the total load

$L = \sum_i \sum_j a_{ij} P_i P_j$ denotes the transmission loss

a_{ij} denotes the transmission loss coefficient

$P_{i,\min}$ denotes the minimum generation power

$P_{i,\max}$ denotes the maximum generation power

In the previous section we discussed how MPT is applied to analyze and optimize portfolios of financial assets. However, in this case the electricity portfolio contains financial and physical assets. In Table 8.2 we summarize limitations of applying MPT to analyze and optimize electricity portfolios.

TABLE 8.2 Some Limitations of the Application of MPT to Electricity Portfolios

Electricity Portfolios	Financial Portfolios
Nonmonetary value associated with power generation assets must be taken into consideration, e.g., consumer preferences.	Monetary and economic value associated with financial assets are taken into consideration
Require consideration of additional criteria: congestion constraints, long-term investment horizon, scheduling, operational, commitment costs	Managed by weighing risk and return
Electric utilities need to manage more than correlation among assets. For example, utilities need to invest in facilities that are equipped and designed for peak demand. This is not captured in MPT (Hickey et al. 2009)	Tools to manage the correlation between securities
Unique characteristics of electricity assets that make it difficult to make probabilistic assumptions to mitigate risk	Probabilistic assumptions made to mitigate risk

More on the ELD problem may be found in (Bisen, 2012), (Farag, 1995) and (Park, 1993). In addition, other applications of MPT to portfolios of electricity assets and derivatives may be found in (Awerbuch, 2003), (Bar-Lev, 1976), (Costello, 2007), Cooper (1999), (Coyle, 2012), (DeLaquil, 2005), (Fleten, 1997), (Hanser, 2007), (Hickey, 2009), (Huang, 2009), (Huisman, 2007), (Humphreys, 1998), (Liu, 2006), (Marinovic (2012), (Omisore, 2012), (Oum, 2006), (Rebennack, 2010), (Stirling, 1998), Stirling (2010), and Yan (2011).

8.3.1 Case Study: Economic Load Dispatch of a Portfolio of Gas-fired Power Plants

In this section we will outline how MATLAB built-in functions may be utilized by energy market participants to perform an ELD of a portfolio of gas-fired power plants (Figure 8.4). As summarized in Figure 8.5 and Table 8.3, this MATLAB case study ties together some key concepts presented in this book:

- Stochastic differential equation (SDE) models for spot prices
- Seasonality of electricity spot prices
- Mean-reversion
- Generation of electricity (a secondary energy source) from gas (a primary source)
- Monte Carlo simulation

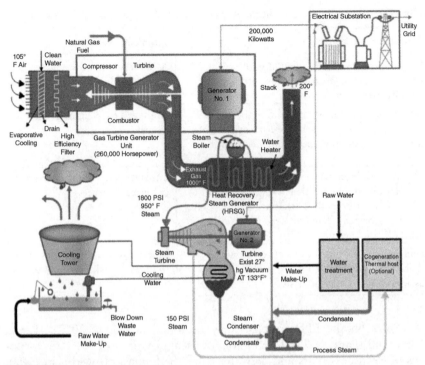

FIGURE 8.4 Gas-Fired Power Plants

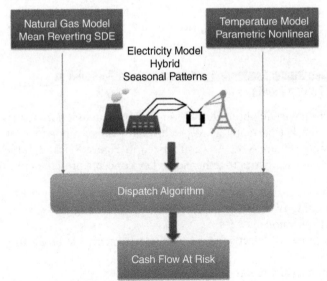

FIGURE 8.5 Economic Load Dispatch of a Portfolio of Gas-Fired Power Plants

TABLE 8.3 MATLAB Case Study Highlights

Simulation	MATLAB Built-In Functions
Natural Gas Prices	Calibrate and simulate a mean-reverting stochastic differential equation (SDE) using MATLAB's code for the Hull-White/Vasicek Model
Hourly Temperature	Parametric (sinusoidal) nonlinear model
Hourly Electricity Prices	Regression tree hybrid model designed with historical data and takes into consideration seasonal patterns
Simulation of Hybrid Electricity Model and Economic Dispatch Model	▪ Load models and data ▪ Simulation for a number of different scenarios ▪ Visualize paths ▪ Visualize multiple paths ▪ Define power plant characteristics ▪ Compute optimal dispatch for single path ▪ Compute optimal dispatch for all paths

MATLAB can be used to compute cash-flow-at-risk for a portfolio of gas-fired plants. For case study highlights, see Table 8.3. More details on this MATLAB case study may be found in MathWorks' "Energy Trading and Risk Management with MATLAB" (2010).

8.4 OPTIMIZATION OF GAS PORTFOLIOS

Suppose we consider a gas portfolio that is comprised of transmission capacities, storage facilities, and delivery and supply contracts. The *gas portfolio optimization problem* can be expressed mathematically as the following linear programming problem:

Objective Function for Gas Portfolio Optimization:
The objective function is cost, which needs to be minimized.

$$C = \sum_{c,t} C_{c,t} \cdot p_{c,t} + \sum_{n,t} VS_{n,t} \cdot S_{n,t} + \sum_{n,m} F_{n,m} \cdot TC_{n,m}$$

Constraints for Gas Portfolio Optimization:
The *node balance equation* ensures that the customer demand does not exceed gas supply at delivery points (nodes).

$$GD_{n,t} \le \sum_{c(n)} C_{c,t} + VS_{n,t} + \sum_{m} \left(F_{m,n,t} - F_{n,m,t} \right) + \sum_{s(n)} \left(W_{s,t} - (1 + I_s) \cdot I_{s,t} \right), \forall (n,t)$$

Where n = gas delivery point (node) (see Figure 8.6)

t = time interval

$GD_{n,t}$ = customer gas demand

$C_{c,t}$ = positive flow variable for long-term contracts

$p_{c,t}$ = contract price

$S_{n,t}$ = spot market price

$TC_{n,m}$ = combined entry and exit tariffs

$F_{n,m}$ = capacity variable

$c(n)$ = index denoting all long-term contracts that have delivery point n

$VS_{n,t}$ = gas volume traded at the spot market

$F_{m,n,t}$ = gas flow from delivery point m to delivery point n during time interval t

$W_{s,t}$ = gas flow out of storage s

$s(n)$ = index denoting storage facilities connected to delivery point n

$I_{s,t}$ = gas flow into storage s

I_s = specific gas consumption of the compressor for the storage

More information on gas portfolio optimization can be found in *Managing Energy Risk* (Burger, Graeber, and Schindlmayr 2007), "Applying Modern Portfolio Theory to Upstream Investment Decision Making" (Orman et al. 1999), and "Stochastic Model for Natural Gas Portfolio Optimization of a Power Producer" (Vaitheeswaran and Balasubramanian 2010).

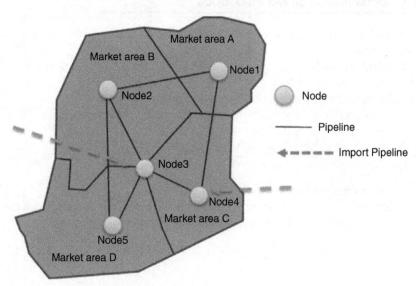

FIGURE 8.6   Gas Delivery Points (Nodes)

TABLE 8.4   Summary of Other Energy Portfolio Management Models

Forecasting Techniques	Electric utilities apply these models to forecast resource supply and customer demand over a specified planning horizon. These forecasting techniques include time series analysis, neural networks, and wavelets (Conejo et al. 2005; Mack 1999).
Unit Commitment Problem	The unit commitment problem involves the scheduling of power generation units in order to serve the load demand at the minimum operating cost while meeting all plant and system constraints (Shobana and Janani 2013; Tseng et al. 2000).
Value at Risk (VaR)-Constrained Portfolio Optimization	VaR-constrained portfolio optimization, with special emphasis on applications in the electric power industry (Kleindorfer and Lide 2004; Min and Felix 2004; Oren 2007; Oum and Oren 2008)
Real Options	A real options framework is combined with portfolio optimization techniques. This framework is used to assess the adoption decision of particular energy technologies under uncertainty (Fortin et al. 2007; Hickey et al. 2009).

8.5   OTHER ENERGY PORTFOLIO MANAGEMENT MODELS

Table 8.4 lists other EPM models that are utilized by energy market participants to analyze and optimize energy portfolios. One of the modeling processes presented in Table 8.4 is real options valuation (ROV). Recall, real options were discussed in Chapter 4. In addition, a more detailed real options case study will be presented in Chapter 9.

8.6   CHAPTER WRAP-UP

In this chapter we discussed how energy market participants can apply portfolio theory to determine a mix of assets and projects that provide the minimum risk for a given level of return. We discussed a few key concepts from modern portfolio theory (MPT) and energy portfolio management (EPM) that may be applied to optimize electricity and gas portfolios. In addition, we presented a case study to illustrate how MATLAB built-in functions may be utilized to optimize a portfolio of gas-fired power plants. Finally, we summarized other EPM models.

REFERENCES

Awerbuch, S., S. Awerbuch and M. Berger 2003. "Energy Security and Diversity in the EU: A Mean-Variance Portfolio Approach." *IEA Research Paper.* www. iea .org/techno/renew/port.pdf.

Bar-Lev, D., and S. Katz. 1976. "A Portfolio Approach to Fossil Fuel Procurement in the Electric Utility Industry." *Journal of Finance* 31(3): 933–947.

Bisen, D., Dubey Hari Mohan, Pandit Manjaree, and B. K. Panigrahi. "Solution of Large Scale Economic Load Dispatch Problem using Quadratic Programming and GAMS: A Comparative Analysis." *Journal of Information and Computing Science* 7(3): 200–11. http://www.worldacademicunion.com/journal/1746-7659JIC/jicvol7no3paper05.pdf.

Burger, M., B. Graeber, and G. Schindlmayr. 2007. *Managing Energy Risk.* Chichester, England: Wiley Finance.

Conejo, Antonio, Javier Contreras, Rosa Espínola, and Miguel A. Plazas. 2005. "Forecasting Electricity Prices for a Day-Ahead Pool-Based Electric Energy Market." *International Journal of Forecasting* 21(3): 435–462. www.sciencedirect.com/science/article/pii/S0169207004001311.

Cooper, R. G., Scott J. Edgett, and Elko J. Kleinschmidt. 1999. "New Product Portfolio Management: Practices and Performance." *Journal of Product Innovation Management* 16(4): 333–351. http://onlinelibrary.wiley.com/doi/10.1111/1540-5885.1640333/abstract.

Costello, K. 2007. "Diversity of Generation Technologies: Implications for Decision-making and Public Policy." *The Electricity Journal* 20(5): 10–21.

Coyle, Thomas. 2012. "Advisers Question Modern Portfolio Theory." *Wall Street Journal.* http://online.wsj.com/article/SB10001424127887323981504578179142854570294.html.

Dantzig, George, and Mukund Thapa. 1997. *Linear Programming 1: Introduction.* Springer-Verlag.

DeLaquil, Pat, and Shimon Awerbuch. 2005. "A Portfolio-Risk Analysis of Electricity Supply Options in the Commonwealth of Virginia." Chesapeake Climate Action Network. https://salsa.democracyinaction.org/o/423/images/va_rps_portfolio_study_report-final_updated.pdf.

Farag, A., S. Al-Baiyat, and Cheng, T.C. 1995. "Economic Load Dispatch Multiobjective Optimization Procedures Using Linear Programming Techniques." *IEEE Transactions on Power Systems* 10(2). http://faculty.kfupm.edu.sa/EE/sbaiyat/richfiles/papers/ECONOMIC%20LOAD%20DISPATCH%20MULTIOBJECTIVE%20OPTIMIZATION.pdf.

Fleten, Stein-Erek, Stein W. Wallace and William T. Ziemba. 1997. "Portfolio Management in a Deregulated Hydropower Based Electricity Market." Norwegian Electricity Federation. http://citeseerx.ist.psu.edu/viewdoc/summary?doi=10.1.1.51.8760.

Fortin, Ines, et al. 2007. "An Integrated CVaR and Real Options Approach to Investments in the Energy Sector." Institute for Advanced Studies, Vienna. www.ihs .ac.at/publications/eco/es-209.pdf.

Hanser, P., and F. Graves. 2007. " Utility Supply Portfolio Diversity Requirements." *The Electricity Journal* 20(5): 22–32.

Hickey, E., J. Lon Carlson, and David Loomis. 2009. "Issues in the Determination of the Optimal Portfolio of Electricity Supply Options." *Energy Policy* 38: 2198–2207. www.csgmidwest.org/MLC/documents/JEPO3951.pdf.

Huang, A. 2009. "Commodity Basket Option/Swaption Valuation: Geometric Conditioning and Moment Matching." PG&E Quant Group. http://207.67.203.54/elibsql05_P40007_Documents/QUANT%20DOCS/GeometricConditioning And%20MomentsMatching_pge_ts.pdf.

Huisman, Ronald, Ronald Mahieu, and Felix Schlichter. 2007. "Electricity Portfolio Management: Optimal Peak / Off-Peak Allocations." *ERIM Report Series Research in Management.* http://repub.eur.nl/res/pub/10775/ERS-2007-089-F%26A.pdf.

Humphreys, Brett, and Katherine McClain. 1998. "Reducing the Impacts of Energy Price Volatility Through Dynamic Portfolio Selection." *The Energy Journal* 19(3). http://sedc-coalition.eu/wp-content/uploads/2011/07/Humphreys-Reducing-the-Impacts-of-Energy-Price-Volatility-1998.pdf.

Kleindorfer, Paul, and Li Lide. 2004. "Multi-Period VaR-Constrained Portfolio Optimization with Applications to Electric Power Sector." *The Wharton School/ OPIM.* http://opim.wharton.upenn.edu/risk/downloads/03-18.pdf.

Mack, Iris. 1999. "Day-Ahead Lunch-Time Electricity Demand Forecasting: Applications to Electricity and Weather Derivatives." Master's thesis, London Business School.

Marinovic, Minja, Dragana D. Makajić-Nikolić, Milan J. Stanojević, and Lena S. Đorđević. 2012. "Optimization of Electricity Trading Using Linear Programming." *Open Access Series in Informatics.* http://drops.dagstuhl.de/opus/volltexte/2012/3550/pdf/11.pdf,.

Markowitz, Harry. 1952. "Portfolio Selection." *Journal of Finance*, 7(1), 77-91.

MathWorks. 2010. "Energy Trading and Risk Management with MATLAB." Matlab Webinar. https://www.mathworks.com/company/events/webinars/wbnr50145.html.

———. 2011. "Portfolio Optimization in Matlab." Matlab Central. www.mathworks.com/matlabcentral/linkexchange/links/3040-portfolio-optimization-in-matlab.

———. 2013. "Linear Programming." Matlab's Optimization Toolbox. www.mathworks.com/products/optimization/description6.html.

Min, Liu, and Felix Wu. 2004. "A Framework for Generation Risk Management in Electricity Markets." *Automation of Electric Power Systems.* http://en.cnki.com.cn/Article_en/CJFDTOTAL-DLXT200413000.htm.

Min, Liu, and Felix Wu. 2006. "Managing Price Risk in a Multimarket Environment." *IEEE Transactions on Power Systems* 21(4). www.eee.hku.hk/people/doc/ffwu/Liu-WuNov06.pdf.

Omisore, Iyiola, Munirat Yusuf, and Nwufo Christopher. 2012. "The Modern Portfolio Theory as an Investment Decision Tool." *Journal of Accounting and Taxation* 4(2): 19–28. www.academicjournals.org/jat/PDF/pdf2012/Mar/Omisore%20et%20al.pdf.

Oren, Shmuel. 2007. "Hedging Fixed Price Load Following Obligations in a Competitive Wholesale Electricity Market." *Energy Systems Modeling Symposium.* www.ise.osu.edu/homepage/ssen/Shmuel%20Oren.pdf.

Orman, M., and T.E. Duggan. 1999. "Applying Modern Portfolio Theory to Upstream Investment Decision Making." *Journal of Petroleum Engineers.* www .aboutoilandgas.com/jpt/print/archives/1999/03/JPT1999_03_management .pdf.

Oum, Yumi, et al. 2006. "Hedging Quantity Risks with Standard Power Options in a Competitive Wholesale Electricity Market." *Wiley InterScience.* www.ieor .berkeley.edu/~oren/pubs/I.A.87.pdf.

Oum, Yumi, and Shmuel Oren. 2008. "VaR Constrained Hedging of Fixed Price Load-Following Obligations in Competitive Electricity Markets." *Risk and Decision Analysis* 1(1), 43-56.

Park, J. H., et al. 1993. "Economic Load Dispatch for Piecewise Quadratic Cost Function Using Hopfield Neural Network." *IEEE Transactions on Power Systems* 8(3). http://web.ecs.baylor.edu/faculty/lee/papers/journal/1993/199308 .pdf.

Rebennack, Steffen, Josef Kallrath, and Panos M. Pardalos. 2010. "Energy Portfolio Optimization for Electric Utilities: Case Study for Germany." *Energy, Natural Resources and Environmental Economics Energy Systems* :221–48. http://link .springer.com/chapter/10.1007%2F978-3-642-12067-1_14.

Shobana, S., and R. Janani. 2013. "Optimization of Unit Commitment Problem and Constrained Emission Using Genetic Algorithm." *International Journal of Emerging Technology and Advanced Engineering* 3(5). www.ijetae.com/files/ Volume3Issue5/IJETAE_0513_62.pdf.

Steinhurst, William, David White, Amy Roschelle, Alice Napoleon, and Rick Hornby. 2006. "Energy Portfolio Management: Tools and Practices for Regulators." *Synapse Energy Economics.* www.naruc.org/Publications/NARUC%20 PM%20FULL%20DOC%20FINAL.pdf.

Stirling, Andy. 1998. "On the Economics and Analysis of Diversity." Working Paper No. 28, *Falmer, Brighton: SPRU Electronic.*

———. 2010. "Multicriteria Diversity Analysis: A Novel Heuristic Framework for Appraising Energy Portfolios." *Energy Policy* 39(4): 1622–34. www.sciencedi-rect.com/science/article/pii/S0301421509000901.

Todd, Michael. 2002. "The Many Facets of Linear Programming." *Mathematical Programming* 91(3), 417-436.

Tseng, C. L., C. A. Li, and S. S. Oren. 2000. "Solving the Unit Commitment Problem by a Unit Decommitment Method." *Journal of Optimization Theory and Applications* 105(3): 707–30. www.ieor.berkeley.edu/~oren/pubs/ud_n_ch02.pdf.

U. S. Environmental Protection Agency (EPA). 2006. "Utility Planning and Incentive Structure." www.epa.gov/statelocalclimate/documents/pdf/guide_action_ chap6_s1.pdf.

Vaitheeswaran, N., and R. Balasubramanian. 2010. "Stochastic Model for Natural Gas Portfolio Optimization of a Power Producer." *Power Electronics, Drives and Energy Systems.* http://ieeexplore.ieee.org/xpl/articleDetails.jsp?reload= true&arnumber=5712549.

Yan, Chang. 2011. "The Optimization of Energy Portfolio Management (EPM): Framework and Simulation." PhD thesis, Southern New Hampshire University, Hooksett, NH.

CHAPTER 9

Hedging Nonlinear Payoffs Using Options

The Case of a New Subsidies Regime for Renewables

*Contributed by Dario Raffaele, Accenture**

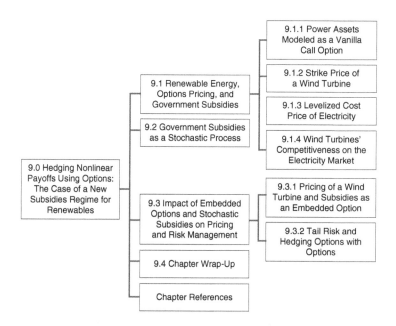

---

* The views expressed in this chapter are wholly those of Dario Raffaele and Iris Mack. They do not in any way reflect official policy by Accenture. Special thanks are extended to Accenture but the coauthors assume responsibility for any error(s) or faux pas contained in the analysis.

A *renewable (or alternative)* energy source is defined to be any naturally occurring, theoretically inexhaustible source of energy that is not derived from fossil or nuclear fuel (examples are biomass, solar, wind, tidal, wave, and hydroelectric power).

Similarly to assets that generate electricity by using fossil fuels, energy market participants who utilize assets that exploit renewable energy sources can apply options pricing theory (as discussed in the previous chapters) for pricing and financial risk management purposes.

In this case study, designed by Dario Raffaele, Msc, CQF of Accenture, we present a real-life game-changing regulatory event that poses an interesting challenge to the application of option pricing theory for the pricing and risk management of renewable energy assets.

RENEWABLE ENERGY SOURCE

A renewable (or alternative) energy source is defined to be any naturally occurring, theoretically inexhaustible source of energy that is not derived from fossil or nuclear fuel.

The discussion presented here will have a different focus than normally found in this body of research. Usually, financial engineering research in the

FIGURE 9.1 An Extensive Wind Park on the way from Gibraltar to Cadiz
Credit: Dario Raffaele photography.

energy industry focuses on the setbacks found in the application of capital markets models to physical assets, for example:

- Analyzing and addressing the shortcomings of the complete markets set of assumptions
- Continuous improvements and the correct implementation of real options theory

For the purpose of this case study, we will utilize a modeling framework based on the following assumptions:

- Continuous delta hedging
- Risk-neutral pricing
- Financial dynamics of renewable assets modeled as vanilla call options

This framework, simplifying some modeling assumptions, allows us to focus and unveil a different type of potential setback in the application of quantitative finance theory to real physical assets. We intend to highlight that even if all modeling hurdles associated with complete markets and real options theory were overcome, there would still be some risks that need to be mitigated by applying different strategies. The analysis will therefore focus primarily on two aspects:

1. Risks arising in embedded optionality: In the case presented, the embedded option leads to tail risk.
2. The need to adopt the principle of hedging options with options, leading to strategic energy portfolio management.

The next section will provide an introductory discussion to pricing and risk management of renewable assets and will serve as a foundation to develop the case study. After providing the necessary basics, the new government regulation for subsidies introduced by the Netherlands will be analyzed and its effects assessed. Thereafter, a pricing framework that appropriately accounts for embedded optionality will be presented and the implications of the associated tail risk analyzed.

9.1 RENEWABLE ENERGY, OPTIONS PRICING, AND GOVERNMENT SUBSIDIES

In this section the basics to introduce the modeling and business framework adopted throughout the chapter are presented. After a general introduction, the discussion will be focused on specific renewable assets: wind turbines. The objective is to provide a practical example and at the same time discuss a *renewable asset* that presents some interesting modeling features. Key topics that are illustrated in this section are as follows:

- Modeling the financial dynamics of a power-producing asset as a vanilla call option
- Strike price of a wind turbine
- Levelized cost price of electricity of a wind turbine
- Competitiveness of the wind turbine in a liberalized electricity market and the role of subsidies

9.1.1   Power Assets Modeled as a Vanilla Call Option

Power producing assets convert an energy source (fossil or renewable) into electricity. The power that is produced can be sold on the electricity market at the price determined by supply and demand dynamics. It may be safely argued that, in principle, assets that have a cost price above the market price would not supply the market. Otherwise, power producers would be operating at a loss.

> *Making a profit when market prices are above a certain threshold resembles a familiar contingent claim: the vanilla call option.*

Making a profit when market prices are above a certain threshold resembles a familiar contingent claim: *the vanilla call option* (described in Chapter 3). *Real option analysis* (introduced in Chapter 4) is a discipline that focuses on the implementation of options pricing theory to model and value real physical assets and projects.

The application of *real options theory* to the problem of modeling and valuing real physical assets often leads to more sophisticated frameworks than the *vanilla call option model*. In this case study, to facilitate the illustration of other modeling setbacks, we will adopt a simplifying assumption and model the financial dynamics of a wind turbine as a vanilla call option.

As anticipated earlier, for the remainder of this section, the analysis will be focused on wind turbines. The reason for choosing specifically wind turbines is based on the fact that wind has some interesting peculiarities, as we will see with the strike price calculation. Moreover wind turbines have drawn considerable attention in public debate, not to mention the remarkable growth these technologies have witnessed in the Netherlands (see Figure 9.5).

9.1.2 Strike Price of a Wind Turbine

Once we accept that the financial dynamics of a renewable energy asset can be modeled as a vanilla call option, we are left with two model elements to determine.

- The form of the process that governs the state variable (and the calibration of the parameters using empirical data)
- The calculation of the strike price

> *Generally a mean-reverting process can be safely used to model the dynamics of electricity prices.*

The first element will not be discussed in great detail in this setting. Generally a mean-reverting process can be safely used to model the dynamics of electricity prices. More interesting modeling questions, beyond the scope of this case study, arise if the market mechanism allows for the formation of negative prices (introduced in Chapter 2), or if we allow the long-term mean to be stochastic or to be governed by a regime-switching model.

Regarding the calculation of the strike price, we face an interesting problem. For power plants running on fossil fuels, generally the strike price is normally set to the marginal cost (that is, the cost of producing one more unit of a good.) Turning to the practical case we are analyzing, wind turbines, the situation is peculiar. *The marginal cost of a wind turbine is virtually zero* and most of the cash outflow is represented by the investment for the realization and maintenance of the asset.

To convince oneself that the strike price of the wind turbine is indeed zero, it is sufficient to attempt to estimate the cost generated by an additional unit of wind, and other unit variable costs (mainly maintenance), to produce an additional unit of electricity. Wind obviously does not have a cost impact. For maintenance, it may be safely argued that the costs induced by producing an additional unit of electricity are either negligible or totally absent, in circumstances when maintenance is performed independently of operations hours.

Therefore the choice will be made to estimate the strike price of a wind turbine as being zero.

9.1.3 Levelized Cost Price of Electricity

An important measure used in electricity markets is the *levelized cost price of electricity* (LCOE). As expressed by the U.S. Energy Information Administration, the LCOE is a convenient summary measure of the overall competiveness of different generating technologies. In essence it represents the unit cost of building and operating a power plant. The inputs for the calculation of the LCOE are, among others, the capital, financing, fuel, and operation and maintenance costs.

> As expressed by the U.S. Energy Information Administration, the LCOE is a convenient summary measure of the overall competiveness of different generating technologies.

We will use the LCOE to analyze the competitiveness of wind turbines, and set the scene for the discussion presented in the next section about the role of government subsidies.

It is not straightforward to determine an exact cost figure that includes both the investment and maintenance required for a wind turbine. This is because there aren't two identical development projects, and data is not easily available. Some publications and organizations provide some input to the calculations. However, by varying slightly arbitrarily determined parameters, such as investment horizon and number of yearly full load hours, the cost price may be quite different.

In order to determine the LCOE of the wind turbine, we perform a sensitivity analysis as illustrated in Table 9.1. The input parameters displayed

TABLE 9.1 Sensitivity Analysis of the Levelized Cost Price of a Wind Turbine in Euros/MWh

Investment cost* (per MW installed)	Full load hours (yearly percentage)	8 Years (investment horizon)	10 Years (investment horizon)	12 Years (investment horizon)
1,250,000 (on-shore wind)	20%	110.59	92.75	80.86
	30%	73.73	61.83	53.91
	40%	55.29	46.38	40.43
1,750,000 (on-shore wind)	20%	154.82	129.85	113.20
	30%	103.22	86.57	75.47
	40%	77.41	64.93	56.60
2,250,000 (off-shore wind)	20%	224.74	192.64	171.23
	30%	149.83	128.42	114.16
	40%	112.37	96.32	85.62

*To be added on top of the investment cost is a yearly maintenance cost calculated as 5 percent of the investment cost for off-shore wind and 3 percent for on-shore wind.

below are based on information provided by the websites of two Dutch agencies: *the National Institute for Energy Innovation (ECN) and the Netherlands Wind Energy Association (NWEA).*

As anticipated, the sensitivity analysis shows how varying assumptions with regards to investment cost per MW installed, yearly percentage of full load hours, and investment horizon, result in differing LCOE for a wind turbine. The data presented in the table should be read looking separately at the three investment cost scenarios. The first and second scenarios should be representative of an on-shore wind turbine investment (1.25 million and 1.75 million respectively), whereas the third scenario should be representative of an off-shore wind turbine investment. We are able to make the following interesting observations:

- The arithmetic average of the LCOE for an on-shore wind turbine, in the first scenario, adds up approximately to 82 euros/MWh; whereas the arithmetic average of the LCOE for an off-shore wind turbine is approximately 140 euros/MWh. Therefore even accounting for higher full-load hours in a year, an off-shore wind turbine has higher LCOE than an on-shore LCOE.
- As the investment horizon is extended, the *LCOE becomes substantially lower.* However, due to regulatory and technology uncertainty (threat of potential disruptive innovations), an investor is unlikely to feel comfortable with a 20-year investment horizon. For this reason we have set the maximum investment horizon to 12 years.
- It might not be sensible to compute an average LCOE for wind technology as a whole. This is because the input parameters used in the calculation differ strongly between different investment scenarios.

9.1.4   Wind Turbines' Competitiveness on the Electricity Market

Figure 9.2 illustrates the APX average monthly spot price between 2000 and 2011. We can observe that a power generation cost price above 80 euros per MWh, which we computed as the lower LCOE bound for different wind technologies, is substantially higher than the average spot price.

> *Electricity generated by wind is considerably more expensive than market prices.*

The fact that electricity generated by wind is considerably more expensive than market prices is also confirmed by Figure 9.3, based on data taken from the NWEA website. (The graph on the NWEA website extends the projection beyond 2014 until 2020.)

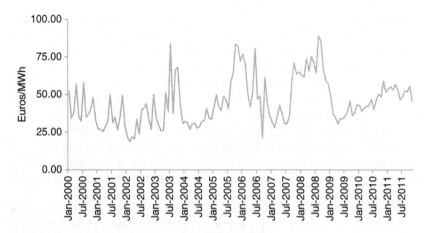

FIGURE 9.2   APX Historical Average Monthly Spot Price
Data source: APX.

> *An interesting question is how many hours in a year will a wind turbine be able to supply power and make a profit?*

However a wind turbine will not always sell at the average market price. Therefore an interesting question is how many hours in a year will a wind turbine be able to supply power and make a profit? To answer that question we present an analysis that shows the percentage price density for which a wind turbine would be in-the-money (ITM), with respect to the LCOE.

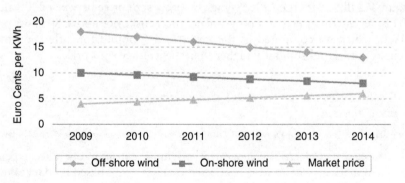

FIGURE 9.3   Cost Price of Wind Energy per kWh
Source: Netherlands Wind Energy Association.

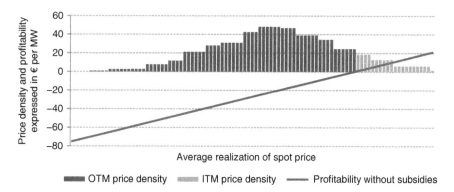

FIGURE 9.4 Wind Asset Payoff and In-the-Money (ITM) versus Out-of-the-Money (OTM) price density with respect to the Levelized Cost Price of Electricity (LCOE)

A conclusion that can be drawn from Figure 9.4 is that a wind turbine would be most of the time *out-of-the-money (OTM)*, with respect to the LCOE, and not able to make a sufficient profit. However, one needs to be very careful with concluding that a wind turbine would be able to fully capture all those opportunities to profitably supply the market. In fact, wind is a variable element and wind turbines' electricity generation cannot be steered as power plants fuelled by fossil fuels. There is no guarantee that for every hour that the market price is above the LCOE, a wind turbine will be able to deliver a full load. More recent research actually shows that during hours with strong wind production, the market prices are on average lower. It may be therefore argued that the competitiveness, and the ability to generate profits, for wind turbines is probably even less encouraging than illustrated in Figure 9.4.

> *There is no guarantee that for every hour that the market price is above the LCOE, a wind turbine will be able to deliver a full load.*

The facts presented so far explain why wind turbines, as most renewable energy currently, need to be subsidized in order to be competitive on the liberalized market and generate a return for investors. In the next section we will look in detail at a recent regulation introduced in the Netherlands. This new regulation introduces some valuable elements of control for public finances and mechanisms to stimulate improvements in renewable technologies. However, it also introduces some complexities that need to be properly evaluated and managed by investors in renewable energy assets.

> *The facts presented so far explain why wind turbines, as most renewable energy currently, need to be subsidized in order to be competitive on the liberalized market and generate a return for investors.*

9.2   GOVERNMENT SUBSIDIES AS A STOCHASTIC PROCESS

> *The SDE introduces added complexity from a pricing and risk management perspective.*

In the present case study we discuss the impact of the *SDE* government regulation on subsidies to renewable energy, introduced in the Netherlands. SDE in this chapter denotes "Stimulerings duurzame energieproductie" and translates to "Stimulus to sustainable energy production." Noteworthy about the SDE is the fact that, in its current formulation, it allows the Dutch government to control the budgetary expenses to stimulate and finance renewable energy projects. However, as we shall see, it also introduces added complexity from a pricing and risk management perspective for owners of renewable

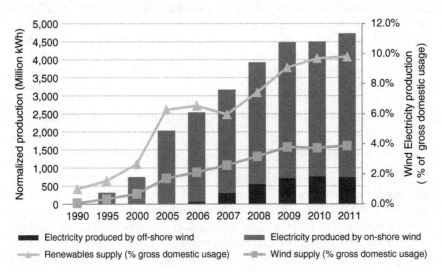

FIGURE 9.5 Increase in Wind Production and Renewables Production as Share of Domestic Usage
Based on data provided in the 2011 report of the Central Bureau of Statistics in the Netherlands

energy assets. Also, please note that the use of "SDE" in this case study should not be confused with the use of this acronym in previous chapters to denote "stochastic differential equations".

SDE: STIMULUS TO SUSTAINABLE ENERGY PRODUCTION

SDE denotes "Stimulerings duurzame energieproductie" and translates to "Stimulus to sustainable energy production."

The Netherlands is a country that has been explicitly committed to supporting renewable energy generation. A strong increase in installed capacity of Dutch renewable energy sources was observed between 1990 and 2011.

In brief the SDE regulation can be described as follows:

- The government uses subsidies (referred to as the *SDE contribution*), in order to bridge the difference between the cost price of renewable energy (referred to as *basis amount*) and the price of gray energy (generated from fossil fuels).
- The price of gray energy is referred to as the *correction amount*, and is currently determined as the yearly nonweighted APX average.
- In order to control the expenses on behalf of the government, the subsidy payout is limited by introducing a floor price for the *correction amount*. The floor is referred to as the *basis energy price* and it is determined once at the outset of the subsidy period for its entire duration.

Figure 9.6 shows a diagram taken from official Dutch government documentation explaining the regulation of subsidies under the SDE. It is

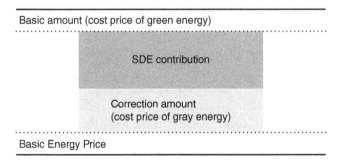

FIGURE 9.6 Translated Extract from the Official SDE Brochure
Source: Bureau of Statistics in the Netherlands. (Translated from the Dutch government website www.agentschap.nl).

important to stress that while the *correction amount* is established on a yearly basis, the *basis energy price* is determined once for the entire duration of the subsidy period. Therefore, over time, the *correction amount* can change due to changing market dynamics while the *basis energy price* remains fixed. These changes, as we discuss later on, can be adverse to the beneficiary of the subsidies, and introduce tail risk.

In order to streamline the discussion that follows, we will simplify the terminology and graphical illustration representing the *SDE regulation*. For the purpose of our analysis, we will use fewer parameters, without compromising the working and dynamics of the regulation as it is currently formulated:

- K will denote the maximum amount of markup paid by the government on top of the arithmetic average of the APX spot price over the year (corresponds to the difference between the *basis amount* and the *basis energy price*).
- K^+: threshold above which no subsidies at all are paid by the government (corresponds to the basis amount).

By using these two parameters we are able to describe the payoff of the subsidy in Figure 9.7 as a long capped Asian put option (defined and illustrated in Chapter 4). On the x-axis we find the arithmetic average of the APX price over the year. On the y-axis we find in euros/MWh, the subsidy payout (which is a function of the arithmetic average over the year).

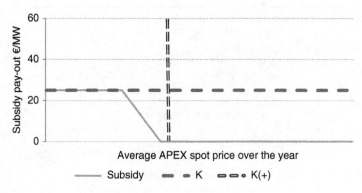

FIGURE 9.7   Payoff of the Subsidies According to the SDE

We are now able to draw some important conclusions:

- Since the subsidy payout is dependent on market price dynamics, which are stochastic, the subsidies payout also become a stochastic process.
- Subsidies should be modeled as a long capped Asian put embedded in the vanilla call option represented by the renewable asset power generation. The payoff of the embedded option is represented in Figure 9.7.
- These features make the pricing and risk management of renewable assets more complex than traditional subsidy schemes.

9.3 IMPACT OF EMBEDDED OPTIONS AND STOCHASTIC SUBSIDIES ON PRICING AND RISK MANAGEMENT

In the previous section we illustrated that under the new regulation, subsidies for renewable assets follow a stochastic process and should be modeled as an embedded option. In this section we discuss how pricing and risk management of a renewable asset are impacted when we include the embedded option. There are two key discussion points we elaborate on:

- The valuation framework needs to correctly incorporate the pricing of the embedded option.
- Within the correct valuation framework, there is still tail risk that cannot be managed by delta hedging. The compound option needs to be hedged by using another option.

9.3.1 Pricing of a Wind Turbine and Subsidies as an Embedded Option

The approach used in this chapter to model the financial dynamics of a wind turbine was introduced in Section 9.1 and further discussed in Section 9.2. In summary, this consists of accepting the complete markets assumptions and analyzing what happens when we model government subsidies as an embedded option, which takes the form of a long capped Asian put.

The proposed formulation avoids loss of generality and allows applicability of the framework proposed to other renewable sources.

Before proceeding with the mathematical formulation, a word needs to be said on the choice made to interpret the government subsidies as a factor that lowers the strike price of the renewable asset. In the mathematical formulation below, it will be seen that the subsidies, in one case labeled as $K(S)$ and later on $F(S(T))$, are subtracted from the strike price. This choice, in the specific case of the wind turbine, may seem counterintuitive, because as discussed earlier, the strike price of the wind turbine is zero. The reasons for proposing the formulation are as follows:

- The proposed formulation is consistent with the economic reasoning that subsidies allow renewable assets to be competitive on the liberalized market by lowering their marginal costs.
- The proposed formulation avoids loss of generality and allows applicability of the framework proposed to other renewable sources.
- From a mathematical perspective, adding a positive number or subtracting a negative one leads to the same result. Therefore this choice does not affect the result.
- Proceeding with the pricing framework, the value of a vanilla call option can be expressed, using the Martingale approach, as:

$$V(S,T) = e^{-r\ (T-t)} * E^{\mathbb{Q}} \left[\text{Max}(S - E, 0) \mid \mathcal{F}_t \right] \tag{9.1}$$

Where V denotes the value of the option

S denotes the underlying state variable (on which the option value depends)

E denotes the strike price

$E^{\mathbb{Q}}$ denotes the expectation under the risk neutral measure $\mathbb{Q}$

T denotes the time to maturity

t denotes the time at which we value the option (time of acquisition)

r denotes the risk-free interest rate

$\mathcal{F}_t$ denotes the filtration at time t

> *The Martingale approach consists in valuing the option as the expectation of the present-valued cash flows under the risk neutral probability measure $\mathbb{Q}$.*

The Martingale approach consists in valuing an option as the expectation of the present-valued cash flows under the risk neutral probability measure $\mathbb{Q}$. A concept that may be new to the reader, by introducing the Martingale approach, is the concept of Filtration. Intuitively, the reader may see the Filtration as a means of modeling the increasing information flow over time. In the case of a stochastic process as time progresses an increasing amount of information is available. Technically, the Filtration is the collection of σ-fields $\mathcal{F}_t \geq 0$, it defines the probability space in which we operate, and allows us to take advantage of the convenient properties of Martingales to perform valuation under risk neutrality. (Hull 2011; Wilmott 2006).

This valuation framework presented in Equation 9.1 can be used provided that government subsidies are constantly bridging the difference between the real strike price of the wind turbine, E^*, and a target strike price E, which allows the wind turbine to be competitive on the market. This is shown in Equation 9.2:

$$E = E^* - K(S) \tag{9.2}$$

However, as illustrated in Section 9.3, under the new government regulation, subsidies to wind assets need to be modeled as a long capped Asian put. Therefore Equation 9.2 cannot be used and Equation 9.3 presented below is the appropriate one to model subsidies.

$$F(S(T)) = e^{-r(T-T_p)} * E^{\mathbb{Q}}\left[\text{Max}\left[\text{Min}\left(K^+ - \left(\frac{1}{T-T_p} * \int_{T_p}^{T} S(\tau)d\tau \right), K \right), 0 \right] \mid \mathcal{F}_{T_p} \right] \tag{9.3}$$

Where $F(S(T))$ denotes the value of the long capped Asian put that represents the subsidies

K^+ denotes the maximum amount that the government intends to finance

K denotes the markup above the spot price that the government is willing to subsidize

t denotes the starting time at which we value the vanilla call option

T_P denotes the starting time at which we value the embedded option

T denotes the expiry date of the vanilla call option and the embedded option

$\mathcal{F}_{T_p}$ denotes the filtration at time T_P

Equation 9.3 describes the payoff diagram depicted in Figure 9.7. By applying this formulation, we model government subsidies as an embedded option, which follows the stochastic process F, which in turn depends on another stochastic process S.

Finally, expressing subsidies following Equation 9.3, we can formulate the proper valuation framework for the wind turbine taking into account the embedded option:

$$G(S, S(T), \tau) = e^{-r(T-t)} * E^{\mathbb{Q}}[\text{Max}(S - (E - e^{r(T-T_p)}F(S(T))), 0) \mid \mathcal{F}_t] \qquad (9.4)$$

9.3.2 Tail Risk and Hedging Options with Options

As introduced in Section 9.1 and later elaborated in Section 9.3, the SDE regulation allows the government to control the financing of renewable energy. However, it also introduces an element of tail risk for the subsidy beneficiary. If market dynamics were to change in the course of the subsidy period, and the price of gray energy would decrease, then the subsidy beneficiary would end up taking a loss.

The pricing Equation 9.4 presented at the end of the previous section can be important in determining what an investor should be willing to pay for the wind turbine. Reasoning is that it can allow one to incorporate in the pricing of the tail risk introduced by the SDE regulation. For such a purpose it would be advisable to attempt, provided a mean-reverting process is chosen, to model the long-term mean as stochastic process or by using a regime switching model.

> *If market dynamics were to change in the course of the subsidy period, and the price of gray energy would decrease, then the subsidy beneficiary would end up taking a loss.*

However, Equation 9.4 does not by itself lead to a solution to mitigate the tail risk. To understand why this is the case it is important to discuss what the consequences might be of a structural change in electricity markets. Electricity markets are characterized by a relatively inelastic demand curve and by a supply curve that is shaped by the generation portfolio, which is costly and takes time to replace. It is reasonable to argue that a structural change would alter the competitive dynamics for a sustained amount of time. Note that 'elasticity' measures how responsive supply and demand curves are to price changes.

> *Electricity markets are characterized by a relatively inelastic demand curve and by a supply curve that is shaped by the generation portfolio, which is costly and takes time to replace.*

Let's hypothesize the following set of events and evaluate the impact:

- Suppose a structural change occurs in electricity markets that significantly reduces the price of gray energy, below the floor price established by the SDE regulation.
- This may be argued to be a disruptive change to the supply-demand dynamics in the electricity markets.
- Within the current formulation of the SDE, as the floor price is hit, the renewable asset owner would not receive additional subsidies above the maximum amount established at the outset of the subsidy period.
- The renewable asset would move more out of the money, as it becomes less competitive on the liberalized electricity market.
- *Delta hedging* would not allow us to solve the issue. The instruments traded on the market are of shorter maturity than the duration of the exposure. Therefore as the market enters into a new paradigm delta hedging does not allow one to offset the cap in subsidies payout.
- It may be argued, on the last point, that by increasing the size of the delta, it would be possible to make up for the cap in the subsidies, in case market prices drop below the floor price. However, one needs to bear in mind the risks posed by hedging long-term exposure with short-term instruments. As we previously discussed in Chapters 5 and 6, *Metallgesellshaft is an often cited example* of a company that lost $1.6 billion by applying a stack-and-roll strategy to hedge a long-term exposure (Kuprianov 1995).

> *The instruments traded on the market are of shorter maturity than the duration of the exposure.*

To be precise, the risk of a mishap by attempting to manage the long-term exposure, created by the SDE regulation, using short-term instruments would be triggered by a different factor. In the case of Metallgesellshaft, the loss was essentially triggered by substantial margin calls in a contango market. However, in the case of the SDE regulation, if a situation occurs where market prices enter a structural decreasing trend, increasing the size of the delta, after the floor price (basis energy price) has been hit, would not lead to the desired offsetting effect that delta hedging usually has. Ultimately the renewable asset would simply be less and less competitive as market prices drop.

A *feasible alternative* that is left in this case is to manage the tail risk on an electric utility company portfolio level (as discussed in Chapter 8). This is achieved by adding to the portfolio an asset that has an offsetting payoff to the tail exposure that needs to be mitigated. In the specific case of the wind turbine, one may consider the following structures:

- A swap with a large *industrial client*
- An investment that would be a natural hedge to the actual payoff of the wind turbine

In simple words, the objective is to hedge a real asset by using another real asset.

The concept of hedging an option's nonlinear payoff using another option has already been extensively used by options market makers in capital markets. According to Nassim Taleb, as he explains in an interview by Espen Haug, this is actually the way to really hedge the exposure created by an option. Taleb goes on to elaborate that only a residual, tiny fraction of the exposure may be managed by rebalancing the delta (Haug 2007).

Perhaps this conclusion may be drawn for energy markets as well. This may be particularly true in cases when market participants need to hedge risks of longer and more complex nature than the instruments that are traded on the market.

A concluding remark, therefore, may be that since the dynamics that govern energy markets can change rapidly and have an unexpected radical impact, the nonlinear payoffs characterizing energy assets need to be managed using options, both physical and financial, on a company portfolio level.

9.4 CHAPTER WRAP-UP

In this case study we discussed a specific challenge of the application of traditional financial engineering concepts and models to the energy markets. Practitioners applying quantitative finance theory to energy markets need to be critical, and scrutinize beyond the usual modeling hurdles posed by the capital markets assumptions and by the implementation of real options theory.

> *The recommendation is to hedge the nonlinear exposure created by the optionality of a physical asset, by adding to the portfolio another physical (or financial) asset with an offsetting payoff structure.*

We have seen that the introduction of the SDE regulation allows the government to better control the budgetary expenses relative to stimulating and financing renewable energy projects. However, it also introduces tail risk for the beneficiaries of subsidies to renewable energy.

The tail risk that is introduced can be priced accordingly using a proper valuation framework. However, it cannot be managed by delta hedging in the case that the market enters a new paradigm characterized by unfavorable dynamics for the subsidy beneficiary.

The best resort is to apply the concept of hedging options with options and manage the tail risk on a utility company portfolio level. Therefore, the recommendation is to hedge the nonlinear exposure created by the optionality of a physical asset, by adding to the portfolio another physical (or financial) asset with an offsetting payoff structure.

The present case study has focused on highlighting this challenge. A thorough description and analysis of the models and alternatives available to manage strategically the assets and investments portfolio of a utility company was beyond the scope of this chapter. However, the development and critical evaluation of modeling alternatives to perform portfolio management with a strategic focus, within the framework of options pricing theory, promises to be a very valuable and interesting field of research.

REFERENCES

Haug, Espen. 2007. *Derivatives Models on Models*. Hoboken, NJ: John Wiley & Sons.

Hull, John. 2011. *Futures, Options and Other Derivatives*, 8th ed. Englewood Cliffs, NJ: Prentice Hall.

Kuprianov, Anatoli. 1995. "Derivatives Debacles: Case Studies of Large Losses in Derivatives Markets." *FRB Richmond Economic Quarterly* 81(4): 1–39. http://papers.ssrn.com/sol3/papers.cfm?abstract_id=2129302.

Wilmott, Paul. 2006. *Paul Wilmott on Quantitative Finance*, 2nd ed. Hoboken, NJ: John Wiley & Sons.

CHAPTER 10

Case Study: Hydro Power Generation and Behavioral Finance in the U.S. Pacific Northwest

Contributed by Bill Dickens

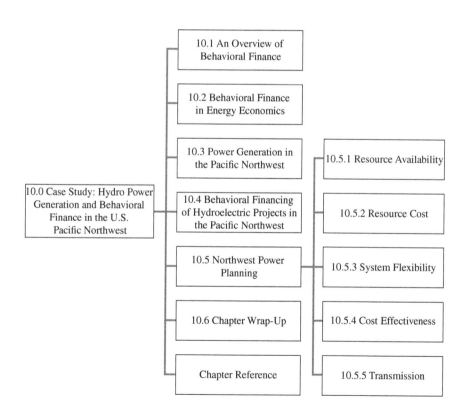

10.1 An Overview of Behavioral Finance

10.2 Behavioral Finance in Energy Economics

10.3 Power Generation in the Pacific Northwest

10.0 Case Study: Hydro Power Generation and Behavioral Finance in the U.S. Pacific Northwest

10.4 Behavioral Financing of Hydroelectric Projects in the Pacific Northwest

10.5 Northwest Power Planning

10.6 Chapter Wrap-Up

Chapter Reference

10.5.1 Resource Availability

10.5.2 Resource Cost

10.5.3 System Flexibility

10.5.4 Cost Effectiveness

10.5.5 Transmission

A primary component of integrated resource planning is determining a utility's long-term load-resource balance. The load-resource balance identifies both the timing and magnitude of potential future power resource deficits. This information is fundamental to assessing whether the electric utility needs additional resources.

In the Pacific Northwest, integrated resource planning for a utility's load-resource balance is covered over three time frames: annual, monthly, and peak. This assessment indicates that new cost-effective conservation coupled with existing supply resources will likely be sufficient to meet retail load under *critical water* conditions. Critical water is a sequence of streamflows under which the regional hydro system could produce an amount of power equal to that which could have been produced during the historical critical period given today's generating facilities and constraints.

> A *primary component of integrated resource planning is determining a utility's long-term* **load-resource balance.**

Given the region's unique climate and ecological constraints in generating electric power, behavioral finance models are needed to provide a plausible tool to assist in long-range power planning decisions. Financing power generation involves activities typically not reflected in the stochastic financial engineering models discussed in the previous chapters. Power planning needs are constrained by ecological conditions such as fish migration and environmental conditions (e.g., minimal elevation levels needed for water flow). Such factors imply that agents in energy markets in the Pacific Northwest will not be faced with the same power constraints that agents in other parts of the United States face. Since the constraints are different in the Northwest, the behavioral responses to energy planning and policy should be different as well.

In this chapter we present a brief introduction to behavioral finance. In addition, we present a case study designed by Bill Dickens, Sr. Economist for Tacoma Power* and Adjunct Professor of Economics at Florida A&M University. This case study illustrates the value of behavioral finance for the Pacific Northwest region. It may serve as the focal point for a primer or case study of Pacific Northwest energy planning decisions.

---

*The views expressed in this chapter are wholly those of Bill Dickens and Iris Mack. They do not in any way reflect official policy by Tacoma Power. Special thanks are extended to the Northwest Power & Conservation Council but the authors assume responsibility for any error(s) or faux pas contained in the analysis.

10.1 AN OVERVIEW OF BEHAVIORAL FINANCE

Behavioral economics is the combination of psychology and economics used to investigate what happens in markets in which some of the agents display human limitations and complications.

Behavioral finance is an epistemological variation of a branch of behavioral economics. It can be defined as an application of behavioral modeling techniques to financial markets.

BEHAVIORAL FINANCE

Behavioral finance is an epistemological variation of a branch of behavioral economics. It can be defined as an application of behavioral modeling techniques to financial markets.

BEHAVIORAL ECONOMICS

Behavioral economics is the combination of psychology and economics used to investigate what happens in markets in which some of the agents display human limitations and complications.

In its attempt to model financial markets and the behavior of firms, modern finance theory starts from a set of normatively appealing axioms about individual behavior. Specifically, people are said to be risk-averse expected utility maximizers and unbiased Bayesian forecasters, that is agents make rational choices based on rational expectations. The rational paradigm may be criticized, however, because

1. The assumptions are descriptively false and incomplete.
2. The theory often lacks predictive power.

One way to make progress is to characterize actual decision-making behavior. Efforts along these lines are made by behavioral economists and psychologists (Mullainathan and Thaler 2000).

Some behavioral finance models are listed in Table 10.1. Such models typically address a particular market anomaly and modify standard models by describing decision makers as using heuristics and subject to framing

TABLE 10.1 Behavioral Finance Models

Heuristics	Framing	Anomalies: Economic Behavior	Anomalies: Market Prices and Returns
■ Prospect Theory ■ Loss Aversion ■ Disappointment ■ Despair ■ Status Quo Bias ■ Gambler's Fallacy ■ Self-serving Bias ■ Money Illusion	■ Cognitive Framing ■ Mental Accounting ■ Anchoring	■ Disposition Effect ■ Endowment Effect ■ Inequity Aversion ■ Reciprocity ■ Intertemporal Consumption ■ Present-Biased Preferences ■ Momentum Investing ■ Greed and Fear ■ Herd Behavior ■ Sunk-Cost Fallacy	■ Equity Premium Puzzle ■ Efficiency Wage Hypothesis ■ Price Stickiness ■ Limits to Arbitrage ■ Dividend Puzzle ■ Fat Tails ■ Calendar Effect

effects. In general, finance continues to sit within the neoclassical framework, the standard assumption of rational behavior is often challenged.

The behavioral finance models listed in Table 10.1 may be applied to address the following issues:

Despair occurs when a trading model is in a major, prolonged drawdown. Hence, many investors may feel great pressure to shut down the model completely. More confident investors with a reckless bent may do the opposite. They may double their bets on their losing models, hoping to recoup their losses eventually, if and when the models rebound. Despair may lead to overleveraging because a trader may try to recoup the losses by adding fresh capital.

Example: In 2006 the fund Amaranth Advisors succumbed to the temptation of overleveraging. This fund eventually failed. The leverage employed on one single strategy (natural gas calendar spread trade) due to one single Amaranth energy trader (Brian Hunter) was so large that a $6 billion loss was incurred, wiping out the fund's equity.

Greed, traditionally used by traders and market commentators, has become a topic of economic research about investor irrationalities (cognitive and emotional biases). It is the more usual emotion when the model is having a good run and is generating lots of profits. The temptation is to increase the leverage quickly in order to get rich quickly. Greed can also lead to overleveraging.

Example: A power trader may add capital too quickly after initial successes with an options trading strategy.

The *status quo bias* is defined as a cognitive bias for the status quo. In other words, individuals tend not to change an established behavior unless the incentive to change is compelling.

Example: The status quo bias is an effect that causes some investors to hold on to a losing position for too long because they demand much more to give up a financial asset than what they would pay to acquire it.

The *endowment effect* (also known as divestiture aversion) is a hypothesis that people value a good or service more once their property right to it has been established. In other words, people place a higher value on objects they own than objects that they do not. The endowment effect is described as inconsistent with classical economic theory that asserts that an individual's willingness to pay for a product should be equal to their willingness to accept compensation to be deprived of the good. This is an effect that may cause some investors to hold on to a losing position for too long because they give too much preference to the status quo.

Example: People demand a higher price for a commodity that has been given to them but put a lower price on one they do not yet own.

Loss aversion refers to people's tendency to strongly prefer avoiding losses to acquiring gains. Some studies suggest that losses are twice as powerful, psychologically, as gains. Such behavioral biases cause investors to hold on to losing positions even where there is no rational reason to do so.

Example: A trader expects trending behavior. However, the trend is such that the positions will lose even more.

10.2 BEHAVIORAL FINANCE IN ENERGY ECONOMICS

Modern portfolio theory and behavioral finance represent differing schools of thought that attempt to explain investor and producer behavior. Perhaps the easiest way to think about their arguments and positions is summarized in Table 10.2. Having a solid understanding of both theory and reality are indispensable for energy planners.

TABLE 10.2 Behavioral Finance versus Modern Portfolio Theory

Behavioral Finance	How financial markets work in the real world
Modern Portfolio Theory	How financial markets would work in the ideal world with stable heuristic assumptions

Generating electric power from a dam can impact fish, wildlife, and the environment. While the power is associated with virtually zero carbon emissions, the attendant *general equilibrium costs* can be significant. These general equilibrium costs imply that standard rational agent based economic models will not fully capture the actual costs needed to understand planning decisions under hydro assumptions. Behavioral finance may be viewed as a tool to help capture the actual costs and thus allow for informed planning decision making.

10.3   POWER GENERATION IN THE PACIFIC NORTHWEST

The 2011 hydro season began earlier and lasted significantly longer than in recent years, well into the summer months. Hydroelectric generation in the Pacific Northwest is typically highest in the late winter and spring when river flows are high because of snowpack melt. This low-cost energy contributed to an average 18 percent decline in wholesale electricity prices compared to prices in 2010 at Mid-Columbia, a major Northwest wholesale pricing hub near the Washington-Oregon border (Figures 10.1 and 10.2).

Although electricity prices were lower in 2011 compared to 2010 in much of the country, the drop in the price at Mid-Columbia was striking. Prices were near multiyear lows throughout most of 2011. Further, the increased hydroelectric output also lowered prices in California and at major electric power hubs as significant levels of power flowed throughout the Western Interconnection (WI). The WI is one of the two major alternating current (AC) power grids in North America. The other major wide area synchronous grid is the Eastern Interconnection. The service territory for the WI extends from Canada to Mexico. It includes the provinces of Alberta and British Columbia, the northern portion of Baja California, Mexico, and all or portions of the 14 Western states across nearly 1.8 million square miles.

An unusual combination of warm and wet weather in the second half of January and early February melted low-elevation snow, filling hydroelectric dam reservoirs on the Columbia and Snake Rivers. The increased precipitation and high water levels at reservoir dams resulted in high hydro generation.

The Pacific Northwest has enormous hydroelectric capacity, and the variable cost of producing electricity from this capacity is minimal because there is no fuel cost. Consequently, when the water flow to generate large amounts of hydro power is available, wholesale electricity prices drop. But peak water flow is typically a seasonal event driven by snowpack melt, so the price-reducing effect of hydro power normally lasts only a few months each year, typically in the spring and early summer.

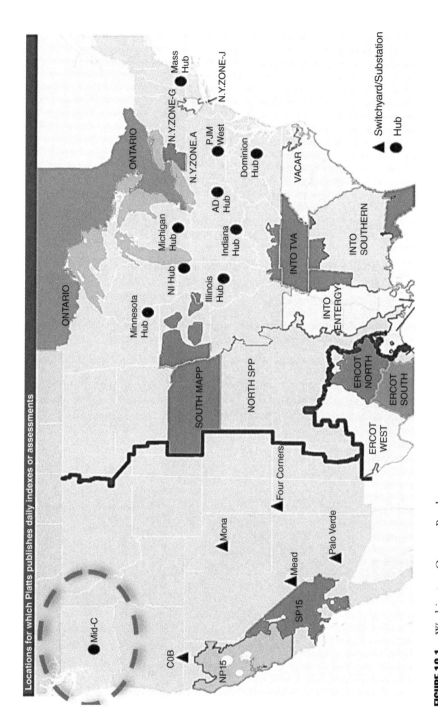

FIGURE 10.1 Washington-Oregon Border

Source: www.Platts.com.

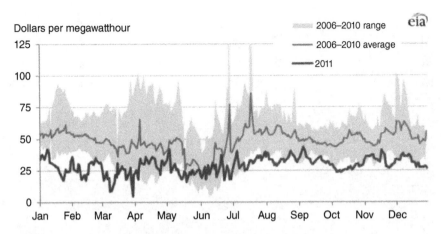

FIGURE 10.2 Mid-Columbia Daily On-Peak Wholesale Electric Prices
Source: U.S. Energy Information Administration, based on SNL Energy.

> *When the water flow to generate large amounts of hydro power is available, wholesale electricity prices drop.*

However, in 2011 high water flows persisted through the summer, as illustrated by the water flow at the Dalles dam on the Columbia River, a centrally located run-of-river hydroelectric plant (see Figure 10.3). The

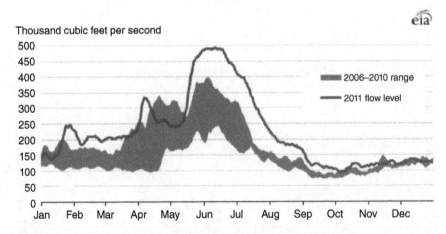

FIGURE 10.3 Water Flow at the Dalles Dam on the Columbia River
Source: U.S. Energy Information Administration, based on U.S. Army Corps of Engineers, Northwestern Division.

difference in 2011 was the persistent rainfall throughout the late spring and summer, prolonging the hydro season well into the summer months and driving down wholesale power prices.

Abundant hydroelectric supply also crowded out natural gas-fired generation compared to 2010 and previous years. Natural gas generation, for example, dropped almost to zero during the third week of May. In 2011, natural gas use for power generation in the Pacific Northwest was down 46 percent, or an annual average of 260 million cubic feet per day, relative to 2010 levels. Other thermal electric power plants as well as wind generators in the region also curtailed supply in favor of hydroelectric generation.

10.4 BEHAVIORAL FINANCING OF PROJECTS IN THE PACIFIC NORTHWEST

The generation, transmission, and distribution of energy are extremely capital intensive. The planning decisions are made based on a future flow of discounted benefits and costs to key energy stakeholders (shareholders and utility rate payers). Given the capital acquisition and upgrades necessary to ensure safe, reliable, low-cost power in the Northwest, utility planners must seek financing for these projects in organized debt or equity markets. The flexibility of hydro power generation has made it an increasingly viable option for regions or corporations hoping to reduce their carbon footprint and diversify their generation portfolio. But growing legislation and costs are putting a brake on new capacity installations and making operational risk management more complex.

> *The flexibility of hydro power generation has made it an increasingly viable option for regions or corporations hoping to reduce their carbon footprint and diversify their generation portfolio.*

Hydroelectric energy is just one of numerous sources of electricity around the world today while financing and funding hydro power project developments will be in demand well into the next century and beyond. This is because the world's needs will persist while we still have an abundance of running water. There are advantages to using this power source. It is sustainable, renewable, clean, and it controls the river's water flow and prevents or controls flood situations. Some disadvantages of damming rivers are that they can harm many life species that live in the vicinity, the land around the dam can be destroyed, and the action of the turbines can kill fish and other wildlife.

To better understand how investments in renewable energies can be fostered, one needs to better understand financial decision making. When an investment object is chosen a variety of criteria is taken into account and the more information available the more probable investors will take an investment decision. The risk-to-return relationship is crucial. Institutional investors in Pacific Northwest electric projects utilize a step-by-step process of investment decision making. Such decisions are driven by a set of factors which include a large variety of relevant market and non-market criteria combined with psychological forces like instincts and intuition. In particular, external sources of information, that is, external agencies or other investors, play an important role.

To attract more capital suppliers of alternative energies, it is necessary to take investors' requirements into account.

- The more information available for investors, the more detailed their assessment can be. Thereby, uncertainty and perceived risk are reduced and the investment probability increases. Open communication with investors and a transparency of company data are essential in this regard. Recommendations especially from research or consulting companies, but also from other investors, are important aspects that also reduce the perceived risk. Renewable energy producers are therefore advised to take care of their image and ensure a consistent track record of prior performance.
- Reliance on subsidies should be reduced to a minimum since investors favor investments that are as self-sufficient as possible. Investors consider company-related information much more intensely than they consider regulatory aspects. Therefore, renewable energy producers should aim at proving their autonomy and profitability without dependence on political support.
- The risk associated with the technology used to produce energy needs to be reduced. This can be done by informing investors and the public about state of the art and future developments.

Reliance on external recommendations certainly reduces decision complexity and is therefore an adequate measure to reduce investment risk. Nevertheless, an individual risk assessment should not be foregone to avoid herding tendencies and unidirectional influences.

As described, institutional investors play an important role for the growth of the renewable energy industry as they provide the means to finance new technological developments, advancements of existing companies, and the emergence of new players. For them, the results of the study indicate the following recommendations: Reliance on external recommendations certainly reduces decision complexity and is therefore an adequate measure to reduce investment risk. Nevertheless, an individual risk assessment should not be foregone to avoid herding tendencies and unidirectional influences.

There is an increasing urgency related to the production of sustainable, renewable green energy throughout the world. Financing hydro power projects and funding hydroelectric dam developments will continue to be leading contributors to clean power of this type. Hydro contributes one-fifth of the world's electricity production. The historical significance of water as a resource to humanity can be evaluated by its early uses, which was primarily for irrigation, turning mill stones for grinding grains, textile mills, and the powering of sawmills and other mechanical devices. Ancient Rome was among the first civilizations to employ the efficient use of taking energy from moving water such as water-powered mills, which produced flour from grains. Also, in the Far East, hydraulically operated pot wheel pumps raised water into irrigation ditches.

By providing financing for hydroelectric projects and funding hydro power developments the new capital markets can capitalize on water as a sustainable, renewable green energy source. Hydro processes, wind- and coal-fired power facilities produce electricity similarly to some extent. All three require a power source that turns a turbine. This turbine then turns a drive shaft in an electric generator, which is the actual motor that produces electricity. A coal-fired power plant uses steam; wind mills utilize the wind whereas a hydro plant uses moving water to turn the turbine.

> *One of the first steps in the process for the lender or investor's due diligence in hydro power funding and hydroelectric financing is to perform an in-depth analysis of the sponsor's business plan or pro forma.*

Water is among the top of the list of nature's most precious resources. Life is impossible without it. We drink it, wash with it, use it in industry, irrigate crops and landscaping and thousands of other practical uses including power generation. An optimum damsite is one on a river that has a substantial drop in elevation. Few flatland regions offer acceptable terrain for hydro dams. The dam backs up and stores huge amounts of water in the reservoir it creates. Somewhere near the lower portion of the dam wall, there is the water intake gate. Gravity pulls the water through the penstock or intake gate inside the dam. Towards the end of the penstock there is a turbine propeller, which is turned as the moving water passes through it. The turbine shaft spins the generator, which produces the electricity. The electricity feeds the grid, which supplies electricity to homes, businesses, and factories in its market. The water then continues unpolluted past the dam into the river for use by water owners downstream (Figure 10.4).

One of the first steps in the process for the lender or investor's due diligence in hydro power funding and hydroelectric financing is to perform an in-depth analysis of the sponsor's business plan or pro forma. They may even have to hire an independent contractor to conduct a feasibility or other study for the due diligence approval. These studies will analyze the environmental data as well as provide substantiation of the financial viability of the business plan.

These reports will also spell out the technical, architectural design, financial, and other aspects of the entire plan. These elements are very important to the source of capital in its evaluation of the total risk. The assets of the development may or may not be secured. Depending on the investor, there may or may not be a requirement of a lien on the facilities and real property. Other sources underwrite solely on the offtake agreements or power purchase agreement (PPA) secured by assignment of ongoing operating revenues and minimum capacity guarantees. Still some capital providers require

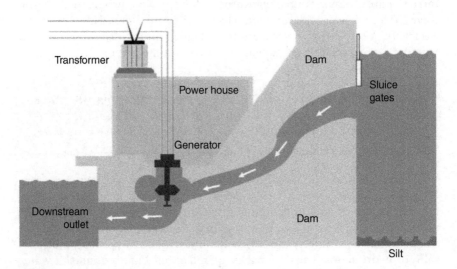

FIGURE 10.4 Hydroelectric Power Production
Source: USGS.gov.

liens on all personal property; and assignment of agreements and permits, including any letters of credit or performance guarantee bonds to which the sponsor is the beneficiary.

10.5   NORTHWEST POWER PLANNING

To meet the power needs for power customers in Oregon, Washington, Idaho, and western Montana requires a coordinated effort among many entities like investor-owned utilities, municipal utilities, public utility districts, and the Bonneville Power Administration. The advent of variable resources, such as wind, makes the coordinated efforts that much more complicated due to the coexistence of hydro as a "fuel" for power generation. The ability to develop and integrate the amount of new wind power requires balancing risk, costs, and renewable compliance. This also includes actions for resolving uncertainties associated with large-scale wind power development during times when the region is oversupplied creating stress on the region's bulk power grid. The much larger amount of renewable resources possibly resulting from continuation of current development trends may raise additional issues and challenges. Several are outlined below.

10.5.1   Resource Availability

Continuation of current trends could require as much as 3,500 average megawatts of renewable energy in addition to the wind power assumed to occur over the next ten years. Up to about 2,500 average megawatts might be obtained from geothermal, biomass, and new hydro in the region's portfolio risk analysis. The balance could likely be obtained from additional conservation, higher cost wind power, imports from other regions, and high-efficiency cogeneration.

10.5.2   Resource Cost

The cost of wind power plants increased substantially in early deployment, but in recent years cost trends have shown a decline due to improvements in wind turbine engines. The forecast delivered power costs for wind projects in Washington and Oregon (for 2012) is approximately $100.00 per megawatt hour compared to new projects (for 2012) of $60.00 (Northwest Power & Conservation Council April 2013). Despite the environmental appeal of wind, from a strict production cost perspective, hydro remains a superior resource option because of the lower system-wide levelized costs.

Please note that the *levelized cost of energy* (LCOE, also called *levelized energy cost* or LEC) is a cost of generating energy (usually electricity) for a particular system. It is an economic assessment of the cost of the energy-generating system including all the costs over its lifetime:

- Initial investment
- Operations
- Maintenance
- Cost of fuel
- Cost of capital

A net present value calculation is performed and solved in such a way that for the value of the LCOE chosen, the project's net present value becomes zero. This means that the LCOE is the minimum price at which energy must be sold for an energy project to break even. Typically LCOEs are calculated over 20- to 40-year lifetimes, and are given in the units of currency per kilowatt hour, for example USD/kWh or EUR/kWh or per megawatt hour.

Example: If a solar energy system costs \$10,000 to install (after all rebates) and it provides 100,000 kWh of electricity over its life, then the Levelized Cost of the solar energy system is \$10,000/100,000 kWh = \$0.10 per kWh.

Many of the factors that have led to recent increases in wind power costs are cyclical, and are expected to reverse within several years. Moreover, analysis conducted during the development of the plan indicates that even if wind power costs fail to drop in real terms over the long-term, wind would remain a cost-effective component of a low-risk resource portfolio. A further cost issue that has been voiced is that demand resulting from state renewable portfolio standards (RPS) requirements force a permanent seller's market. However, most economists in the Northwest predict that sustained demand would create more competition among suppliers, eventually forcing down costs.

10.5.3   System Flexibility

Wind, solar, wave, and tidal current resources produce power intermittently. The intermittent power production places additional demands on system frequency regulation and load-following resources ("system flexibility"). While existing system flexibility has been adequate to support existing wind power development, concerns have been raised regarding the ability

> *Wind, solar, wave, and tidal current resources produce power intermittently.*

to integrate the new wind generation, estimated to be 1,500 to 2,000 mega-watts, expected within the next two to three years.

10.5.4 Cost Effectiveness

As discussed above, wind delivers less value than its cost. However, the hedge value provided by wind against uncommon but potentially costly risk events resulted in the full 5,000 megawatts of wind power being cost-effective. The cost-effectiveness of larger amounts of wind power requires additional testing. The results of such sensitivity analysis are designed to test whether or not with declining wind costs and the larger amounts of wind, or other renewable resources providing similar risk protection at comparable cost would be cost-effective relative to hydro power.

Please note that the use of the word "hedge" in the context of this hydro case study has a different meaning from that used in the previous chapters. When we speak of the 'hedge value of wind' this is in reference to the carbon mitigating value that wind offers vis-à-vis traditional fossil fuel generation technologies like coal or natural gas. Minimizing the total cost of electric power in a carbon-neutral environment implies that greenhouse gas emissions must be reduced to its lowest level. This is simply an optimization problem where the objective is to minimize power generation costs subject to a vector of non-linear constraints, e.g., hydro water flow, lake levels, FERC licensing and CO_2 or carbon price.

10.5.5 Transmission

Near-term renewable resource development is unlikely to be constrained by bulk long-distance transmission capacity limits. Larger-scale development in the longer term, however, is expected to require expansion of bulk transmission capacity. The issue is complicated by the relatively low capacity factor of the wind projects expected to comprise the majority of this capacity.

10.6 CHAPTER WRAP-UP

This case study provided an overview of the role of behavioral finance in energy economics and how it is applied to a specific area in the country, Pacific Northwest. Pacific Northwest utilities are energy constrained because of water uncertainty. The problem has been exacerbated in recent years due to the increased attention devoted to fish management issues and state compliance with renewable portfolio standards. These constraints imply that normal cost of capital models underestimate the true cost of capital by not taking into consideration how agents behave under these specific circumstances. Behavioral finance can be a helpful tool in integrating the role of psychology with economic analysis to capture the complex nature of hydroelectric generation. While more is needed to refine the modeling process, the new paradigm of behavioral finance offers an informed and insightful strategy for Northwest energy planners.

REFERENCE

Mullainathan, Sendhil, and Richard H. Thaler. 2000. "Behavioral Economics," NBER Working Paper No. 7948, National Bureau of Economic Research. www .nber.org/papers/w7948.

Bibliography

Alberta Treasury Branches (ATB) Financial. "Alberta Natural Gas: Basis Swap," 2012. www.atb.com/business/corporate/commodities-and-foreign-exchange/Pages/natural-gas-basis-swap.aspx.

Alexander, C., and A. Venkatramanan. "Analytic Approximations for Spread Options." ICMA Centre, University of Reading, 2007. www.icmacentre.ac.uk/files/pdf/dps/dp_200711.pdf.

Aragones, J., C. Blanco, and K. Dowd. "Incorporating Stress Tests into Market Risk Modeling." *Institutional Investor* (2001). www.fea.com/resources/a_stresstest.pdf.

Awerbuch, S., Martin Berger. "Energy Security and Diversity in the EU: A Mean-Variance Portfolio Approach." *IEA Research Paper* (2003). www. iea.org/techno/renew/port.pdf.

Aydin, N., and C. Kucukozmen. "Stress Testing of Energy-Related Derivative Instruments Based on Conditional Market Risk Models." *Enerji, Piyasa ve Düzenleme* (Cilt:1, Sayı:2, Sayfa 121–144), 2010. http://epddergi.org/articles/2010-2/Aydin-Kucukozmen.pdf.

Bank for International Settlements (BIS). "Exchange Traded Derivatives Statistics," 2012. www.bis.org/statistics/extderiv.htm.

Bar-Lev, D., and S. Katz. "A Portfolio Approach to Fossil Fuel Procurement in the Electric Utility Industry." *Journal of Finance* 31, no. 3 (1976): 933–947.

Barone-Adesi, G., and R. Whaley. "Efficient Analytic Approximation of American Option Values." *Journal of Finance* 42, no. 2 (1987): 301–320.

Barroll, Daniel, and Yumi Oum. "Spark Spread Option Deltas Compared to Probability of Operation," 2009. http://207.67.203.54/elibsql05_P40007_Documents/QUANT%20DOCS/Delta%20vs%20MWh%20Summary_pge_ts.pdf.

Bessembinder, H., and M. Lemmon. "Equilibrium Pricing and Optimal Hedging in Electricity Forward Markets." *Journal of Finance* 57, no.3 (2002), 1347-1382. www.tapir.caltech.edu/~arayag/PriHedFws.pdf.

Birge, J., C. Ning, and S. Kou. "A Two-Factor Model for Electricity Spot and Futures Prices." Texas Quantitative Finance Festival, 2010. http://www2.mccombs.utexas.edu/conferences/tqff/TQFF_Program.pdf.

Bisen, D., Dubey Hari Mohan, Pandit Manjaree, and B. K Panigrahi. "Solution of Large Scale Economic Load Dispatch Problem using Quadratic Programming and GAMS: A Comparative Analysis." *Journal of Information and Computing Science* 7, no. 3 (2012): 200–211. http://www.worldacademicunion.com/journal/1746-7659JIC/jicvol7no3paper05.pdf.

Bjerstaf, Olof, and Juna Sodergren. "On the Topic of Energy Risk Management." Financial Risk—MSA400, 2012. www.math.chalmers.se/~rootzen/finrisk/OlofBjerstafJunaSodergrenEnergyRisk.pdf.

Black, F. "The Pricing of Commodity Contracts." *Journal of Financial Economics* 3 (1976): 167–179. http://ideas.repec.org/a/eee/jfinec/v3y1976i1-2p167-179.html.

Black, Fischer, and Myron Scholes. "The Pricing of Options and Corporate Liabilities." *Journal of Political Economy* 81, no. 3 (1973): 637–654. https://www.cs.princeton.edu/courses/archive/fall02/cs323/links/blackscholes.pdf.

Borovkova, Svetlana, and Ferry Permana. "Asian Basket Options and Implied Correlations in Energy Markets," 2010. www.feweb.vu.nl/nl/Images/AsianBasketOptions_tcm 96-194677.pdf.

Bouchentouf, Amine. *Commodities For Dummies*, 2nd ed. Hoboken, NJ: John Wiley & Sons, 2011.

Boyarchenko, S. I., and S. Z. Levendorskii. "Perpetual American Options under Levy Processes." *SIAM Journal on Control and Optimization* 40, no. 6 (2002): 1663–1696. http://epubs.siam.org/doi/abs/10.1137/S0363012900373987?jour nalCode=sjcodc.

Brajkovic, Jurica. "Real Options Approach to Investment in Base Load Coal Fired Plant." Energy Institute Hrvoje Pozar, 2010. http://papers.ssrn.com/sol3/papers .cfm?abstract_id=1603919.

Breen, R. "The Accelerated Binomial Option Pricing Model." *Journal of Financial and Quantitativve Analysis* 26 (1991): 153–164.

Brennan, M. J. "The Pricing of Contingent Claims in Discrete Time Models." *Journal of Finance* 34 (1979, March): 53–68.

Brennan, M., and E. Schwartz. "Finite Difference Methods and Jump Processes Arising in the Pricing of Contingent Claims." *Journal of Finance and Quantitative Analysis* 13 (1978): 462–474.

Broadie, M., and J. Detemple. "American Option Valuation: New Bounds, Approximations, and a Comparison of Existing Methods." *Review of Financial Studies* 9, no.4 (1996): 1211–1250.

Bunn, D., and N. Karakatsani. "Forecasting Electricity Prices." London Business School 1 (2003).

Burger, M. *Risk Measures for Large Portfolios and Their Applications in Energy Trading*. Karlsruhe, Germany: EnBW Trading GmbH, 2011.

Burger, M., B. Graeber, and G. Schindlmayr. *Managing Energy Risk*. Chichester, England: Wiley Finance, 2007.

Caflisch, R. "Monte Carlo and Quasi-Monte Carlo Methods." *Acta Numerica* (1998): 1–49.

Caflisch, R., W. Morokoff, and A. B. Owen. "Valuation of Mortgage-Backed Securities Using Brownian Bridges to Reduce Effective Dimension." *Journal of Computational Finance* 1 (1997): 27–46.

California ISO (CAISO). "Congestion Revenue Rights," 2013. www.caiso.com/market/Pages/ProductsServices/CongestionRevenueRights/Default.aspx.

Caporale, G., and M. Cerrato. "Valuing American Put Options Using Chebyshev Polynomial Approximation." London Metropolitan University Working Paper, 2005.

Carmona, R., M. Coulon, and D. Schwarz. "The Valuation of Clean Spread Options: Linking Electricity, Emission and Fuels," 2012. http://arxiv.org/pdf/1205.2302.pdf.

Carmona, Rene, and Valdo Durrelman. "Pricing and Hedging Spread Options." *SIAM Review* 45, no. 4 (2003): 627–685. www.cmap.polytechnique.fr/~valdo/papers/siam.pdf.

Carmona, Rene, and Nizar Touzi. "Optimal Multiple Stopping and Valuation of Swing Options." *Mathematical Finance* 18, no. 2 (2008): 239–268. http://onlinelibrary.wiley.com/doi/10.1111/j.1467-9965.2007.00331.x/abstract.

Carpenter, Guy. "Energy Market Convergence: Time to Review Trading Strategies, Risk Management and Operations." Oliver Wyman Group, 2007. www.oliverwyman.de/deu-insights/energy_mkt_convergence_ERC_0206.pdf.

Carr, Peter. "Dynamic and Static Hedging of Exotic Equity Options." NationsBanc Montgomery Securities, 1999. www.math.columbia.edu/~smirnov/over99.pdf.

Carr, P., and D. Faguet. "Fast Accurate Valuation of American Options." Working Paper, Cornell University, Ithaca, NY, 1996.

Chicago Board Options Exchange (CBOE). "Options Dictionary," 2012. www.cboe.com/LearnCenter/Glossary.aspx.

Clewlow, L., and C. Strickland. "A Multi-Factor Model for Energy Derivatives." *Quantitative Finance Research Centre*, University of Technology, Sydney, Australia, 1999. http://ideas.repec.org/p/uts/rpaper/28.html.

———. *Energy Derivatives, Pricing and Risk Management.* London: Lacima, 2000.

CME Group. "Block Trades." Trading Practices, 2013. www.cmegroup.com/clearing/trading-practices/block-trades.html.

———. "CME Commodity Trading Manual." Chicago Mercantile Exchange, 2006. http://gpvec.unl.edu/files/Futures/CME%201%20Commodity%20Trading%20Manual.pdf.

———. "Energy Products," 2013. www.cmegroup.com/trading/energy.

———. "Fundamentals of Energy Trading." CME Group Education, 2010. www.cmegroup.com/education/interactive/webinars-archived/fundamentals-of-energy-trading.html.

———. "Glossary," 2013. www.cmegroup.com/education/glossary.html.

———. "Heating Oil Crack Spread Average Price Option," 2013. www.cmegroup.com/trading/energy/refined-products/heating-oil-crack-spread-average-price-options_contract_specifications.html.

———. "Henry Hub Natural Gas Futures." Energy Products, 2013. www.cmegroup.com/trading/energy/natural-gas/natural-gas.html.

———. "Introduction to Crack Spreads." How the World Advances, 2012. www.cmegroup.com/trading/energy/files/EN-211_CrackSpreadHandbook_SR.PDF.

———. "Light Sweet Crude Oil (WTI) Futures and Options: The World's Most Liquid Crude Oil Benchmark." Energy, 2011. www.cmegroup.com/trading/energy/files/en-153_wti_brochure_sr.pdf.

———. "Power Industry Terminology." Education, 2013. www.cmegroup.com/education/interactive/webinars-archived/power-industry-terminology.html.

———. "RBOB Gasoline Crack Spread Option." *NYMEX Rulebook,* 2009. www.cmegroup.com/rulebook/NYMEX/3/387.pdf.

————. "RBOB Gasoline Options." Energy Products, 2013. www.cmegroup.com/trading/energy/refined-products/rbob-gasoline_contractSpecs_options.html.

Cohan, Peter. "Big Risk: $1.2 Quadrillion Derivatives Markets Dwarfs World GDP," 2010. www.dailyfinance.com/2010/06/09/risk-quadrillion-derivatives-market-gdp/.

Conejo, Antonio, Javier Contreras, Rosa Espínola, and Miguel A. Plazas. "Forecasting Electricity Prices for a Day-Ahead Pool-Based Electric Energy Market." *International Journal of Forecasting* 21, no. 3 (2005): 435–462. www.sciencedirect.com/science/article/pii/S0169207004001311.

Cooper, R. G., Scott J. Edgett, and Elko J. Kleinschmidt. "New Product Portfolio Management: Practices and Performance." *Journal of Product Innovation Management* 16, no. 4 (1999): 333–351. http://onlinelibrary.wiley.com/doi/10.1111/1540-5885.1640333/abstract.

Costello, K. "Diversity of Generation Technologies: Implications for Decision-making and Public Policy." *The Electricity Journal* 20, no. 5 (2007): 10–21.

Cox, J., S. Ross, and M. Rubinstein. "Option Pricing: A Simplified Approach." *Journal of Financial Economics* 7 (1979, September): 229–263.

Coyle, Thomas. "Advisers Question Modern Portfolio Theory." *Wall Street Journal*, 2012. http://online.wsj.com/article/SB10001424127887323981504578179142854570294.html.

Curran, Michael. "Beyond Average Intelligence." *Risk* 5, no. 10 (1992): 60.

D'Ecclesia, Rita. "Commodities and Commodity Derivatives: Energy Markets," 2012. www.ems.bbk.ac.uk/for_students/msc_finance/comm1_emec054p/energy_12.pdf.

d'Halluin, Y., P. A. Forsyth, and G. Labahn. "A Penalty Method for American Options with Jump Diffusion Processes." *Numerische Mathematik* 97, no. 2 (2004): 321–352.

Dantzig, George, and Mukund Thapa. *Linear Programming 1: Introduction.* Springer-Verlag, 1997.

Dash, S., and Skyba, E. "Inside the Oil Markets." TradeStation Group, 2012. http://www.tradestation.com/education/labs/analysis-concepts/inside-the-oil-markets.

DeLaquil, Pat, and Shimon Awerbuch. "A Portfolio-Risk Analysis of Electricity Supply Options in the Commonwealth of Virginia." Chesapeake Climate Action Network, 2005. https://salsa.democracyinaction.org/o/423/images/va_rps_portfolio_study_report-final_updated.pdf.

Deng, S. J., and S. S. Oren. "Electricity Derivatives and Risk Management." *Energy* 21 (2006): 940–953. www.ieor.berkeley.edu/~oren/pubs/Deng%20and%20Oren-86.pdf.

Deryabin, Mikhail. "On Implied Volatility Reconstruction for Energy Markets." *International Journal of Human and Social Sciences* 5 (2010):13. www.waset.org/journals/ijhss/v5/v5-13-128.pdf.

Dorr, Uwe. "Valuation of Swing Options and Examination of Exercise Strategies by Monte Carlo Techniques." PhD thesis, Oxford University, UK, 2003. https://www.maths.ox.ac.uk/system/files/private/active/0/ox_udo_04.pdf.

Drajem, Mark. "Methane in Water Seen Sixfold Higher Near Fracking Sites." *Bloomberg*, 2013. www.bloomberg.com/news/2013-06-24/methane-in-water-seen-sixfold-higher-near-fracking-sites.html.

Edwards, Lin. "Fracking Risks to Ground Water Assessed." PHYS.org, 2013. http://phys.org/news/2013-05-fracking-ground.html.

Engdahl, F. William. "Perhaps 60% of Today's Oil Price is Pure Speculation." *Oil Economy*, 2008. www.engdahl.oilgeopolitics.net/Financial_Tsunami/Oil_Speculation/oil_speculation.HTM.

Ernst & Young (E&Y). "Derivative Instruments and Hedging Activities." Ernst & Young Financial Reporting Developments, 2013. www.pwc.com/us/en/cfodirect/publications/accounting-guides/guide-to-accounting-for-derivative-instruments-and-hedging-activities-2013-edition.jhtml.

European Federation of Energy Traders (EFET). "Towards a Single European Energy Market," 2012. www.efet.org/Cms_Data/Contents/EFET/Folders/Documents/Home/~contents/GPC2TV6X8L2STWT8/Highlights-II-Final.pdf.

European Federation of Energy Traders (EFET). "Towards a Single European Energy Market," 2012. www.efet.org/Cms_Data/Contents/EFET/Folders/Documents/Home/~contents/GPC2TV6X8L2STWT8/Highlights-II-Final.pdf.

Eydeland, A., and K. Wolyniec. *Energy and Power: Risk Management*. Hoboken, NJ: Wiley Finance, 2003.

Fackler, P. L., and Y. Tian. "Volatility Models for Commodity Markets." Proceedings of the NCR-134 Conference on Applied Commodity Price Analysis, Forecasting, and Market Risk Management, Chicago, IL, 1999. www.farmdoc.illinois.edu/nccc134/conf_1999/pdf/confp16-99.pdf.

Falloon, William, and David Turner. "The Evolution of a Market." In *Managing Energy Price Risk*. London: Risk Books, 1999.

Farag, A., S. Al-Baiyat, and T.C. Cheng. "Economic Load Dispatch Multiobjective Optimization Procedures Using Linear Programming Techniques." *IEEE Transactions on Power Systems* 10, no. 2 (1995). http://faculty.kfupm.edu.sa/EE/sbaiyat/richfiles/papers/ECONOMIC%20LOAD%20DISPATCH%20MULTI-OBJECTIVE%20OPTIMIZATION.pdf.

Fattouh, Bassam. "Speculation and Oil Price Formation." *Review of Environment, Energy and Economics* (2012). www.feem.it/userfiles/attach/201253159474Re3-B.Fattouh-2012902.pdf.

Federal Energy Regulatory Commission (FERC). "Energy Primer: A Handbook of Energy Market Basics." The Division of Energy Market Oversight, Office of Enforcement, Federal Energy Regulatory Commission, July 2012. www.ferc.gov/market-oversight/guide/energy-primer.pdf.

———. "Industries: LNG." Federal Energy Regulatory Commission, June 2013. http://ferc.gov/industries/gas/indus-act/lng.asp.

Figlewski S., B. Gao, and D. H. Ahn. "Pricing Discrete Barrier Options with an Adaptive Mesh Model." *Journal of Derivatives* 6, no. 4 (1999): 33–43.

Fleming, J., and B. Ostdiek. "The Impact of Energy Derivatives on the Crude Oil Market." *Journal of Energy Economics* 21 (1999): 135–167. http://ideas.repec.org/a/eee/eneeco/v21y1999i2p135-167.html.

Fleten, Stein-Erek, Stein W. Wallace, and William T. Ziemba. "Portfolio Management in a Deregulated Hydropower Based Electricity Market." Norwegian Electricity Federation, 1997. http://citeseerx.ist.psu.edu/viewdoc/summary?doi=10.1.1.51.8760.

Forero, Juan. "Oil Boom in the Americas Shifts Energy Geopolitics." Global Association of Risk Professionals, 2012. www.garp.org/risk-news-and-resources/risk-headlines/story.aspx?newsid=47220.

Fortin, Ines, et al. "An Integrated CVaR and Real Options Approach to Investments in the Energy Sector." Institute for Advanced Studies, Vienna, 2007. www.ihs.ac.at/publications/eco/es-209.pdf.

Franken, Jason, and Joe Parcell. "Cash Ethanol Cross-Hedging Opportunities." Working Paper AEWP 2002-9, Department of Agricultural Economics, University of Missouri-Columbia, 2002. http://ageconsearch.umn.edu/bitstream/26035/1/aewp0209.pdf.

Galuschke, Holger. "Technical Analysis Applied on Energy Markets." E.ON Energy Trading, 2010. www.bbv-online.org/downloads/eonpraes.pdf.

Garner, C. *Trading Commodities, Commodity Options and Currencies*. Upper Saddle River, NJ: FT Press, 2012.

GasLand. Directed by Josh Fox. Hollywood, CA: 2010. http://www.amazon.com/GasLand-Josh-Fox/dp/B005C0DHEY/ref=sr_1_1?ie=UTF8&qid=1393640152&sr=8-1&keywords=gasland.

Geske, Robert. "The Valuation of Compound Options." *Journal of Financial Economics* 7 (1979): 63–81.

Geske, R., and H. E. Johnson. "The American Put Option Valued Analytically." *Journal of Finance* 39 (1984): 1511–1524.

Good, Allison. "New Possibilities Are Opening for Louisiana's Energy Industry." *The Times Picayune*, 2011. www.nola.com/business/index.ssf/2011/08/new_possibilities_are_opening.html.

Graves, Frank, and Steven Levine. "Managing Natural Gas Price Volatility: Principles and Practices Across the Industry." The Brattle Group, Inc., 2010. www.cleanskies.org/wp-content/uploads/2011/08/ManagingNGPriceVolatility.pdf.

Greenspan, Alan. "Remarks by Chairman Alan Greenspan." http://www.federalreserve.gov/boarddocs/speeches/2000/20000504.htm.

Han, Jun. "Pricing Some American Multi-Asset Options." Department of Mathematics, Uppsala University, Sweden, 2011. http://uu.diva-portal.org/smash/record.jsf?pid=diva2:302011.

Hanser, P., and F. Graves. " Utility Supply Portfolio Diversity Requirements." *The Electricity Journal* 20, no. 5 (2007): 22–32.

Harvey, Scott, and William Hogan. "California Electricity Prices and Forward Market Hedging." Center for Business and Government, Harvard University, Kennedy School of Government, 2000. www.hks.harvard.edu/fs/whogan/mschedge1017.pdf.

Haug, Espen. "Asian Options with Cost of Carry Zero," 2006. www.espenhaug.com/AsianFuturesOptions.pdf.

———. *The Complete Guide to Option Pricing Formulas*, 2nd ed. New York: McGraw-Hill, 2006.

———. *Derivatives Models on Models*. Hoboken, NJ: John Wiley & Sons, 2007.

He, Yizhi. "Real Options in the Energy Markets." Dissertation, University of Twente, The Netherlands, 2007. http://doc.utwente.nl/58482/1/thesis_He.pdf.

Henn, Markus. 2013. "Evidence on the Negative Impact of Commodity Speculation by Academics, Analysts and Public Institutions." WEED, 2013. www2.weed-online.org/uploads/evidence_on_impact_of_commodity_speculation.pdf.

Hickey, E., Lon Carlson, and David Loomis. "Issues in the Determination of the Optimal Portfolio of Electricity Supply Options." *Energy Policy* 38 (2009): 2198–2207. www.csgmidwest.org/MLC/documents/JEPO3951.pdf.

Hikspoors, Samuel. "Multi-Factor Energy Price Models and Exotic Derivatives Pricing." PhD thesis, University of Toronto, Canada, 2008. www.osti.gov/eprints/topicpages/documents/record/148/2540353.html.

Hodges, S. D., and M. J. P. Selby. "On the Evaluation of Compound Options." *Management Science* 33, no. 3 (1987): 347–355.

Hsu, M. "Spark Spread Options Are Hot." *The Electricity Journal* (1998). www.researchgate.net/publication/223110881_Spark_Spread_Options_Are_Hot!.

Huang, A. "Commodity Basket Option/Swaption Valuation: Geometric Conditioning and Moment Matching." PG&E Quant Group, 2009. http://207.67.203.54/elibsql05_P40007_Documents/QUANT%20DOCS/GeometricConditioningAnd%20MomentsMatching_pge_ts.pdf.

Hsu, Michael. "Perpetual American Options." PG&E Quant Group, 2008. http://207.67.203.54/elibsql05_P40007_Documents/QUANT%20DOCS/PerpetualOptions_pge_ts.pdf.

———. "Remarks on Mean Reverting Processes." PG&E Quant Group, 2012. http://207.67.203.54/elibsql05_P40007_Documents/QUANT%20DOCS/MeanRevertHedgeB_pge_ts.pdf.

———. "Spark Spread Options Are Hot." *The Electricity Journal* (1998). www.researchgate.net/publication/223110881_Spark_Spread_Options_Are_Hot!.

Huang, Alex. "Commodity Basket Option/Swaption Valuation: Geometric Conditioning and Moment Matching." PG&E Quant Group, 2009. http://207.67.203.54/elibsql05_P40007_Documents/QUANT%20DOCS/GeometricConditioningAnd%20MomentsMatching_pge_ts.pdf.

———. "Perpetual American Options." PG&E Quant Group, 2008. http://207.67.203.54/elibsql05_P40007_Documents/QUANT%20DOCS/PerpetualOptions_pge_ts.pdf.

Huang, Alex, and Sean Yang. "Digital Exchange Option." PG&E Quant Group, 2007. http://207.67.203.54/elibsql05_P40007_Documents/QUANT%20DOCS/Digital%20Exchange_pge_ts.pdf.

Huisman, Ronald, Ronald Mahieu, and Felix Schlichter. "Electricity Portfolio Management: Optimal Peak / Off-Peak Allocations." *ERIM Report Series Research in Management* (2007). http://repub.eur.nl/res/pub/10775/ERS-2007-089-F%26A.pdf.

Hull, John. *Futures, Options and Other Derivatives*, 8th ed. Englewood Cliffs, NJ: Prentice Hall, 2011.

Humphreys, Brett, and Katherine McClain. "Reducing the Impacts of Energy Price Volatility Through Dynamic Portfolio Selection." *The Energy Journal* 19, no. 3 (1998). http://sedc-coalition.eu/wp-content/uploads/2011/07/Humphreys-Reducing-the-Impacts-of-Energy-Price-Volatility-1998.pdf.

Ibanez, A. "Valuation by Simulation of Contingent Claims with Multiple Early Exercise Opportunities." *Mathematical Finance* 14, no. 2 (2004): 223–248.

Imai, Junichi, and Mutsumi Nakajima. "A Real Option Analysis of an Oil Refinery Project." *Financial Practice and Education* 10, no. 2 (2000): 78–91. www.ae.keio.ac.jp/lab/soc/imai/JIMAI/paper/imai_nakajima.pdf.

Intercontinental Exchange (ICE). "Delisting of Cleared Only Swaps," 2011. https://www.theice.com/publicdocs/futures_us/exchange_notices/ExNotDelisting-Swaps.pdf.

———. "Swaps to Futures," 2012. https://www.theice.com/s2f_products.jhtml.

Intertek. "Crude Oil Grades and Types," 2013. www.intertek.com/petroleum/crude-oil-types.

ISO/RTO Council. "Working Together to Power North America," 2001. www.isorto.org.

Jaillet, P., E. Ronn, and St. Tompaidis. "Valuation of Commodity-Based Swing Options." *Management Science* 50, no. 7 (2004): 909–921. http://mansci.journal.informs.org/content/50/7/909.abstract.

James, T. *Energy Markets: Price Risk Management and Trading*. Hoboken, NJ: Wiley Finance, 2007.

Johnson, H. 1983. "An Analytical Approximation for the American Put Price." *Journal of Financial & Quantitative Analysis* 18 (1983): 141–148.

Johnson B., and G. Barz. "Energy Modeling and the Management of Uncertainty." In *Selecting Stochastic Processes for Modelling Electricity Prices*. Risk Publications, 1999.

Ju, N., and R. Zhong. "An Approximate Formula for Pricing American Options." *Journal of Derivatives* 7, no.2 (1999): 31–40.

Kaminski, Vincent. "The U.S. Power Market." In *The Challenge of Pricing and Risk Managing Electricity Derivatives*, 149–171. London: Risk Publications, 1997.

Kemna, A. G. Z., and C. F. Vorst. "A Pricing Method for Options Based on Average Asset Values." *Journal of Banking and Finance* 14 (1990): 113–20.

Kennedy, Joseph. "The High Cost of Gambling Oil." *New York Times*, 2012. www.nytimes.com/2012/04/11/opinion/ban-pure-speculators-of-oil-futures.html.

Klassen, T. R. "Simple, Fast, and Flexible Pricing of Asian Options." *Journal of Computational Finance* 4 (2001): 89–124.

Kleindorfer, Paul, and Li Lide. "Multi-Period VaR-Constrained Portfolio Optimization with Applications to Electric Power Sector." *The Wharton School/OPIM*, 2004. http://opim.wharton.upenn.edu/risk/downloads/03-18.pdf.

Kluge, Tino. "Pricing Swing Options and Other Electricity Derivatives." PhD thesis, Oxford University, UK, 2006. http://eprints.maths.ox.ac.uk/246/1/kluge.pdf.

Knupp, Wayne. "The Importance of Fundamental Analysis." Energy-Koch Trading, 2011. http://www.docstoc.com/docs/68419267/The-Importance-of-Fundamental-Analysis.

Kowalski, Chuck. "Futures Quote and Chart Websites." About.com Commodities, 2013. http://commodities.about.com/od/understandingthebasics/tp/futures-quotes-charts.htm.

KPMG Energy Reform Implementation Group. "Review of Energy Related Financial Markets: Electricity Trading," 2006. http://www.ret.gov.au/energy/Documents/erig/Financial_markets_review_KPMG20070413120316.pdf.

Kristiansen, T. "Markets for Financial Transmission Rights." *Energy Studies Review* 13, no. 1 (2004). http://digitalcommons.mcmaster.ca/cgi/viewcontent.cgi?article=1250&context=esr.

Kroner, Kenneth F., Devin P. Kneafsey, and Stijn Claessens. "Forecasting Volatility in Commodity Markets." Research Working Paper WPS 1226, *The World Bank*, 1993. http://econ.worldbank.org/external/default/main?pagePK=64165259&theSitePK=469072&piPK=64165421&menuPK=64166322&entityID=000009265_3961005141748.

Kuprianov, Anatoli. "Derivatives Debacles: Case Studies of Large Losses in Derivatives Markets." *FRB Richmond Economic Quarterly* 81, no.4 (Fall 1995): 1–39. http://papers.ssrn.com/sol3/papers.cfm?abstract_id=2129302.

Le, Duong. 2009. "Implied Volatility in Crude Oil and Natural Gas Markets." *ResearchGate.* www.researchgate.net/publication/228425050_Implied_Volatility_in_Crude_Oil_and_Natural_Gas_Markets.

Leising, Matthew. 2013. "Energy Swaps Migrating to Futures on Dodd-Frank Rules." Bloomberg. www.bloomberg.com/news/2013-01-25/energy-swaps-migrating-to-futures-as-dodd-frank-rules-take-hold.html.

Levy, Edmond. 1992. "Pricing European Average Rate Currency Options." *Journal of International Money and Finance* 14: 474–491. www.ret.gov.au/energy/Documents/erig/Financial_markets_review_KPMG20070413120316.pdf.

Linetsky, V. "Spectral Expansions for Asian (Average Price) Options." *Operations Research* 52, no. 6 (2004): 856–67. http://users.iems.northwestern.edu/~linetsky/asian.pdf.

Liu, M., and F. Wu. "Managing Price Risk in a Multimarket Environment." *IEEE Transactions on Power Systems* 21, no. 4 (2006). http://www.eee.hku.hk/people/doc/ffwu/Liu-WuNov06.pdf.

Longstaff, F. A., and E. S. Schwartz. "Valuing American Options by Simulation: A Simple Least-Squares Approach." *Review of Financial Studies* 14, no. 1 (2001): 113–147.

Mack, Iris, and Harrison Rowe. 1981. "Coupled Modes with Random Propagation Constants." Radio *Science Journal*, 16(4), 485-493, July-August 1981.

Mack, Iris. "Block Implicit One-Step Methods for Solving Smooth and Discontinuous Systems of Differential/Algebraic Equations: Applications to Transient Stability of Electrical Power Systems." PhD diss., Harvard University Press, 1986.

———. "Day-Ahead Lunch-Time Electricity Demand Forecasting: Applications to Electricity and Weather Derivatives." Master's thesis, London Business School, 1999.

Mack, Iris, and Sloan School of Management. 2011a. "Generalized Picard-Lindelf theory." (White paper). Available at http://amzn.to/1fbHxEX.

Mack, Iris, and Sloan School of Management. 2011b. "Convergence analysis of block implicit one-step methods for solving differential/algebraic equation." (White paper). Available at http://amzn.to/1igEnaF.

MacMillan, W. "Analytic Approximation for the American Put Option." *Advances in Futures and Options Research* 1 (1986): 119–139.

Margrabe, W. "The Value of an Option to Exchange One Asset for Another." *Journal of Finance* 33 (1978): 177–186.

Maribu, K., A. Galli, and M. Armstrong. "Valuation of Spark-Spread Options with Mean Reversion and Stochastic Volatility." *International Journal of Electronic Business Management* 5, no. 3 (2007): 173–181. http://ijebm.ie.nthu.edu.tw/IJEBM_Web/IJEBM_static/Paper-V5_N3/A02.pdf.

Marinovic, Minja, Dragana D. Makajić-Nikolić, Milan J. Stanojević, and Lena S. Đorđević. "Optimization of Electricity Trading Using Linear Programming." *Open Access Series in Informatics* (2012). http://drops.dagstuhl.de/opus/volltexte/2012/3550/pdf/11.pdf.

MarketsWiki. "Physical Delivery," 2012. www.marketswiki.com/mwiki/Physical_delivery#cite_note-0.

MarketWatch. "Potential Hidden Opportunities in the Fracking Industry." *Wall Street Journal*, 2013. www.marketwatch.com/story/potential-hidden-opportunities-in-the-fracking-industry-2013-02-05.

Markowitz, Harry. 1952. "Portfolio Selection." *The Journal of Finance,* 7(1), 77-91. http://links.jstor.org/sici?sici=0022-1082%28195203%297%3A1%3C77%3APS%3E2.0.CO%3B2-1

MathWorks. "Energy Trading and Risk Management with MATLAB." Matlab Webinar, 2010. https://www.mathworks.com/company/events/webinars/wbnr50145.html.

———. "Linear Programming." Matlab's Optimization Toolbox, 2013. www.mathworks.com/products/optimization/description6.html.

———. "Portfolio Optimization in Matlab." Matlab Central, 2011. www.mathworks.com/matlabcentral/linkexchange/links/3040-portfolio-optimization-in-matlab.

McElroy, Michael, and Xi Lu. "Fracking's Future." *Harvard Magazine*, 2013. http://harvardmagazine.com/2013/01/frackings-future#article-images.

McKean, H. P. "A Free Boundary Problem for the Heat Equation Arising from a Problem in Mathematical Economics." *Industrial Management Review* 6, no. 2 (1965): 32–39.

McLean, Bethany, and Peter Elkind. *The Smartest Guys in the Room: The Amazing Rise and Scandalous Fall of Enron.* New York: Penguin Books, 2004.

McMahon, Chris. "Financial Settlement vs. Physical Delivery." *Futures* (2006). www.futuresmag.com/2006/07/25/financial-settlement-vs-physical-delivery.

Meinshausen, N., and B. Hambly. "Monte Carlo Methods for the Valuation of Options with Multiple Exercise Opportunities." *Mathematical Finance* 14, no. 4 (2004): 557–583.

Merton, Robert. 1976. "Option Pricing When Underlying Stock Returns are Discontinuous." *Journal of Financial Economics* 3: 125–144.

———. "Theory of Rational Option Pricing." *Bell Journal of Economics and Management Science* 4, no. 1 (1973): 141–183.

Metropolis, N., and Ulam, S. "The Monte Carlo Method." *Journal of American Statistical Association* 44 (1949): 335–341.

Min, Liu, and Felix Wu. "A Framework for Generation Risk Management in Electricity Markets." *Automation of Electric Power Systems* (2004). http://en.cnki.com.cn/Article_en/CJFDTOTAL-DLXT200413000.htm.

Min, Liu, and Felix Wu. "Managing Price Risk in a Multimarket Environment." *IEEE Transactions on Power Systems* 21, no. 4 (2006). www.eee.hku.hk/people/doc/ffwu/Liu-WuNov06.pdf.

Mullainathan, Sendhil, and Richard H. Thaler. "Behavioral Economics," NBER Working Paper No. 7948, National Bureau of Economic Research, 2000. www.nber.org/papers/w7948.

NCDEX. "Physical Delivery Guide, v. 1.1," 2012. www.ncdex.com/Downloads/ClearingServices/PDF/Physical_delivery_Guide_15022012.pdf.

Nearing, Brian. "Report Finds Little Drilling Damage." *GARP* (2012). www.garp.org/risk-news-and-resources/risk-headlines/story.aspx?newsid=46723.

New York ISO (NYISO). "Transmission Congestion Contracts," 2013. www.nyiso.com/public/markets_operations/market_data/tcc/index.jsp.

New York Mercantile Exchange (NYMEX). *Crack Spread Handbook* (2000). http://partners.futuresource.com/marketcenter/pdfs/crack.pdf.

———. "A Guide to Energy Hedging," 2011. www.docstoc.com/docs/84385167/A-GUIDE-TO-ENERGY-HEDGING.

NGV Communications Group. "Worldwide NGV Statistics." *NGV Journal* (2010). www.ngvjournal.dreamhosters.com/en/statistics/item/911-worldwide-ngv-statistics.

Nicolosi, Marco. "Wind Power Integration, Negative Prices and Power System Flexibility—An Empirical Analysis of Extreme Events in Germany." EWI Working Paper, No. 10/01, EWI Institute of Energy Economics at the University of Cologne, March 2010. www.ewi.uni-koeln.de/fileadmin/user_upload/Publikationen/Working_Paper/EWI_WP_10-01_Wind-Power-Integration.pdf.

Omisore, Iyiola, Munirat Yusuf, and Nwufo Christopher. "The Modern Portfolio Theory as an Investment Decision Tool." *Journal of Accounting and Taxation* 4, no. 2 (2012): 19–28. www.academicjournals.org/jat/PDF/pdf2012/Mar/Omisore%20et%20al.pdf.

Oren, Shmuel. "Hedging Fixed Price Load Following Obligations in a Competitive Wholesale Electricity Market." Energy Systems Modeling Symposium, 2007. www.ise.osu.edu/homepage/ssen/Shmuel%20Oren.pdf.

Organization of the Petroleum Exporting Countries (OPEC). "OPEC Share of World Crude Oil Reserves 2012," 2013. www.opec.org/opec_web/en/data_graphs/330.htm.

Orman, M., and T.E. Duggan. "Applying Modern Portfolio Theory to Upstream Investment Decision Making." *Journal of Petroleum Engineers* (1999). www.aboutoilandgas.com/jpt/print/archives/1999/03/JPT1999_03_management.pdf.

Ornstein, L. S., and G. E. Uhlenbeck. 1930. "On the Theory of the Brownian Motion." *Physical Review* 36, no. 5 (1930): 823. doi:10.1103/PhysRev.36.823.

Oum, Yumi, and Shmuel Oren. "VaR Constrained Hedging of Fixed Price Load-Following Obligations in Competitive Electricity Markets," 2008. https://ixquick-proxy

.com/do/spg/highlight.pl?l=english&c=hf&cat=web&q="VaR+Constrained +Hedging+of+Fixed+Price+Load-Following+Obligations+in+Competitive+ Electricity+Markets."&rl=NONE&rid=LBLNSNRTSMPP&hlq=https:// startpage.com/do/search&mtflag_ac=0&mtabp=-1&mtcmd=process_search& mtlanguage=english&mtenginecount=1&mtx=20&mty=17&mtcat=web&u=h ttp%3A%2F%2Fwww.pserc.wisc.edu%2Fdocuments%2Fpublications%2Fpa pers%2F2008_general_publications%2Fvar_yumi_040108.pdf.

Oum, Yumi, Shmuel Oren, and Shijie Deng. "Hedging Quantity Risks with Standard Power Options in a Competitive Wholesale Electricity Market." *Wiley Inter-Science* (2006). www.ieor.berkeley.edu/~oren/pubs/I.A.87.pdf.

Palmer, Brian. "Why Do We Call Financial Instruments 'Exotic'?" *Slate* (2010). www.slate.com/articles/news_and_politics/explainer/2010/07/why_do_we_ call_financial_instruments_exotic.html.

Park, J. H., Srikrishna Subramanian, and Ganesan Sivarajan. 1993. "Economic Load Dispatch for Piecewise Quadratic Cost Function Using Hopfield Neural Net-work." *IEEE Transactions on Power Systems* 8, no. 3 (1993). http://web.ecs .baylor.edu/faculty/lee/papers/journal/1993/199308.pdf.

Pilipovic, Dragana. *Energy Risk: Valuing and Managing Energy Derivatives*, 2nd ed. New York: McGraw-Hill, 2007.

PJM. "Financial Transmission Rights." PJM Markets and Operation, 2013. www .pjm.com/markets-and-operations/ftr.aspx.

Pointon, James. "EU Commodity Markets and Trading: Exotic Derivatives." CALYON Corporate and Investment Bank, 2006. www.isda.org/c_and_a/ppt/ 8-JamesPointon-EU-Commodity-Markets-Trading-Exotic-Derivatives.pdf.

PriceWaterhouse Coopers (PwC). "Glossary of Terms Used in Trading of Oil and Gas, Utilities and Mining," 2008. https://www.pwc.com/gx/en/energy-utilities-mining/pdf/eumcommoditiestradingriskmanagementglossary.pdf.

Rebennack, Steffen, Josef Kallrath, and Panos M. Pardalos. "Energy Portfolio Optimization for Electric Utilities: Case Study for Germany." *Energy, Natu-ral Resources and Environmental Economics Energy Systems* (2010):221–48. http://link.springer.com/chapter/10.1007%2F978-3-642-12067-1_14.

Reiner, Eric, and M. Rubenstein. "Breaking Down the Barriers." *Risk* 4, no. 8 (1990): 28–35.

Rendleman, R., and B. Bartter. "Two-State Option Pricing." *Journal of Finance* 34 (1979): 1093–1110.

Riedhauser, Chuck. "The American Cash-or-Nothing Option," 2001. http://207.67 .203.54/elibsql05_P40007_Documents/QUANT%20DOCS/Am_CON_pge.pdf.

———. "Average Price Options," 2001. http://207.67.203.54/elibsql05_P40007_ Documents/QUANT%20DOCS/APO_pge_ts.pdf.

———. "Fast Spread Option Evaluation," 2000. http://207.67.203.54/elibsql05_ P40007_Documents/QUANT%20DOCS/fast_spread_pge_ts.pdf.

———. "A Forward Curve Model Tutorial." PG&E PEC-Energy Procurement-Quantitative Analysis Group, January 3, 2003. http://pge.com/quant.

———. "Green Function Solution for Barrier Options," 1997. http://207.67.203.54/ elibsql05_P40007_Documents/QUANT%20DOCS/Green_function_pge_ts.pdf.

————. "Single Barrier and Double Barrier Rebates." July 21, 1995. http://207.67.203.54/elibsql05_P40007_Documents/QUANT%20DOCS/Green_function_pge_ts.pdf.

————. "Terminal Correlation in a Spread Option," 2002. http://207.67.203.54/elibsql05_P40007_Documents/QUANT%20DOCS/Spread_correlation_pge_ts.pdf.

————. "Valuation of Compound and Partial Barrier Options," 1997. http://207.67.203.54/elibsql05_P40007_Documents/QUANT%20DOCS/partial_barrier_pge_ts.pdf.

————. "Weighted Average Price Options." PG&E PEC-Energy Procurement-Quantitative Analysis Group, January 9, 2004. http://207.67.203.54/elibsql05_P40007_Documents/QUANT%20DOCS/Weighted%20average%20price%20options.pdf.

Rohlfs, W., and R. Madlener. "Multi-Commodity Real Options Analysis of Power Plant Investments: Discounting Endogenous Risk Structures." Institute for Future Energy Consumer Needs and Behavior (FCN), FCN Working Paper No. 22/2011, 2011.

Roll, R. "An Analytic Valuation Formula for Unprotected American Call Options on Stocks with Known Dividends." *Journal of Financial Economics* 5 (1997): 251–258.

Rubinstein, Mark. 1991. "Double Trouble." *Risk* 5, no. 1 (1991): 73.

Ryabchenko, V., and S. Uryasev. "Pricing Energy Derivatives by Linear Programming: Tolling Agreement Contracts." *Journal of Computational Finance* 14, no. 3 (2011): 73–126. www.risk.net/digital_assets/4231/v14n3a3.pdf.

Sanders, Bernie. "Stop Excessive Oil Speculation," 2012. www.sanders.senate.gov/newsroom/recent-business/stop-excessive-oil-speculation.

Saravia, Celeste. "Speculative Trading and Market Performance: The Effect of Arbitrageurs on Efficiency and Market Power in the New York Electricity Market." University of California, 2003. www.ucei.berkeley.edu/PDF/csemwp121.pdf.

Schneider, Stefan. "Power Spot Price Models with Negative Prices." *The Journal of Energy Markets* 4 (Winter 2011/2012): 77–102. www.risk.net/digital_assets/6064/jem_schneider_web.pdf.

Shobana, S., and R. Janani. "Optimization of Unit Commitment Problem and Constrained Emission Using Genetic Algorithm." *International Journal of Emerging Technology and Advanced Engineering* 3, no. 5 (2013). www.ijetae.com/files/Volume3Issue5/IJETAE_0513_62.pdf.

Shu, Cheng-Hsiung. "Pricing Asian Options with Fourier Convolution." Thesis, Department of Computer Science and Information Engineering, National Taiwan University, 2006. www.csie.ntu.edu.tw/~lyuu/theses/thesis_r93922111.pdf.

Siclari, M., and G. Castellacci. "Beyond the Spark Spread Option—Fuel Switching." *Energy Risk International* (2011). www.olf.com/software/energy-commodities/articles/energy-risk-beyond-the-spark-spread-option-fuel-switching.pdf.

Skantze, Petter, and Marija Ilic. "The Joint Dynamics of Electricity Spot and Forward Markets: Implications of Formulating Dynamic Hedging Strategies."

Energy Laboratory Report No. MIT-EL 00-005, 2000. http://web.mit.edu/energylab/www/pubs/el00-005.pdf.

Smith, W. "On the Simulation and Estimation of the Mean-Reverting Orstein-Uhlenbeck Process: Especially as Applied to Commodities Markets and Modeling." Commodity Models, 2010. http://commoditymodels.files.wordpress.com/2010/02/estimating-the-parameters-of-a-mean-reverting-ornstein-uhlenbeck-process1.pdf.

Soronow, D., and C. Morgan ."Modeling Locational Spreads in Natural Gas Markets." Financial Engineering Associates, 2002. http://www.fea.com/resources/a_modeling_locational.pdf.

Standard & Poor's (S&P). "U.S. Oil And Gas Sector Makes Extensive Use Of Commodity Derivatives." Standard & Poor's Ratings Services, 2012. www.ratingsdirect.com.

Steinhurst, William, David White, Amy Roschelle, Alice Napoleon, and Rick Hornby. "Energy Portfolio Management: Tools and Practices for Regulators." *Synapse Energy Economics* (2006). www.naruc.org/Publications/NARUC%20PM%20FULL%20DOC%20FINAL.pdf.

Stirling, Andy. "Diversity and Ignorance in Electricity Supply Investment." *Energy Policy* 22, no. 3 (1994): 195–216.

———. "Multicriteria Diversity Analysis: A Novel Heuristic Framework for Appraising Energy Portfolios." *Energy Policy* 39, no. 4 (2010): 1622–1634. www.sciencedirect.com/science/article/pii/S0301421509000901.

———. "On the Economics and Analysis of Diversity." Working Paper No. 28, Falmer, Brighton: SPRU Electronic, 1998.

Stoft, S., T. Belden, C. Goldman, and S. Pickle. "Primer on Electricity Futures and Other Derivatives." Environmental Energy Technologies Division: Ernest Orlando Lawrence Berkeley National Laboratory, LBNL-41098, UC-1321, 1998. http://eetd.lbl.gov/ea/emp/reports/41098.pdf.

Taleb, Nassim. *Dynamic Hedging: Managing Vanilla and Exotic Options*. New York: John Wiley & Sons, 1997.

Thomsett, Michael. 2012. "Black-Scholes—The Wrong Assumptions Make This Model Fatally Flawed—Updated." *Thomsett Options*. http://thomsettoptions.com/black-scholes-the-wrong-assumptions-make-this-model-fatally-flawed-updated.

Thomson Reuters. "Reuters Electronic Trading." Automated Dealing, 2008. http://thomsonreuters.com/content/financial/pdf/s_and_t/RET_AutomatedDealing.pd.

Thoren, Stefan. "A Monte Carlo Solver for Financial Problems." Master's thesis, Stockholm Royal Institute of Technology, 2005. www.nada.kth.se/utbildning/grukth/exjobb/rapportlistor/2005/rapporter05/thoren_stefan_05114.pdf.

Todd, Michael. "The Many Facets of Linear Programming." *Mathematical Programming* 91, no. 3 (2002), 417-436.

Tractebel Engineering. "Study on Interaction and Dependencies of Balancing Markets, Intraday Trade and Automatically Activated Reserves, Final Report." Katholieke Universiteit Leuven, TREN/C2/84/2007, 2009. http://ec.europa.eu/energy/gas_electricity/studies/doc/electricity/2009_balancing_markets.pdf.

Tseng, C. L., C. A. Li, and S. S. Oren. "Solving the Unit Commitment Problem by a Unit Decommitment Method." *Journal of Optimization Theory and Applications* 105, no. 3 (2000): 707–730. www.ieor.berkeley.edu/~oren/pubs/ud_n_ch02.pdf.

Turnbull, S. M., and L. Wakeman. "A Quick Algorithm for Pricing European Average Options." *Journal of Financial and Quantitative Finance* 26 (1991): 377–389.

U.S. Commodities Futures Trading Commission (CFTC). "Dodd-Frank Wall Street Reform and Consumer Protection Act." U.S. Congress, H.R. 4172, 2010. www .cftc.gov/ucm/groups/public/@swaps/documents/file/hr4173_enrolledbill.pdf.

U.S. Energy Information Administration (EIA). "Derivatives and Risk Management in the Petroleum, Natural Gas, and Electricity Industries," 2002. www.eia.gov/ oiaf/servicerpt/derivative/chapter3.html.

———. "Louisiana: Profile Overview," 2012. www.eia.gov/state/?sid=la.

———. "Natural Gas Weekly Update," 2013. www.cmegroup.com/education/files/ eia-natural-gas-weekly-update-2013-04-17.pdf.

U. S. Environmental Protection Agency (EPA). "Utility Planning and Incentive Structure," 2006. www.epa.gov/statelocalclimate/documents/pdf/guide_action_ chap6_s1.pdf.

Vaitheeswaran, N., and R. Balasubramanian. "Stochastic Model for Natural Gas Portfolio Optimization of a Power Producer." *Power Electronics, Drives and Energy Systems* (2010). http://ieeexplore.ieee.org/xpl/articleDetails.jsp?reload= true&arnumber=5712549.

Vasicek, Oldrich. "An Equilibrium Characterization of the Term Structure." *Journal of Financial Economics* 5 (November 2, 1977): 177–188. doi:10.1016/0304-405X(77)90016-2.

Vorst, T. "Prices and Hedge Rations of Average Exchange Rate Options." *International Review of Financial Analysis* 1, no. 3 (1992): 179–194.

Wang, Muhu. "A Finite-Element Approach for Pricing Swing Options Under Stochastic Volatility." PhD thesis, University of Houston, Texas, 2010.

Wasenden, O-H. "Supervision and Regulation of Energy Derivatives Trading: An Introduction to the Main Legislation and Some of the Challenges in Practice." Florence School of Regulation, Brussels, May 23, 2012. www.florence-school .eu/portal/page/portal/FSR_HOME/ENERGY/Policy_Events/Workshops/2012/ EU%20Energy%20Law%20%20Policy/120523_Wasenden_Odd-Harald.pdf.

Weron, R., and A. Misiorek. "Forecasting Spot Electricity Prices with Time Series Models." International Conference of The European Electricity Markets EEM-05, 2005. www.mendeley.com/research/forecasting-spot-electricity-prices-time-series-models.

Weron, R. A. "Market Price of Risk Implied by Asian-style Electricity Options," 2008. http://128.118.178.162/eps/em/papers/0502/0502003.pdf.

Wilcox, D. "Spread Options Enhance Risk Management Choices." *NUMEX Energy in the News* (Autumn 1991): 9–13.

Wilmott, Paul. *Paul Wilmott Introduces Quantitative Finance*, 2nd ed. Chichester, England: Wiley Global Finance, 2007.

———. *Paul Wilmott on Quantitative Finance*, 2nd ed. Hoboken, NJ: John Wiley & Sons, 2006.

————. "The Problem with Derivatives, Quants, and Risk Management Today," 2010. www.qfinance.com/capital-markets-viewpoints/the-problem-with-derivatives-quants-and-risk-management-today?page=6.

Wisniewski, D. "Mathematical Models and Measurement." *Rasch Measurement Transactions 5*, no. 4 (1992): 184.

Wittwer, J. W. "Monte Carlo Simulation Basics." Vertex42.com, 2004. www.vertex42.com/ExcelArticles/mc/MonteCarloSimulation.html.

Woo, Chi-Keung, Ira Horowitz, Arne Olson, Andrew DeBenedictis, David Miller, and Jack Moore. "Cross Hedging and Forward-Contract Pricing of Electricity in the Pacific Northwest." *Managerial and Decision Economics 32*, no. 4 (2011): 265–279. http://onlinelibrary.wiley.com/doi/10.1002/mde.1533/abstract.

Yan, Chang. "The Optimization of Energy Portfolio Management (EPM): Framework and Simulation." PhD thesis, Southern New Hampshire University, Hooksett, NH, 2011.

Yu, Carisa, and Hung Hom. "Pricing American Options without Expiry Date." Hong Kong Polytechnic University, 2004. www.soa.org/library/proceedings/arch/2004/arch04v38n1_7.pdf.

Zhang, P. G. "Section 15.3." In *Exotic Options*, 2nd ed. World Scientific, 1998.

Zhang, Xian. "Exotic Options Bundled with Interruptible Electricity Contracts." The 7th International Power Engineering Conference (IPEC), 2005. http://ieeexplore.ieee.org/xpl/mostRecentIssue.jsp?punumber=10834.

Zhao, Lu. "Risk Management of Energy Derivatives." Department of Mathematics and Statistics, University of Calgary, 2007. www.pptuu.com/show_676745_5.html.

Index